JOCK LEWES

Here is a House that armours a man
  With the eyes of a boy and the heart of a ranger
And a laughing way in the teeth of the world
  And a holy hunger and thirst for danger.

Hilaire Belloc

JOCK LEWES

CO-FOUNDER OF THE SAS

by

JOHN LEWES

With a Foreword by

THE RT HON
THE EARL JELLICOE

KBE, DSO, MC, FRS

LEO COOPER

First published in Great Britain in 2000
and reprinted in this format in 2001, 2007 and 2016 by
PEN & SWORD MILITARY
An imprint of
Pen & Sword Books Ltd
47 Church Street
Barnsley, South Yorkshire
S70 2AS

ISBN 978 1 84415 615 3

A CIP catalogue record for this book is
available from the British Library

Printed and bound in England
By CPI Group (UK) Ltd, Croydon, CR0 4YY

Pen & Sword Books Ltd incorporates the Imprints of Aviation, Atlas,
Family History, Fiction, Maritime, Military, Discovery, Politics, History,
Archaeology, Select, Wharncliffe Local History, Wharncliffe True Crime,
Military Classics, Wharncliffe Transport, Leo Cooper, The Praetorian Press,
Remember When, Seaforth Publishing and Frontline Publishing.

For a complete list of Pen & Sword titles please contact
PEN & SWORD BOOKS LIMITED
47 Church Street, Barnsley, South Yorkshire, S70 2AS, England
E-mail: enquiries@pen-and-sword.co.uk
Website: www.pen-and-sword.co.uk

This book is dedicated to my parents, David and Daphne Lewes: Life-givers, nurturers and storytellers, and in memory of the 'Originals', 'L' Detachment, SAS.

Contents

Acknowledgements

I am most grateful to Leo Cooper and Brigadier Henry Wilson, my publishing manager, for their help and support, and also Alan Moore who introduced my story of Jock to them at the time of its writing in 1998, and undertook the lion's share of checking the typescript. I also owe special thanks to many scholars who have helped me with their encouragement, advice and suggestions: Michael Bloch read over the book and Philip Warner helped with the history of the SAS; Giles MacDonogh and Nicholas O'Shaugnessy looked over the chapters on Jock's writing from Berlin; Peter Yeend supported me with material from the museum at the King's School, Parramatta, in Australia; Roland Wilcock, OBE, encouraged with research material and advice; Mark Seaman and Alan Hoe also gave me their advice. Discussions with Jeff Holbrook and David Birt, who both helped with reading the typescript, have also been most instructive. Tom Hartman's wit, enthusiasm and guidance were invaluable and much appreciated.

I owe many debts of gratitude to the following people, who knew Jock Lewes and who have been unstinting with their time and support. In particular, I offer my deepest thanks to those who knew Jock: Major Jim Almonds, MM; Douglas Arnold; Dr M. Ashby, FRCP; Bob Bennet, BEM; Ernie Bond, OBE; Group Captain Owen Dibbs, OBE; Joan Fitzhardinge;

John Garton, CBE; Major Sandy Gordon, DFC; Angelica Guyon de St Prix; Charlie Hackney; Brian Hodgson, CMG; The Rt Hon. Earl Jellicoe, KBE, DSO, MC, FRS; Dr David Lewes, FRCP; Sir Carol Mather, MC; Elizabeth McArthur; David Mynors, OBE; Major Pat Riley, DCM; Reg Seekings, MM, DCM; and Jimmie Storie.

I am also indebted to a host of guides and helpers: Alkin Books Ltd.; Edith Baird; Esme Barrett; Ieda Basualdo; Paulo Baigent and Speak To Me Gabriel Co.; Lisa Blemmer; Thomas Boyd; Barbara Bramall; Paula Brennan; Mike and Jane Caffrey; Stephen Carroll; Amanda Crompton; Charles Cuddon; John Delaney; Vivaldo Dorretto; Jane Fish; Richard Fishlock; Elizabeth Garton; Kay Gladstone; James and Geoffrey Hadfield; Leslie Hope; Joanna Jaaniste; Jacqueline Kington; Wendy Legg; The Hon. Hugh Lawson-Johnston; Jane Lewes; Professor Eric and Monica Newbigging; Charlie McArthur; Ian and Elma McArthur; Virginia Lewes-Malandrakis; Gordon Marsden, MP; Major Anthony Maycock; Terry MacDonogh; Professor Andrew O'Shaugnessy; Gilbert Pleuger; Patricia Powell; The Countess of Ranfurly; Hilary Roberts; Paul Sargeant; Stephen Rouse, Becky Sear; Jenny Spencer-Smith; Gordon Stevens of Television South; Rosemary Tudge; Michael, Amanda, Simon and Tara Wagstaff; Simon Wells; Laurence Whistler; Paul Wilson-Bonder; The late Viscount Whitelaw, MC; Roni Wilkinson; Michael Wise; Andi Wright; David Wright; Susie Wright; Jessica Woollard; Sarah Woollard; William Woollard; and Drs George and Margaret Yerbury.

I am grateful to the following institutions and their staff, who have greatly assisted me: The British Council; The Imperial War Museum's Reference Library, Research and Information, Film, Photographic and Sound units; The National Army Museum; The Reference Library at Colindale; The Public Record Office at Kew; and the Outward Bound centre in Aberdovey, Wales.

My thanks go also to the following publishers and authors

for permission to quote from their works: Little, Brown and Company, *David Stirling* by Alan Hoe; Little, Brown and Company, *Joy Street:A Wartime Romance in Letters, 1940–1942,* edited by Michael Wise.

Thanks also to the following periodicals and publications: *Isis,* 13 and 20 May 1936; *The Lady,* 8 December 1938; *The Times,* 16 April 1937; *The Times,* 17 April 1937; *Scottish Daily Express,* 24 August 1944; *John Bull,* 9 March 1957; *Sunday Times,* 27 December 1993; *Spectator,* 20 May 1995; *Boston Sunday Globe,* 2 July 1995; *Independent,* 10 April 1999; and *The Spectator,* 9 November 1999.

———

To my darling wife, Anna, for her help, and for her forbearance well beyond the call of the marriage vows, and my children, Christina Daphne and David Michael Steel for their patience.

Foreword

by

THE RT HON THE EARL JELLICOE

KBE, DSO, MC, FRS

Many, many books have been written about the SAS – rather too many, in fact, about its recent operations. That said, I believe that this informative biography, written by his nephew, of Jock Lewes, who made so vital a contribution to the early SAS, is greatly to be welcomed.

David Stirling, the Commanding Officer of the early SAS, has of course a unique place in the history of this remarkable Regiment. Never in a fairly long life have I known someone with such a special quality, so great a gift, of leadership. However, David always very rightly stated that there were three Co-Founders with him of the early SAS – Paddy Mayne, Georges Bergé and Jock Lewes.

The part which Mayne played in those early days – the untold damage which he wreaked behind the enemy lines in the Western Desert, his role thereafter as CO of 1 SAS, his four DSOs – is well known. Less well known is the role of that splendid Free French Officer, Bergé, who brought his excellent French Squadron to join the SAS when, following its disastrous initial raids in November 1941, the SAS had been reduced to a mere five Officers and twenty-one Other Ranks.

I believe that the quite outstanding role which Jock Lewes played in those early days in the history of the SAS is also too little known and too little appreciated. That is a principal reason why I welcome this biography. As it happens I served with Jock in No. 8 Commando in the early days of the war but never got to know him well and he met his death before I joined the SAS. It has been fascinating for me to learn more about this quite remarkable personality.

In preparing this long-overdue biography of a particularly distinguished young soldier and a most unusual man the author consulted a multitude of sources. He was also lucky to come across some 450 letters from Jock, always a prolific writer, to his parents.

As a result, we learn about Jock's boyhood and school life in Australia – that Australian upbringing which gave him, as a friend has written, 'besides a fine physique and presence, a bounding energy and strength and great skill of eye and hand'. We learn about the special interest which as a schoolboy he shared with his younger brother in chemistry – an interest which later culminated in the Lewes Bomb. And we learn from a schoolboy contemporary how in the school Cadet Corps they together 'discussed and developed what was to become known as the Commandos; highly trained, light arms and ammunition, disguise, etc'.

There is also a fascinating account of Jock's very full life at Oxford and of what he gave to rowing there and how, with his skill, experience and powers of leadership, he, as President of the Oxford University Boat Club, ended a Cambridge run of thirteen successive Boat Race victories.

We gain from this biography, above all, far more knowledge than has hitherto been generally available of the very special contribution which this quite exceptional young officer made in the early stages of the war, be it as a Training Officer with the Welsh Guards, be it with No. 8 Commando or be it later with the early SAS. We learn also of his disenchantment with Layforce following its arrival in the Middle East, despite his admiration for its Commanding Officer, Bob Laycock, who was later to succeed Mountbatten in command of Combined Operations Headquarters.

Like David Stirling, Jock had come to believe soon after his arrival in the Middle East and after taking part in or witnessing a number of unsuccessful operations by Layforce, that success in raiding operations behind the enemy lines would lie with highly trained, small and select forces rather than with larger, more cumbersome groups. He succeeded – no mean achievement in itself – in obtaining permission to form a small parachute detachment, the immediate forerunner of the early SAS, which could have proved a great success had its operations not been cancelled by higher military authority. Thereafter he joined a small group from No. 8 Commando (by then expecting disbandment) in Tobruk – carrying out with considerable acumen and great courage a number of highly successful raiding operations.

All this is well described in this biography. Equally well and fully described is all that Jock brought with him to the unit (L Detachment, SAS Brigade) which David Stirling had gained permission to form at Kabrit in the Canal Zone. He brought with him the fine 'Tobruk Four' who had served with him in Tobruk and he brought, above all, his experience of raiding operations, his ability to organize, manage and enthuse, his vision and a high degree of dedication. It was there that he invented the Lewes Bomb and it was there that he initiated an astonishingly rigorous and intensive training programme which served to mould the early SAS. At that time Jock wrote of David Stirling in one of his letters to his parents, 'Together we made a combination that could hardly be bettered.' This is true and it is described with skill and authority in this biography.

It is sad that this great and most unusual man was killed so early in the war. He still had much to give the SAS and to our wartime effort. I also believe that he would have had a valuable contribution to make to our peacetime world. It is good that his short, albeit intensely full and valuable life is commemorated so well in this biography.

Introduction

During the Second World War, when newspaper articles referred to activities of the SAS, they often did so by claiming that the élite force's escapades 'were conceived and created by two young officers, Lieutenant David Stirling, Scots Guards, and Lieutenant Jock Lewes, Welsh Guards'. Since 1945 there has been a plethora of books on the SAS and its origins, and more recently many works refer to Jock Lewes as 'the practical academic' and 'SAS expert' of what was then an embryonic Brigade that became a Regiment in 1942.

For nearly fifty years Jock's role in the inception of the SAS Regiment has tended to be superseded by the stories in biographies and general histories that concentrated on the lives of other soldiers. This was understandable as these soldiers were fascinating characters in their own right, and there appeared to be much more information on them than on Jock Lewes, who had often seemed elusive to even his own men. Jock seemed to be as invisible in the stories of the SAS as he had mostly succeeded in being to Axis forces in the North African desert.

Clues to Jock's story lay in various files and papers in a very cluttered attic and garage at my father's home. The portrait of Jock Lewes by Rex Whistler, so generously given to my father after Rex's death, dominated the family hearth, and there was no escaping the presence of the young war leader. A story was waiting to be written. Jock had said so himself with the words he wrote to his parents in late 1941: 'The tale must wait until the censor graciously condescends to release it from suppression. In the meantime you will be able to make up all sorts of stories about me and think them true until you know otherwise.' Many of Jock's contemporaries considered him to be a savant, and these words do seem prophetic in the sense that a significant part of Jock Lewes's work in the desert has still not seen the light of day.

In 1993 a period of 'resting' as an actor gave me the opportunity to search for Jock's military journal to his parents, and this complemented Michael Wise's discovery of Jock's love letters to Mirren Barford, Michael's mother. These would be later published by Little, Brown and Company as *Joy Street: A Wartime Romance in Letters, 1940–1942*. Michael Wise had initiated the 'release' of Jock's life in the desert with a wonderful but tragic exposé of the two parted lovers: Jock was in the Middle East when Mirren wrote to him from Oxford. They envisioned a great love in letters that also hinted at the origins of the concepts that we now associate with the SAS. The hunt to find a full picture of the background of Jock's plans and operations behind enemy lines was now on! As the leader of the SAS who was present in their base camp at Kabrit during its foundation in 1941, Jock was responsible for censoring his own letters, which he did, yet he also left important clues behind as to the nature of his and David Stirling's enterprise.

Yet how to write a life of Jock Lewes? Perhaps more papers might be found among my grandparents' letters, which I travelled to Scotland to collect. The answer came after Pen and Sword made a commitment to publish Jock's story, which might have been rather short but for the fortunate detection in August 1998 of more of his correspondence. Dr David Lewes, my father and Jock's younger brother, knew that some of Jock's letters had probably been stored in the outhouse of the farm that belonged to their sister, Elizabeth McArthur.

The McArthurs kindly pointed me in the right direction: this room too needed clearing. The barn was damp – had the letters survived? I removed the dust of half a century. The paper and ink that Jock had used was of good quality; the ink remained dry and legible in a bold hand. Every letter was dated and not one was damaged, still intact in its original envelope. By the time I had finished my hunt, I had discovered 450 letters written by Jock between 1924 and 1941; he had written to his parents almost weekly since adolescence. Of these a number are long, many well-penned and of interest to students of this era. Perhaps as few as two or three of the original SAS men at their Kabrit camp kept diaries in 1941 and Jock was one of them. This makes him a key witness to the creation and foundation of the Special Air Service. His letters have not been paraphrased or summarized for several reasons. Some portraits of well-known sportsmen and soldiers of his day may well be unique and better left intact to avoid distortion. I preferred direct quotation from his reports on Tobruk, propaganda, politics, strategy, and from the rare records of his own self-assessments in his relations with one of two women that he fell in love with. With such documents a life of Jock Lewes was truly possible.

The further discovery of David Stirling's chivalrous letter of 1942 to Jock's father, Arthur Lewes, when he found the time to write in the thick of fighting, was a revelation that helped to solve the conundrum of why Jock was so essential to the foundation of the SAS. This primary source material, in addition to Jock's military journal, meant that both officers mutually but independently confirmed each other's account of how the blend of their capabilities and qualities gave the impetus that ensured the formation of their unit. That both men corroborate each other's story is a fact of the greatest importance in giving an objective view of the origins of the SAS. They formed an amalgam of the rarest kind that guaranteed some of the most daring exploits of the Second World War.

Prologue
The Art of War

In his book *The War of the Flea* Robert Taber drew attention to Sun Tzu, who set out a number of important principles on guerrilla strategy and tactics in the oldest known writing on the subject in his essay on *The Art of War*. In the light of the work of the SAS, some of these codes now have a familiar ring about them:

> All warfare is based on deception.
> When near, make it appear that you are far away; when far away, that you are near.
> When he concentrates, prepare against him.
> Anger his general and confuse him.
> Keep him under a strain and wear him down.
> When he is united, divide him.
> Attack where he is unprepared; sally out when he does not expect you.
> These are the strategist's key to victory.

Jock certainly admired Eastern philosophies and ideas, but it is not certain whether he had read *The Art of War* or knew anything about it. In some senses Jock was a natural successor to Sun Tzu well over two thousand years later in the Western Desert.

David Stirling once recalled a conversation when Jock

raised the subject of the Ranger, Major Robert Rogers, who fought for the British in North America during the wars against the French in the late eighteenth century. It is likely that Jock knew something about Rogers' Rangers, because, in his discussions with David Stirling, he mentioned that Rogers, fighting behind enemy lines 'with small teams', was not a 'new concept'. As a young man Jock had been inspired to adopt bold tactics when raiding the 'enemy' in school cadet camp operations in Australia. Perhaps Major Rogers was the source of that inspiration.

Rogers developed a set of his own principles while fighting the Red Indians and their French allies. His 'twenty-eight commonsense rules' and 'nineteen standing orders' covered everything from marching and retreating to night operations. Whether Jock knew the detail of these or not, it is clear that some of his pioneering work on many of the ideas we associate with the SAS in 1941 and today was similar to that of the New Hampshire Major, even if the harsh terrain where both men operated was different.

Both men led and trained troops who were considerably outnumbered by their respective enemies. In spite of that, the two leaders 'took the fight' to their opposition. Partly due to the shortage of manpower, both SAS and Rangers split into sub-units of ten men or fewer. In September and October 1758 barely 100 Rangers challenged the combined forces of 700 French and Abenaki Indians by the St Francis River. On poles in the nearby Abenaki Indian settlement hung between 600-700 English scalps. Another horrendous fate seemed to await Englishmen in North Africa over two hundred years later, when the Italians, though hardly capable of the brutality of the North American Indians in Rogers' day, nevertheless appeared to have the capability of bringing about a crushing defeat on the Allies: in 1939 a million Italians were posted in the Middle East where there were less than 40,000 British troops facing them.

SAS and Rangers endured terrible conditions in order to

harass their combatants deep behind enemy lines with success out of all proportion to their numbers; both used surprise to its greatest potential. In late 1757 and late 1941 their respective troops marched over 200 miles in order to prepare and complete their strikes at the heart of the superior forces who opposed them. One force had endless miles of dense spruce swamps to contend with, the other burning days and freezing nights in featureless terrain. One hundred and forty of Rogers' Rangers killed over one third of the Indians that they ambushed and suffered far fewer casualties. The SAS in their first fortnight of raids destroyed over sixty planes, twenty trucks, and petroleum without losing any of their own men.

Though the era of Rogers was simpler than the present one, the skills required to become an élite soldier were often similar. Jock Lewes and Robert Rogers trained their men to become individualists who could operate on their own if necessary. They were both great motivators and often pushed their men well beyond the expected limits of their endurance.

When he arrived in Egypt, it wasn't long before Jock was aware of an appalling stalemate – or much worse – if troops like his Commando units weren't utilized in an inventive and bold way to counter superior mechanized armies and numbers of German and Italian forces.

It could be said that Middle Eastern Headquarters quickly needed to reinvent the art of war, but somehow, with all their military training and experience, or perhaps because of it, they had forgotten how. Like Major Roberts, Jock was neither a general nor a statesman, he commanded no great army and won no major conflict. However, this book is about a young Lieutenant whose great inventiveness, vision and daring showed his generals the art of war.

John Lewes August 1999

PART 1

Childhood and Youth in Sydney, Australia

1

Parent and Child

'The child is father to the man'

Jock was greatly influenced by his father, Arthur Lewes. An explanation of the make-up of a dour but doting parent high-lights the character of young Jock's mould. Victorian Puritanism was impressed upon him from an early age after Arthur had completed his service as a senior partner of Lovelock and Lewes, the Calcutta chartered accountants. Arthur settled for early retirement to be with his young family at the Lewes home just outside Sydney in Bowral, NSW; he was only fifty-three and still in the prime of his life. His own strict upbringing had a powerful impact on his family. Arthur's own father had only ever expressed love for his sixth and last child on his deathbed with a 'dear boy' as his parting words, and Arthur's mother, who gave birth to him at the age of fifty-four, became a somewhat remote figure since she was self-conscious at having become pregnant in the first place.

In spite of the maturity of his mother, all the evidence suggests that Arthur was the legitimate son of both his parents rather than the illegitimate and adopted offspring of a daughter or a niece. Eyebrows were raised. Today the ability to conceive late in life has become a laudable activity; in 1869 members of the local congregation regarded late conception as impropriety. If you spent your time playing shove-half-penny and indulging in the physical pleasures, such feats of fertility were entirely possible, but not if you purported to be

7

a member of the genteel society of Lewisham where Arthur's ancestors had been Chief Victuallers to the Royal Navy at Greenwich, London, since the time of Samuel Pepys.

It seems that the last in the line of Leweses was regarded as a 'mistake' at home in Lewisham and an embarrassment abroad; Arthur was a pest to a growing family. Thus Jock's grandparents quickly found a governess and nanny to whisk his unfortunate father out of sight and, to all appearances, out of mind; these were not easy times for the smallest of a very able bunch of siblings. Arthur's nanny, 'Fanny', was the provider of love and care and ultimately the one who was responsible for nurturing his emotional intelligence; she had plenty of opportunities to do so since she stayed with the family for sixty years. Her sense of Christian duty was probably easier for Arthur to stomach, but it did not prevent him from running away from school three times. As he grew up, he discovered that in his family he was expected to do everything that he was told. When his older brother Samuel ignored a warning to return home punctually in the evenings, Arthur discovered that at 10 p.m. one night the door had been locked and Samuel informed by a notice that he was not welcome. Young Arthur never saw him again; this prodigal son did not return. It is possible to see that Arthur in turn could be a remote role model for his own children, but any love and affection that he had received as a lad he was determined to pass on to his own children and, it seems, to Jock in particular.

Jock Lewes was born on 21 December 1913 in Calcutta and he, his elder sister Elizabeth and his mother, Elsie Lewes, travelled to Elsie's native Australia to settle in the new family home of 'Fernside' when he was only two years of age. Jock's father took leave from Lovelock and Lewes every two years to visit his family in the face of the quiet disapproval from some of Elsie's sisters that a newly wed mother deserved a husband who was nearer at hand. Arthur was repeating a family tradition that his parents had set in the previous generation, except that any distance that he might have felt in his relations with his wife and children were exacerbated by his decision to work in an entirely different continent.

Arthur's move to Calcutta from Oxford enabled him to meet Elsie. It was 1895 when Arthur joined his brother Herbert in Calcutta at the Lovelock and Lewes firm that Arthur later chaired. After leaving Oxford Arthur had set his heart on a career in the civil service, but he had not taken a degree in his favourite subject, in which he had excelled at the Royal Naval College. His masters there had exhausted the number of gold medals for classical scholarship which they could award Arthur. Winning a maths scholarship to Oxford, he opted for the mathematics that might have introduced him to remarkable storytellers like Charles Dodgson but brought him little kudos at graduation. Denying himself the first class degree in Classics that the civil service had required, he took a third and settled for the family firm. He had been an excellent classical scholar and an able mathematician, but he did not seek the relative comfort of remaining in Oxford as a don. His morale had been dampened by an uncharacteristic error of being absent from his exam for the civil service. In those circumstances the firm of Lovelock and Lewes was an attractive alternative, however far away it might be. A series of return trips from Calcutta to Southampton created his first meeting with Elsie, then Elsie Robertson. In 1909 Elsie made her voyage from Tilbury to Sydney on the Aberdeen & Commonwealth's vessel, the *Multoon*. She had just completed her postgraduate course at Queen's Square with distinction; the family fold beckoned as her father lay dying of tuberculosis.

Arthur stood out from the rest of the passengers on the *Multoon*. There may well have been ladies' egg-and-spoon races on the ship or protracted sessions of housey-housey, both being popular pastimes. If this was so, then Elsie probably plumped for Mr Lewes's intellect, bearing, good looks and voice which she might have heard on deck, partly because

Arthur was unlikely to be found shouting 'house' below it. On such a trip he finished his twice-yearly leave in England and noted that he had met a 'young lady with whom I talked at length'. In those days the *Multoon's* crossing to Sydney would have taken some six weeks. Arthur had embarked at Marseilles in order to avoid the longer and rougher voyage via the Bay of Biscay, but he would still have had ample opportunity to befriend Elsie before disembarking at Calcutta. Ladies' egg-and-spoon races would have had few heats because most of the passengers on the *Multoon* were men going out to join the Colonial Service. At Port Said many of them trooped off to watch the locals belly-dancing; Arthur remained on board. Elsie delighted in his 'wonderful resonant voice'; her first impressions were that he was either a nobleman or a minister, or an amalgam of the two. The chartered accountant replied that her chosen career of nursing, 'was the noblest profession that a woman could have'. Before Arthur disembarked at Port Said for Calcutta he made a request, 'Miss Robertson, you will let me know how your father is?' It was difficult not to comply.

Jock's parents corresponded almost daily. In those days frequent correspondence was usual, but, even by the standards of the time, theirs was profuse, continuing even when they were apart for only a few days. Elsie, based in Sydney, wrote to Arthur who lived at the Bengal Club in Calcutta. For the next few years correspondence became as lengthy as the conversations on the *Multoon*. Winning a mate can be a risky business, not least for a Victorian gentleman who had been brought up to overcome any vulnerability that he might have felt, except in the face of God. At the Bengal Club, Arthur had whiled away the hours playing duets and chamber music with German bachelor friends of whom he was especially fond. The Club, for all its attractions and mod cons, was unlikely to keep him forever in Calcutta. Eventually, too, Arthur tired of those members that were determined to rot their livers with brandy; but he still made it his base for the next fourteen years. It may not have been easy to give up the comfort of the Club, except on leave. His loyal manservant, his khansamah, attended to most needs and accompanied Arthur to the cooler climes of Darjeeling that afforded a welcome respite from the incredible heat. David Lewes, Jock's youngest sibling, remembered that 'both men gave great respect to one another' and Arthur's khansamah 'never broke one piece of crockery in twenty-five years of service, and never forgot to pay a scribe to write letters of gratitude for his pension during the next twenty-five.'

Moderation was a policy with Arthur. Once married, his accountancy skills kept all household spending in check. Before he wed Elsie in 1911, 'All things in moderation' was a maxim that was taken to extremes when, after two years of happy correspondence with Elsie, Arthur was somewhat economic with the truth about the reason for his projected voyage to Elsie's native Australia. The pretext for his visit was to stay with distant relatives in Melbourne, but 'he never visited his relations but ploughed onto Sydney in order to seek out Elsie Robertson'. Arthur located the young nurse at Dorrigo and 'gave notice of his visit to her sisters with whom she was staying'. Elsie may have been under the impression that Arthur was just making a brief stop along his itinerary. Elsie's mother and sisters were intrigued by the letters that had been arriving from Arthur. On his envelopes the 'E' for Elsie was written with a certain flourish, and he had quickly become known as 'the "E" man'. Elsie protected the nature of the correspondence for a time by announcing, 'Oh, he's a married man.' She was certainly impressed by Arthur's intellectual capacity and politesse; her natural love and affection for him had been sealed in correspondence.

In setting about winning Elsie's hand Arthur had not only to undertake the ocean crossing to Australia, he also had to embrace an entirely new culture in the outback. Dorrigo was a long way from the niceties of the Bengal Club: setting out for Dorrigo meant a journey of some distance by road. Arthur was met by one of Elsie's brothers-in-law, Jack Edgley, recently returned from the war with a DSO. A sartorially elegant Arthur, David remembered, was 'spruced up in his best outfit squeezed into Jack's sulky with pristine leather bags that were bundled into the trap'. The two men broke their journey at an inn and enjoyed their meal; whether Arthur was as enthusiastic about the limited accommodation is less certain: they had to share a double bed. Arthur's youngest child recalls that 'this austere and gentle Englishman took it all in good spirit, spurred on by his objective of winning Elsie's hand'. The journey might have seemed rather testing for Arthur when Jack pulled his shotgun out of the trap, shooting rabbits and other game (for fellow pioneers) as they wound their way to Dorrigo.

Jock was brought up by a father who was parsimonious but also capable of the occasional bout of excess. Arthur and Jack were greeted by the beautiful and well-turned-out Molly Edgley at Dorrigo. Without much ado Arthur proposed to Molly's sister who accepted; the immediate problem was not the cost of the wedding ring 'but when to get married'. Elsie had been sent to Sydney to purchase a ring and later informed Arthur that she had chosen the most beautiful and, incidentally, the most expensive ring in the whole display. After they had married in Strathfield Church, the couple honeymooned in the Blue Mountains. As if there wasn't enough haze already, caused by the eucalyptus vapour that produced the blue light in the region, Arthur decided to pack half a dozen bottles of champagne, breaking once again with his principle of moderation. A suite of rooms was taken at Wentworth Falls. Carping relations, who had warned 'marry in haste and repent at leisure' were royally entertained but also silenced by the delicious food and wine that was served at the Australia Hotel before the newly wedded couple sailed for London to enjoy the remainder of Arthur's leave. On their return to India they rented a little house in Calcutta for the next few years; Elizabeth was born in June 1912 and Jock arrived one and a half years later. The youngest, David, was born in Sydney in 1915.

Jock was named John as a baby and was christened on 24 March 1914. Arthur and Elsie, who were together in Calcutta for their first two years of marriage, might well have noted this day as special. Later on Jock would have certainly made the day of his baptism a red-letter day, because it marked the staging of the Oxford and Cambridge Boat Race when Jock was President of the Oxford crew exactly thirty-three years later. Arthur would have remembered that day also because it was St Thomas's Day: when Elsie brought Jock towards the font of St Paul's Cathedral, Calcutta, the Reverend R.H. Stuart, who was performing the ceremony, had the temerity to suggest that they name their son Thomas after the saint. Arthur dispossessed the Reverend of this idea swiftly and surely, for no son of his would be allowed to present the minister with an opportunity to celebrate a doubting Thomas. The proud parents called their son after the 'graciousness of God', John; they were not bringing their son into the world for faithlessness.

Jock was brought up at a distance by his father, who remained in Calcutta for most of the first eight years of Jock's life. Arthur was conscious of the physical separation that existed between himself and his family and made considerable efforts to share his life in India with Jock and Elizabeth, as his illustrated letters to the children suggest. For someone with his background he showed imagination in attempting to entertain his children from afar. His letters are good learning aids in that they educated Jock in the life of the last days of the Raj; he was allowed into his father's world. The boy received stories of wild animals that tested the bravest of hunters. To an illustration that he had sent Jock, Arthur added his own caption: 'The man with a gun will have to be careful, for if he misses it will be Mr Tiger's turn, and he won't shoot because Father is a long way off and he wants his boy to do it for him.' Arthur did not forget to finish the letter with

'God bless you my son: here is my love and kiss from your loving father.' This was a far cry of hope and affection, but a far cry from the absence of love that Arthur had experienced when he was five. He sent coloured drawings of tigers and crocodiles to his son and tropical flowers to his daughter. Political correctness did not enter into his Edwardian outlook on life, and the children appeared not to suffer from his thoughtful and stimulating missives! His enthusiasm for and love of learning was to make a powerful impact on all his children. Yet Arthur could not monitor all the activities of his sons at school; he was unaware that David's ingenuity had outwitted the requirements of the first public telephone system. The boy had managed to rig up a long piece of cardboard sturdy enough to insert into the phone's coin slot resulting in unlimited calls across hundreds of miles of brand new telegraph poles.

Arthur was not culled like so many of his generation at Gallipoli. When he had presented himself for recruitment in 1914, he slipped through the net of military service when an incorrect medical examination forced him back into 'civvy' street. He had served at Dum Dum barracks where he contracted amoebic dysentery. Later, Elsie's cousin, Ruth Steel, who was in charge of a field hospital at Gallipoli, may well have informed Arthur how fortunate he had been in having a wrong diagnosis: he appeared to be diabetic as there was far too much sugar in his urine sample; military service was out of the question. It was fortunate for Jock that his father possessed all the symptoms of the condition, but in fact only suffered from a low renal threshold. Arthur abstained from sugar for the rest of his life and Jock retained a father who could continue to guide him from the Bengal Club.

Jock learned to endure a spartan regime at home. On his retirement in 1923, Arthur made his last journey to Bowral from Calcutta and his family adjusted to new routines and habits. David observed that the severity of his father's disposition, as Arthur swept into the Serpentine Drive, was such that he 'cleared off quickly, and well out of the way. I think he was a serious–minded man who was so given to abstract thought and contemplation, unmoved in many ways by the trite and trivial aspects of life; he certainly possessed sterling qualities.' He was stern: Elizabeth and her brothers were made to walk the mile and a half to the early service and back 'without passing food to mouth'; this was not uncommon at the time. The combination of walks, faith and abstinence were later to play a great part in Jock's military career.

Jock grew up to respect the needs of others. Arthur often practised what he preached, and ten percent of his sizeable income was automatically donated to the Church each year. In the years of the Depression when the children were just in their teens, Jock never saw a hungry stranger turned away at the door; wandering victims of the economic crash left Fernside after a hearty meal that Elsie gladly provided. David remembered that his parents' unselfishness had a direct influence on Jock who, having a strong sense of selfhood, never forgot the needs of those around him, especially those who were dependants. Arthur and Elsie strove hard to instil into their children their own pursuit of excellence: 'Their integrity, high ideals and generosity to others were captured by Jock and made part of his own nature.' Jock did sometimes challenge the authority of his father, for the boys enjoyed breaking the laws of home and country on more than a few occasions, but David later recalled, 'Jock conformed more easily and consequently absorbed more of the homilies and philosophy. He usually managed to evade punishment through a combination of experience and intelligence,' and more often than not because he did not have to suffer the personality clash that David experienced with his father.

The Lewes family usually enjoyed excellent health. At Fernside Daisy the cow provided fresh milk daily and, although food was never wasted, there was always plenty of everything. Bowral, where the ferns not only provided shade but also a moist environment, was cooler than neighbouring

Sydney; nonetheless the sun was a welcome ingredient in what was mainly an outdoor life. Jock grew stronger each year on the philosophy that his father knew would not fall on deaf ears, and a lifestyle that a wealthy chartered accountant could provide. Elsie Lewes, granddaughter of the Reverend Steel, had trained at the Royal Prince Albert Hospital in Sydney as a nurse and taken a postgraduate course in England at Queen's Square Hospital, which was in the forefront of neurological research. Her love and care of her children with expert skills were needed on more than one occasion. Elsie delivered her youngest herself and David might have died of pneumonia but for Daisy's milk and Mother's nursing. Jock, like David, courted danger from an early age, and a hand that was both benevolent and patient healed wounds inflicted by experiments and pranks conducted by the boys.

The young Jock was surrounded by beauty that would elevate any spirit. He was two when his parents purchased Fernside, and the roughness of the outdoors was complemented by the serenity and charm of the gardens there. The Serpentine Drive was designed by the original owner, a German philosopher called Dr Robinson. The doctor had planted every tree that was mentioned in the Bible, including the Hollyman Tree. This suited Arthur and Elsie well and may have been one reason for Arthur's decision to purchase Fernside. David remembered how the garden 'lifted any heart and mind': it was a treasure for Jock whose great benefit was that he shared it with a family who realized how fortunate they were to enjoy such beauty. The flora and fauna at Fernside have continued to be well appreciated and maintained, and with the skill of other occupants have become one of Australia's most prized gardens; paddocks, fields and ferns continue to provide an ideal place for a boy to grow, and so it was for Jock. Roses adorned the summerhouse; there was a magical walk from the lawns; pond, fir and nut trees overlooked the wilderness where Daisy would graze at the edge of the estate by Captain Broadbent's farm: mythical groves for an idyllic setting for the myriad of fairies to entertain the main characters of Arthur's fairytale, *Hollyman*. Work on Fernside with its sixteen acres was completed by an architect and great friend of the family, Herbert Denis; it was a house that could be afforded in the comfortable days before the Depression. Kerosene lamps were lit by Jock and David before electricity was connected.

Jock, with his eighteen-month seniority, became the clear leader of the two boys, always ready to advise his younger brother: 'He inherited his mother's devotion, caring, unselfishness, and in a sense his mother's subservience to the overriding authority of his father.' Jock shared David's view of their mother, when in adulthood he claimed that his great friend, David Winser, 'possessed a mother who was more thoughtful about others than anyone he knew except Elsie Lewes'. David recalled that 'the discipline that Jock showed in his short life was undoubtedly instilled by my father. We were indeed a David and Jonathan'. The boys would fight occasionally; as a small boy David, who was also the youngest of a large collection of cousins, could be found tied to a tree with the collaboration of an older brother, sister or cousin, but as the years went by Jock would always stand up for his brother's fair treatment irrespective of the size of the antagonist. David remembered Jock's decision-making and initiative. When Jock was sent to Hayfield Preparatory School in Carlingford near Sydney, David missed him greatly. He may have wished that he had the protection of his brother against his own father whose fury could be vented on him, and more so when he was on his own. Sometimes he may have deserved to be on the receiving end of Arthur's spleen as it was he who involved Jock in trouble more than the other way around.

Jock seemed to be carried along by Arthur's narrow gauge of moral conduct while David frequently derailed. Records of behaviour were the most highly prized reports in the Lewes household. Poor conduct was followed by two-hour lectures;

Horatio Nelson's words were often quoted: 'Thank God I have done my duty.' With a half-inch-thick, four-foot-long cane poor conduct was beaten out of the boys; David was the recipient in most cases. On one occasion Arthur's beating led to David losing fingernails on his hand when he had tried to intercept the fourth of the six strokes that he received. Elsie would defend the boys, in spite of being somewhat repressed by the patriarch's powerful intellectual, moral, spiritual and religious influence. She willingly changed her whole nature as a very happy-go-lucky, fun-loving woman to become the servant of this scholarly man who was eleven years her senior. Personal confessions were offered by the children to their mother rather than their father. Jock towed the line fairly punctiliously. Arthur viewed David as a child who would never leave his mother's 'confessional box'. David considered that 'Jock had a more organized life than I did . . . he listened to my father and clearly followed my father's moral behaviour without kicking over the traces and the trouble that ensued.' It was not that the older brother did not have plenty of courage, but rather that he was good at listening; the messages were mostly worth listening to. David concluded, 'The discipline moulded Jock's character to a remarkable degree, to the extent that he owed his father a great debt, hard and harsh though some of these messages were.'

Arthur and Elsie made their children's way straight. It may well have been the horror of the Great War that helped Arthur Lewes to fire the imagination of his children, in order to protect them from the incredible disillusion and despair that much of the world suffered long after the Armistice. Arthur was a voracious reader but soon turned his hand to creative writing as well, and from 1918 his letters home included extracts from his fairytale, *Hollyman*, named after the evergreen shrub which adorned his beautiful Fernside garden in Bowral. In the serialized story this was no ordinary Holly, but a magical imp who helped to serve and guide two children, Peter and Mary. Performing magic in the beautiful grounds of Fernside, Hollyman shrank in size and led the children inside the mysterious garden by shrinking them too, but not without first providing them with a moral template with which to return to their usual blessed state of life. This was a story of the quest for earthly paradise in the great tradition of Parsifal and Sir Gawain and the Green Knight.

Thirty years before, Arthur had been introduced to Alice Liddell by her father who was Dean and Head of Arthur's Oxford College, Christ Church. Arthur was acquainted with 'Lewis Carroll', Charles Dodgson, who was a fellow mathematician as well as the celebrated author of *Alice In Wonderland*. Dodgson, the scholar and don, had inspired a convert to the fairy tale without ever knowing it; Arthur's collection of extracts to Jock, his sister and brother were privately published in Calcutta in 1923. The absentee father of three children might have appeared to put chartered accountancy before family, but if that was so he was spending most of the leisure hours that God gave him to encourage the young Leweses to live up to their family motto, 'As Wise as a Serpent and as Gentle as a Dove.'

2

Youth

'As Wise as a Serpent and as Gentle as a Dove'
– Lewes family motto.

Jock seemed to have absorbed his father's fairy tales and homilies because in late February 1926 he wrote that:

> I have not forgotten my eight points, because I say them over each night. They are as follows:
>
> Love God as our father
> Keep your face to the light
> Tell the truth at all costs
> Think of others
> Forget yourself
> Stick up for the weak
> Play the game
> Take your beating like a man

It was not extraordinary for such strictures to be preached to adolescent boys. What was perhaps rare was a youth's desire to be so committed to the rules of guidance as young Jock seems to have been. Arthur probably enumerated his edicts when Jock was a lad of ten or eleven. Jock may have become aware of their importance in late 1925 for he informed his father that 'the days of last term were very slow because I was lazy'. It was as if he guessed that his father wished to be both parent and minister rolled into one – a father-confessor who expected Jock to be honest about his shortcomings. This relationship between father and son, mirrored in Jock's correspondence, was established early on in Jock's life at home when the two were separated. The previous September he had drawn a Star of David representing Arthur's Eight Points at the bottom of his letter with a little note, 'I remember.' Jock's parents needed to know his heart and mind and he responded in what was then a short fortnightly letter in large well formed handwriting. The eldest son still managed to have some fun in between reciting family codes and tables because he proudly proclaimed in December 1925 that, 'at the end of term everyone dresses up and I am going as a pirate'. The escapist role as a marauder would have been a welcome break from the discipline exerted from afar.

Arthur had a sense of being destined for greatness, and imparted it. He was guided more by the Stoics than by his own parents and steered by his love of the classics. He relied heavily on Christian mores, even if they had not always been upheld by the chorus of disapproval that had met his birth. From an early age Jock would listen to his father who would read Plato and Aristotle in the original. Owen Dibbs, a school friend of Jock's, recently wrote of Arthur's scholarship:

> I was most impressed by his reading: he would wait till we were all settled down for the night, then retire to his study and his special desk with the current volume propped on a reading stand. It was always one of the Greek classics – I wondered why he would want to read anything that solid for the second or third time! I think he usually read till around dawn.

To his loyal and supportive wife, Elsie, Arthur would never fail to read aloud a chapter from the Bible every day. Elizabeth, Jock's older sister, recently suggested that her mother endured this well. If mother was so diligent in Bible study, it is not surprising that Jock also absorbed a strong sense of morality. Arthur took comfort in Jock and

Elizabeth's developing 'map' of how the minds of the ancient philosophers worked. A proud father and mother attended prize-giving at the King's School, Parramatta, where the popular but powerful headmaster E.M.Baker awarded fourteen-year-old Jock with the Divinity Prize; prizes were presented with the help of such local dignitaries as Rear Admirals or Generals. This particular prize would have given Arthur great pleasure because he had won the equivalent honours himself a generation before at the Royal Naval College, Greenwich.

These were auspicious and hopeful beginnings for a new generation that still had yet to embrace the aftermath of war. R.C.Sherriff was preparing to write *Journey's End* when the easy optimism about warfare and peacemaking had turned to disillusion. War could never be glorified in the same way but in the face of violence and intolerance duty was still highly prized and 'sticking it because it's the only decent thing a man can do'. Arthur would have approved of such prize-givers since in one of his illustrated letters to his sons he had coloured in a fine portrait of Admiral Beatty and highly recommended that his little boy, David, should emulate the naval leader's qualities: 'His name is David. You must try to be brave and good just like him'. In 1927 Jock received a copy of Hyde's *Favourite Greek Myths* and he won the prize the following year. Over this period it was no accident that Greek and Divinity won him the best accolades in Baker's end-of-term-reports: Arthur's expectations for all his children knew few bounds, and Jock managed to follow in his father's foot-steps. As he progressed at King's, chemistry was another subject in which he excelled with an 'A' grade that was 'better than expected', and an important reason for this was that his other academic mentor was none other than his younger brother David, who was fast becoming a fine chemist and also an alternative but very different influence from Arthur.

Jock was indoctrinated with a Christianity that was tinged sometimes with more than a hint of Puritanism. Learning not to shirk the hardest tasks and chores around the family home was in many ways an invaluable initiation into the demands that life would one day make on him and his siblings. Not all the family found life as wholesome as Arthur, and David, rather than Jock, fought the harsher codes and edicts of their father. Arthur's notes for the speech he gave at his daughter's school, Frensham, reveal that he rose to the occasion when addressing youth in general. He was invited to Frensham to propose the toast of the School and Fellowship and spoke of the opening of their new Hartfield House as 'the breathing space and as one looks back on the ground gained, it presses steadily on'. Perhaps some of Arthur's qualities as a leader, held in abeyance a decade before by his military medical, were unleashed on his largely female audience during his speech on 28 April 1925. He was a fine-looking man with great intellect, and he might well have struck a chord with the ladies present when he reiterated his admiration for the Suffragette Movement. This strong tradition of a Christian ethos within the family was not unusual amongst Arthur's contemporaries, although that April he confided to the Frensham girls and their school mistresses that 'In Church early on this last Easter morning I suddenly realized to my shame that there were at least ten women to one man: that rough proportion, I fear, is no exception but the general rule.' Then again perhaps some of the absentee males had not enjoyed Arthur's good fortune in avoiding campaigns like Gallipoli and of retaining their faith with which they had first entered the war. If that was so, Jock Lewes was also fortunate to possess a father whose convictions, ideals and vision had not been personally shaken to the core.

Jock developed his parents' talent for writing. Letters home survive from as early as 1924 when he wondered if he might join the Navy; he enthused about his career hopes in early March that year. He had enjoyed a school trip to view the fleet at Jervis Bay. For weeks Jock had referred to the proposed visit in his correspondence. Finally the day came in early

April. Afterwards he declared, 'There were not many boys who saw the 15" gun working so I count myself lucky.' This was the time of the Treaty of Locarno when Britain, France and Germany signed pacts guaranteeing their security, the League of Nations no longer able confidently to do so itself. Militarism was alive and well, yet the Kellogg-Briand pact of 1928 would outlaw war three years later and be signed by over sixty countries but hope in the League was already fading when peace in the world was threatened again. There were still places in the Dominion fleet for cadets from King's School, Parramatta. Within a year however, Jock was setting his sights on a scholarly youth and rejected the Navy because 'I want to work hard enough to go to Oxford.' He set to with this enterprise by reading *The Waverley Novels*, 'so I have many good friends.' Three weeks later he informed his parents that '*The Fair Maid of Perth* is simply glorious.'

If Jock did not fully appreciate his good fortune at the time of Arthur's toast at Frensham six years earlier, he must have begun to by 1931, when he sent his parents a full breakdown of his exam timetable, a post-mortem of his answers, and a report on how he had fared, enclosing examples of his exam papers. The reader is left with the impression that he cared very much what his parents thought of him, and that he wanted to express his deep love and gratitude to them. He let them into his world in the same way that they had opened up their lives to him. Jock surely felt that this was expected of him and so in November 1931 he sent the Greek paper, a favourite of Arthur's; he had been asked to translate how Thrasybulus 'resolved to distinguish himself greatly in the war with Sparta and deliver Athens with his small band'. Arthur would no doubt have approved of Professors Woodhouse and Hobbs's choice of the paper's content for the King's School examination.

Jock and David escaped the sometimes oppressive nature of their strict beginnings; the Victorian patriarchy that dominated the home did not always rule supreme. Occasionally

Plato was read aloud for the benefit of non-classicists within the Robertson fold. However, Elsie's cousins and grand-children displayed not only a gaiety but also a force of personality that more than matched Arthur's. Vivacious and earthy cousin Joy, who usually wore the same red hat every day, was cloistered in the dining room with Arthur who was reading from the original Greek when she barked at him, 'Arthur! Put that book away! Put that silly book away!' Jock and David revelled in the fact that their father rather sheep-ishly did so; they were quietly amused, and when cousin Joy was not there to provide a little mirth they created it them-selves by arranging pony rides, picnics or shooting competitions. Each year the two boys would compete for the silver trophy that Arthur provided: the Home Cup was inscribed with the victor of the shooting competition at home and sometimes at the King's School summer cadet camp. Both Jock and David were eligible for the camp in 1931, but Jock followed at least two of his eight points – that he had deter-mined to live by for the past six years – when he offered to support his parents at home:

> It would mean giving up our whole holidays. But that means that you are alone at home. I think the best idea is to let one go for camp and one stay at home. In that case it would be best for me to stay with you at home since I could do more work with you.

Jock and his brother became good amateur jockeys. Creamy Billy, Lassie and Jack were the Lewes's ponies: Jack was fifteen hands high and belonged to Jock, because he was the eldest. Riding on their ponies, the three children were able to taste the freedom of the outback well beyond the Fernside estate. Adventure was a magical element of their lives, and more so in adolescence. As soon as the summer holidays began, Jock and David would catch the train from Parramatta and smoke a whole packet of cigarettes in a foggy compartment.

They would then arrive home to a warm welcome with tea on the lawn laid out on a comfortable rug with none of the adults any the wiser. Daily expeditions would be planned. The Steindl brothers might be invited to stay, and all the boys would look after Elizabeth's friends from Frensham if they visited for the day. Trips would be made to Blue Crane Valley, Cordeaux Creek situated a few miles from Berrima Gaol, Mount Jellore or Fitzroy Falls. These were the favourite picnicking spots of the Lewes children and their cousins, Peggy and Mary, who had lived at Fernside during the war. Expeditions set out at about 10 a.m. with Jock riding Jack, David on Lassie and Elizabeth on Twinkle; after two hours of riding the party watered their beasts in the shade and amused themselves before lunch. Fine views were enjoyed, rabbits chased, pools swum in and mushrooms picked. Cordeaux Creek offered excellent views of the Blue Mountains. The Lewes brothers with their cheap Box Brownie cameras took great pleasure in recording many of their adventures.

Jock and David's ability to make use of their environment allowed them to enjoy glorious days together. Diaries of the period suggest they were well aware of the blessings of their lives at home and school: Elsie would expertly pack a 'plenteous dinner' of sandwiches and chops that could be fried up. At Mount Jellore the ponies would be tethered at Paper Tree Grove, which afforded lush grass and shade. The hot hikes up the mountain were rewarded with a victorious climb on the trig. station that marked the peak; the boys were relieved that 'coming down was a lot easier than going up'. The animals would be watered again and when it became cooler the party would head back in time for supper and an early night so that plans for another trip could be talked through before lights out. Fitzroy Falls offered great opportunities for mushroom picking and a substantial lunch at Fitzroy House; with energy still left the posse of pony riders, sometimes numbering as many as ten, would create human pyramids with the boys usually forming the burdened base. When the group reached home badminton might be set up, competitions held and a fine supper laid out in the summerhouse. If the boys wanted to have adventures at home there was always a rabbit burrow to dig up at Captain Broadbent's farm; rabbits were shot along with the occasional black and poisonous snake.

Arthur wanted his sons to join the professions even at the risk of their becoming dangerously over-qualified. Before he was taught with Jock at the King's School, David was sent off to Hayfield Preparatory rather than to the local school. It was a mixed blessing to be away from home and the love and care of their mother whose apron strings were still not entirely cut. When Jock moved up to the senior school David was temporarily on his own again and left to his own devices; 'Dave' became a promising chemist barely before he was out of shorts and into long trousers at the senior school. His father provided him with the necessary chemicals but was unaware that they were to be used in a series of experiments that escalated in entertainment and danger. Arthur Lewes rarely discovered the exact nature of David's extracurricular activities and showed a great deal of trust in offering his son most of the chemicals that could only be found under lock and key in the King's School laboratory.

It hardly occurred to Arthur that the extra facilities that he had provided would not be used carefully to push forward the frontiers of schoolboy science, aware that he was that some degree of danger was all part of the learning process. The potassium chlorate and hydrochloric acid that both the Lewes brothers used encouraged them to experiment with originality throughout their lives. Their association in using gunpowder was the training ground for Jock's later innovation in developing the 'time-pencil' and 'sticky' or Lewes Bomb in the fledgling SAS in North Africa. David was to take the Hippocratic Oath in his twenties, discover rare heart diseases, and become an inventor himself; NASA took his method of testing heart rates up to space.

The fellow brothers in crime discovered that potassium

chlorate and sulphur produced far more satisfying explosive displays than ordinary gunpowder. 'Performances' were occasionally provided for spellbound schoolboys whose gambling competitions with local snails paled into insignificance when compared with this spectacular entertainment. Old brass .303 cartridges were emptied, percussion caps blown out and packed with the Lewes ingredients, not forgetting the essential trails of gunpowder necessary for detonation. The results were 'tremendous'. At Junior House David recalled that 'the cartridge cases disappeared before my very eyes'. Not content merely to repeat popular and successful displays, David and Jock would diversify and escalate the explosions and so realize Arthur's expectations of the boys' training, or at least a part of it.

'Wait awhile', Arthur's favourite refrain to help his sons develop patience, had little impact on the boys' use of pyrotechnics. Jock usually benefited from the high levels of excitement that were to be gained from taking part in what now were becoming illegal 'demos'. Eventually he and David became casualties. Cartridges were buried below the surface of the ground and then ignited so that if you were standing on the same surface you could look forward to being raised at least 'six inches off the ground'. A demonstration at Junior House one Sunday led to brass shrapnel being dispersed between David's leg and another boy's arm; the fact that David was wounded may well have led to his being shown clemency – with the result that experiments continued to be mounted. He was forgiven and even earned a paragraph in the school magazine.

Jock was still fascinated by this and, although David had been gated at school, the brothers continued learning through trial and error, with almost fatal results. Blowing huge boulders up into the air was less hazardous than making their own cartridge-bombs. At about the age of twelve Jock nearly lost his life packing brass cartridges with the Lewes mixture along with a six-inch nail and a block of wood. The results were devastating. Auntie Molly and Jock's friend, Owen Dibbs, were not far away when they heard a deafening blast. Owen cried out, "I'm hit! I'm hit!" David thought that his brother had lost his left hand which 'looked just like a piece of raw meat'; there was also a deep red rent in his trousers. The instigator of the experiment, David, merely suffered a bit of brass that had nicked his own trousers. Owen Dibbs, later a Group Captain in the Royal Australian Air Force, identified David as the culprit:

> John stayed with us at Wyong River. We had great fun loading our cannon (about 10cm) and trying to sink a roughly made target galleon. We were most careful to use the simple old-fashioned powder: ground charcoal, flowers of sulphur and saltpetre sodium nitrate. This was stable and could be rammed down quite hard when loading. Next holidays David got all upset because we would not let him use our cannon. John discovered David out on the back porch with his own gun: a .303, brass cartridges clipped down to a hunk of wood, and a touchhole he had knocked in with a nail. Nothing would convince him it was dangerous, so John set out to demonstrate, loading it and firing from a long wick. We were sitting opposite each other while he rammed the wad home with a wooden rod. But David had omitted to warn us that he had not used gunpowder, but mixed his own using potassium chlorate instead of saltpetre.

The mixture was very unstable and Lewes bombs were dearly won. David recalled that half of Jock's hand was 'a tangled mess of blood and fingers'. After Dr Harbisson's expert surgery, Jock was only to suffer one shortened little finger. Owen thought it was a miracle because 'Harbisson was a dreadful doctor but cleaned us up well'. Elizabeth announced to her father, when Arthur returned on the day of the explosion, that 'David and John have had a little accident'. True to his nature, Arthur Lewes never moved a muscle when he heard how he had nearly lost a brace of sons. Evidently he became used to the young chemists when some years later he returned home to hear a large explosion half a mile from Fernside, and then confided that he had uttered to himself, 'The boys are gone'.

David had not in fact disposed of himself or his brother, but other activities would certainly keep their parents on their toes. Arthur was much more upset with his sons in an incident when, returning from a business trip, he discovered that Jock and David had helped themselves to his best port and cigars. Then he had punished them by demanding an apology of hundreds of lines that had to be penned in Greek. No such sanctions were imposed on the young Lewes bombers. Jock and David used to ride out on their ponies, armed with small packs of explosive, and would select targets in the neighbourhood of Bowral. Owen Dibbs records that selection of targets was made easy when 'two or three homes in one street objected nastily to the noise we made having gallops past their gates. Revenge comprised getting out at night on the horses, dropping big home-made Chinese crackers in their mailboxes and taking off at full speed.' The saboteurs had clearly been successful at times, because one victim had created a detachable mailbox that could be slid out of its holding post and removed after the mail had arrived. The locale adapted to the spate of destruction, but unpopular neighbours still bore the brunt of their operations. One of the local hotels received twice the weight of explosive because of the patron's superiority complex, and in spite of the fact that the hotel's immediate neighbour was the police station.

The Sydney population had already experienced some of the Lewes mischief. Unsuspecting pedestrians would go along their well-trodden route to shop in the city and unbeknown to them the hedgerows provided adequate cover for two boys, one gas Bunsen burner and a handful of pennies. Coins were heated up and kept red hot until an unfortunate shopper approached; a penny was then tossed on the ground from behind the hedge. Whoops of delight met the cries of the duped citizen after he had tried to pick up the innocent-looking currency; the coin was usually left on the street to be collected later. There was the double risk that the boys would not only be caught but also be out of pocket. However, they usually had an escape route planned, so, at worst, many hours of entertainment could be enjoyed at the cost of a few pennies. Not long afterwards Arthur had discovered the wanton destruction of a dozen croquet mallets whose heads had been blown off by small piles of explosive powder that ignited at a touch. The mind boggles as to how David and Jock managed to explain the mallet heads away. Strangely, Arthur never severely punished them for the chemical experiments, which today would have most parents throwing their hands up in horror.

The school chemistry prizes that David started to win year after year funded the brothers' love of shooting. Two guineas bought him his .22 rifle that enabled him and Jock to compete for the Home Shooting cup. Targets were fixed, positions taken some fifty yards away and the brothers turned themselves into marksmen; Jock undoubtedly benefited from the fact that David was a keen shot. The latter, however, again seemed destined to encourage Jock to join him in putting his life in jeopardy; this time blank cartridges provided entertainment and danger. Sporting a borrowed pistol and a pocketful of blanks, the two climbed the tallest pine at Fernside and proceeded to terrorize the neighbourhood, which was at its wit's end as to the source of the repetition of loud reports from a powerful-sounding gun. As it happened, the Lewes brothers had unwittingly disturbed a poacher in the Fernside paddock, who, seeing the puffs of smoke emanating from the tree, returned accurate live fire from his .22 rifle. Bullets whizzed amongst the branches, but Jock and David emerged later a little wiser and unscathed.

The cadet corps at King's expedited Jock and David's conspicuous interest in things military. Jock climbed the ranks to cadet Lieutenant, and he assisted the commander of the school cadet corps. David remembers Jock's ability to strip a Lewis gun that consisted of a considerable number of parts. He was timed as he stripped and reassembled the weapon at record speed. On cadet camp he developed stamina as well as skills, for during the summer of 1932 he wrote how, 'We mean to work to a timetable that we drew up so that we shall not be over or underworked – so that we first learn to stick to it no matter how tired we are and when we have the grit then we polish up our knowledge and technique'. Owen Dibbs recalled both his and Jock's knowledge and prescience regarding tactics between the World Wars:

> Over the years, John and I, often with one or two stout hearts, had really studied – I think we knew Field Service Manual better than our tables, could clean and reassemble Lewis and Vickers guns blindfold, and all that. We were convinced that the army would go into battle next time with no more ideas or tactics than they finished WW1 with. We discussed and developed the idea of what became known as the Commandos: highly trained, light arms and ammunition, disguise, etc.
>
> At school cadet camps Lewes and I spent many evenings dreaming about the value of lightly armed, superlatively trained intruders behind enemy lines. The two of us organized a small raiding party of the King's School signallers in a series of successful night raids, even managing to capture the neutral judges of these exercises, who immediately deserted to the enemy.

The combination of careful planning and wreaking havoc confirmed in Jock's mind the value of the surprise attacks. This was the stuff of Roger's Rangers. One brave liaison officer tried to prevent the 'King's Commandos' from receiving an 'ear-bashing' by suggesting that the raiders may have spoiled the exercise by signalling its premature end – but wasn't that what it was all about? Shouldn't they be used to demonstrate their kind of warfare to the staff? The answer was no. The cadet Lieutenant experienced more than one dress rehearsal that night: he discovered that new ideas could easily be frowned upon. Over the next ten years, the Army continued to need new ideas, and Jock discovered that it would often greet them with a frown. The initiative of his cadet raiding party may well have confirmed in his mind the importance of the element of surprise in a military engagement, schoolboy or otherwise.

Music and drama remained safer school pursuits. The boys were inspired by the talents of their own father and played Schubert's 'Marche Militaire' on the piano at school concerts with David on the bass and Jock at the treble. They would then swap over and play Moszkovski's 'Spanish Dances' to ring the changes and liven up things yet further. Duets by Glinka were played, in spite of Arthur's previous caveat that 'Glinka is a mediocre composer'. The father changed his mind when he heard the boys' renditions. Drama was enjoyed by the boys, but Arthur was ambivalent about the virtues of the theatre. He regarded theatrical pursuits as a gross indulgence: 'Pushing oneself forward should be frowned upon.' This attitude is at odds with Arthur's keen attendance at the theatre, where his intellect may have been in conflict with more than a streak of Puritanism. Twenty years before he dissuaded his boys from treading the boards Arthur had been a regular visitor at the Garrick Theatre. Apart from seeing the classics he had also managed to watch Mrs Patrick Campbell as Dulcie Larondie in *The Masqueraders* at the end of April 1894, and Miss Blanche Massey as a Gaiety Girl at Prince of Wales Theatre five years later.

Perhaps he considered that an earlier relative of the Leweses, George Henry Lewes, had unwisely 'pushed himself forward' with theatre and free love, and by sharing his mistresses with Leigh Hunt and his name with George Eliot. It is possible Arthur had decided that it was the theatre that, in the wrong hands, could taint the human spirit. Jock's letters

33

to a sympathetic Elsie insisted that he play Mistress Quickly and David give vent to his sense of justice with Portia's courtroom scene. Their English master, P.C. Beaumont, informed them that they had only just obtained their roles 'by the skin of their teeth'. This almost certainly was made possible by the intervention of a more relaxed mother. If Arthur had been somewhat distrustful of his sons' ability to withstand the temptations of the theatre, he changed his mind after seeing the school productions. For John and David had 'achieved fine things on stage'. When Jock played a minor female role in *Macbeth* he wrote in mid-August 1929 that P.C. Beaumont told him, 'I was the best woman he had ever had and I would have been Mrs Macbeth had he known in time!'

Jock and his brother received homilies on women from Arthur, but they were considered somewhat misleading by David. Arthur did not wear his religion on his sleeve, but he did insist on praying, with the boys and any of their guests who would stay over in the evenings. David would often go to sleep in the middle of his father's talks and prayers but it is less likely that he did so when Arthur discussed women, and especially when he insisted that his sons regard any woman as a manifestation of the Virgin Mary. 'He tried to bury the idea that you could enjoy women fully in all senses.' David recalled that, in his anxiety to warn the boys of the dangers of women, Arthur created a gulf between them and females: no liberties of any kind should be taken with them. David viewed this with scepticism, and it had a reverse effect upon him. He was frightened of the opposite sex because of this gulf, but he yearned for them that much more because he had been asked to eschew them at all costs. This well-intentioned advice had in David's opinion a deleterious effect upon himself rather than his older brother. Jock on one occasion was propositioned by a wanton female, but was unable to do anything about it because he had enjoyed too many drinks. So he had not fully absorbed his father's strictures. Jock usually followed the dictum in the book that, 'whatever thy hand find thee to do, do it with all thy might.' In this instance his might did not rise to the occasion of the lady's bedchamber; Jock left in the virginal state in which he had entered.

David believed that his father's stern admonition against the wiles of women had within it the seeds of the wanton planted in himself. For Arthur had fallen in love with a married lady in his bachelor days. Elsie informed David after Arthur's death that his father may have done the very thing that he had advised his boys not to do. His conscience was so pricked by his own experience that he was probably expiating his own errors of commission so that his sons would not follow his example. This paternal inhibition prompted David rather than Jock to go the other way in his youth and take the liberties he had been warned against. However, Arthur did instruct his boys on the transmission of life and the facts of life in a layman's account. For someone who had not been given any such initiation in his own family, Arthur was certainly trying to break one cycle of non-communication. Jock, like most boys and girls, supplemented his knowledge of the 'birds and the bees' at school.

Jock's influence on the school rowing is recorded in his own hand in the King's School Archive, where all the hopes, techniques and training of the crew of 1933 are carefully laid out in diary form. Apart from his letters that return the compliment of writing skills in correspondence to his parents, this is the first indication of Jock the well-organized and gifted writer and recorder. Jock was Captain of Boats that year and he was determined to regain the Public School's Regatta trophy which King's had won the first year that they had entered the competition some ten years before. It is Jock's first journal that has survived and the School Archive Society is justly proud of it. It charts the development of a crew that attempts to match the skills of other school VIIIs that had been rowing with tried and tested rowing style for some time. In late 1932 the King's oarsmen had discussed the possibility of

35

switching their technique to the new 'Fairbairn' style, which was then popular. Orthodox styles emphasized a bright catch and steady slide work, but 'Fairbairn used methods that eliminated body lift, driving solely with the legs and using the slide quickly, carrying the body in a horizontal plane-like fashion.' The Scots and Grammar Schools had been successfully operating this method to their advantage and their crews were gelling well with it. It seems from Jock's account that the King's School benefited from this style, despite the fact that the 1st VIII only spent three and a half months testing it for themselves. Jock was clearly very ambitious and was supported by enthusiastic coaches and a crew who piloted the new orthodoxy.

Ambition and hard work sometimes led to Jock's intolerance of hesitant crew members. When the mock exam results came out in the spring of 1933 the King's bow bowed out of the boat to attend to his studies. Jock must have thought that the bow had lost his nerve, for he was dismissed in the rowing journal as a 'blithering idiot'. Perhaps the bow could not be assured of a place at his father's college of Christ Church as Jock almost certainly was. In the first round of the Great Public School's Regatta, the Maiden VIIIs, Jock's crew surprised writers in the Sydney papers. For the King's School, the lightest crew in the race, came second to Grammar by three feet. 'If the coxwain had not made a slight error in steering, the King's would have won', and the journalist added, 'It is unfortunate that this crew has drawn a heat in which the probable first and second in the final, St Joseph's and Shore, will be racing.' In the Maiden race the King's beat two other Fairbairn crews, Sydney University and Scots. The *Sydney Morning Herald* reported that the fine rowing that day had been 'a triumph for Fairbairners'. Jock's rowing report for the race was concluded with 'Lessons' to be learnt: 'Had we all held our finishes a little harder and longer Grammar would have finished a length behind us.' On 22 April, a few days before the race, the tipsters of the sport could only 'shut your eyes, take a pin and try to pick 'em'. On Wednesday 26 April, the day of race, the captain of the King's crew must have been disappointed for his VIII arrived late on their marks and Jock wrote that 'we failed to make a good start of it and lost a length on all crews . . . it was a good race, we could not have rowed better, the start excepted.'

Jock finished his detailed rowing diary with a brief but apposite epilogue that suggested important refinements necessary for the following year. His 'Hints to the Captain' suggest that some of the King's strong form may well have been smoothed out, not only by the strong encouragement of their committed coach, Mr Ernest Dorsch, who had complete confidence in his captain, but also by Jock's own usually fair but firm leadership:

> Take your job seriously and keep the crew well in hand without appearing to be officious. Talk to the crew in the boat when by yourselves and get them to talk and give their opinions. Always insist on strict discipline in the boat and in the handling of her. Make sure that everybody is content and act as peacemaker in arguments and quarrels. In time preserve the peace and equanimity of the crew. Always give your unbiased opinion to the coach when he asks for it and Never try to be facetious or funny in the boat to the coach, and Never sulk.

This balanced approach to resolving and preventing problems was unusual in a young man who was barely nineteen. Jock's team sports were very important to him and, though he worked very hard at school, recruiting, managing, organizing and encouraging a team with which he mixed was more important to him than studying. Yet he had gained his leaving certificate and, though not a scholar, impressed Gilbert Ryle, the Senior Censor at Christ Church, Oxford. Jock enjoyed his studies and finished his last term with letters about his approach towards the examinations. He wrote enthusiastically of his Oxbridge General Paper, 'See if you can guess which questions I did.' Question 9 concerned a subject that he had mulled over with Owen Dibbs: 'What new methods of warfare are likely to be adopted in the event of another war?' It is likely that he answered it. If the boy hadn't done so on paper, Oxford University would prepare the man before he achieved it on the battlefield.

PART 2

Manhood in Oxford
and Europe

3

Student

'A brighter lustre and a richer tone' – J.S.Lewes

Jock, a brown-haired, blue-eyed and lissom six foot, boarded the Aberdeen and Commonwealth Line's *Larg's Bay* in late August 1933. He teamed up with school friends, Nigel Piquet and Peter Willsallen, and the trio cleaned up most of the sporting trophies offered during the five-week voyage. Elizabeth, Jock's sister, in a recent interview, maintained that her elder brother modelled himself on Christ. Anyone who embraced the spartan regime of discipline at school and at home with Jock's tenacity might well have had to. Yet young Lewes seems to have enjoyed his sea passage to Southampton, as his letters home indicate. A year later his brother David made the same journey to England in the *Jervis Bay* before it was used in the heroic defence of Malta; David had finished a rugby tour of New South Wales but had not written about it or his own voyage to his older brother. Jock made fun of David's lack of correspondence by writing that he 'hoped you have had a stinking voyage. I'm looking forward to giving you a bloody good fist in the eye for not writing', and added that in compensation he wanted a 'ball by ball account each week'. By the end of his own travels Jock had cleared a whole room of teenage 'raucous raiders' with a fire extinguisher, dealing several of the party blows to the stomach. Information was proffered to his mother rather than to his father. The party had attempted to plunge Jock into a cold bath wearing only his underpants; the group had of course made sure this youthful celebration was witnessed by at least a bathroom full of teenage girls. Jock outwitted his opponents, preserved his modesty intact and subsequently helped lead the crazy gang into another unfortunate's cabin.

Perhaps Jock did sound all of his nineteen years when he wrote on 19 August, 'Peter has at last started to calm down and he is enjoying it immensely – silly boy – he should have realized it long ago; he used to wonder how I could enjoy myself so much, and although I repeatedly told him, he did not take any notice.' Jock and Peter would sometimes play the ship's officers at bucket quoits and deck-tennis, but Jock refused to play quoits with the vessel's doctor because 'he is such a bad sport'. The school sporting trio overcame such obstacles with Jock winning the tennis singles, 6–2; Jock and Nigel Piquet, losing the doubles final, 4–6; Nigel winning the deck billiards and Peter winning bucket quoits. Competitions over, there was more time for Jock to read his copy of *The Golden Treasury* on deck; favourite verse became the subject of conversation with a Major Adams. Jock and the major read each other their favourite verses. After listening to a rendition of 'The Burial of Sir John Moore at Corunna', Jock quizzed Major Adams on qualifying for the Army. The young man was pleased to hear that playing rugger for the school would no doubt compensate for his flat feet. Jock wrote to his father and informed him that 'the major had thought I was right to abandon my idea of joining the frontier cavalry in India'.

Jock had enjoyed most of the calls to port along the way. Adelaide and Melbourne had been exciting with 'such an enormous number of faces that we did not know which way to look'. Natives in Colombo were considered much more welcoming than the people in Port Said. Malta was one of Jock's last rests before arriving at Southampton. He was not High Church and did not like the elaborate art in the Cathedral, but he defended the Maltese right to use it: 'I could not but admire the loving work that all the delicate gilding and painting had meant.' Little did Jock know that he would be back in this part of the world again seven years later. Then he would be instrumental in defending much more than the Cathedral's paint work. He would be playing an innovative and active role in masterminding the destruction of the Axis aeroplanes that came so near to achieving the blockade and starvation of the Maltese.

As soon as Jock arrived in Oxford he appeared to land on his feet. David recalled how Jock 'typically managed to find the most excellent rooms in Christ Church, in Canterbury 2.vii.' Apart from Tom Quad that was occupied by the Canons of Christ Church and Mr Dundas, the Senior Tutor, Canterbury 2.vii offered some of the finest rooms, views and locations. Mr Dundas occupied the same rooms where Lewis Carroll was inspired to write his tales of Alice In Wonderland. In that room the tiles around the fireplace still depict the rabbit and other animals that had so fired Carroll's imagination. Jock was now in the heart of his father's old stamping ground. It was here that Arthur's own imagination had been so captured by Carroll, the place of Hollyman's origins. In February 1934 students at Oxford University Union shocked the older generation by voting 275–153 that they would not fight 'For king and country'. The previous October when Jock made himself comfortable in Canterbury 2.vii was the month that Hitler stormed out of the League of Nations. It was not long before Jock took sides over the burning issues of the day, so clearly demonstrated by the famous Union debate, by wearing a blue and white badge that simply read, 'For king and country'.

Jock's bills at Blackwell's Bookshop, 'where a lot of my money will go', revealed that if he was profligate, it seemed to arise from his desire to educate himself. He had purchased, among other books, Strowski's *Nationalisme ou Patriotisme*, and his later writing indicates that it may have helped him reflect on the intensifying international situation. After visiting his Uncle Herbert in Folkestone, Jock spent his week in Oxford enjoying several plays and the latest film from Hollywood, *King Kong*. He enjoyed the technical effects but dismissed one of Hitler's favourite films as 'blood and thunder'. A trip to Appleshaw outside Andover a few days later on 4 October enabled him to try and be a model pupil to his old Headmaster and calm the retired E.M.Baker's disquiet that the latter's successor at the King's School, Mr Parkinson, might be making changes that were too rapid. The task of reassuring the formidable E.M.Baker, 'whose word was law' according to David, was no mean feat. Jock wrote to his father that, 'I tried to let him see, very tactfully, I hope, that I was confident that Mr Parkinson would make a success of it eventually.'

Tact was a useful quality to have as a freshman in a college as grand as Christ Church, Oxford. It took a while to work out who was a freshman and who was not. It may have been rather overwhelming in those first few days, even for someone as well-informed as Jock clearly was. He had enjoyed travelling around before term started, but he had not entirely landed on his feet, for one month later he conceded to his mother that the first few days at Oxford were 'bitter'. He felt more than a tinge of despondence. He wrote that, 'I moped about till 10 waiting and wishing for something, for someone to knock . . . a notice, or card to dispel my loneliness and then realising what a foolish little self-important schoolboy I was I went out and had a good walk. I am going to love this place.'

After a term of writing regularly to his parents Jock observed that his letters to them 'have taught me more about myself in the last few weeks than I ever knew before'. At the same time as he determined to take a leaf out of his own book and 'Not Sulk', he was unaware that the Senior Censor at Christ Church would not allow him to be inveigled into any big college organizations that did not include rowing pursuits. Not long after his walk 'a tall good-looking chap breezed past me and then turned quite suddenly and asked me if I was John Lewes – it was Gilbert Ryle, the Senior Censor, the first man to speak to me of his own accord in Oxford. You have no idea how much better I felt; it was like drink to a man lost in the Sahara!' It seemed that the pleasure was also Gilbert Ryle's for Jock was soon invited to lunch to talk of rowing. Ryle was the Christ Church rowing coach and with his rowing pedigree Jock would be indispensable for the college VIII. Arthur had 'prophesied' that by Jock's second evening the various college secretaries would visit one by one requesting his membership of their societies. Jock had been correct in his anticipation of visitors and knocks on the door, but to these welcome interruptions he told them 'that I had promised to row, and they sighed'. The irony was not lost upon Jock that he had not yet won a single rowing race, and he confided as much to his parents.

Within the fortnight Jock was forced to unlearn many things, everything from rowing and riding to mixing with his peers. The young student was a good amateur jockey and found the riding techniques of Oxford University Officer Training Corps (OUOTC) cumbersome to say the least; he noted that 'it is just as if the blooming horse were a motor car with "Directions for Use" on the cardboard cover . . . what bunkum, piffle, perfect rot to anybody that has developed the horse sense . . . I flatter myself that I have acquired a little.' He might well have tired of an aching backside by late October because he was hard at the task of rowing with a fixed rowing seat in the 'orthodox style' to which he was unaccustomed. However, he was determined 'to relearn my methods of life and I shall relearn them too!' He closed his letter to Arthur with some self-mockery to add to the jibes aimed at the OUOTC: 'After this outburst of feeble complaining I shall retire me to bed and weep into my pillow and so arise with a stiff neck tomorrow which will not help me in my struggle for humbleness of mind.' Jock expressed concern for the 'poor blighters' who were forced to rise to a trot even though they had never been on a horse in their life. During the evening when he wrote his weekly diary home, he enjoyed domesticity at college: he might content himself with a new 12-inch Ropp pipe, nibble biscuits from his silver christening bowl, and sip a very good 1924 claret.

By 21 December Jock writes of his approach to his diary entries to his parents that 'I try to exaggerate nothing, I hide nothing.' The young student was taking a measure of the way others attempted to relax and content themselves. Tea time in England was, however, not an activity that enhanced his own sense of happiness and contentment. Jock may well at times have suffered from something not unlike cabin fever, especially when he was pinned into a drawing-room seat in a claustrophobic setting:

> I never feel quite at home with a cup of tea in the hand and a plate with a squashy cake in the other trying to decide how to go, and when I do decide, to find that someone has been talking to me for some time, taking my grunts of distress as indications that I am following him, and is now waiting for my answer or views on the subject, and I always find conversation is so forced. They are never content to just sit and be together but seem to get panicky at every silence and start talking about the most inane subjects or cracking drawing-room jokes at which the whole company is convulsed with polite mirth. I would much prefer to be in the open air drinking Billy tea out of a tin mug and munching a greasy and blackened chop.

The undergraduate may well have considered how fortunate were the days when he had been able to roam the bush back at home whilst fishing for yabbies which he would cook in a kerosene tin of salted water over sticks. Instead, Jock arranged an 'all day picnic' with his sister Elizabeth the following Sunday after the early service. These 'expeditions' by bicycle rather than pony in England became a fairly regular feature of the two Lewes's stay abroad. He may have belittled one great English tradition, but in the same week Jock commented on his pleasure at reading the 'wonderful' *Times* newspaper, and by the end of term he had adopted Oxford clothing regulations with ardour when he wrote that 'suede shoes are worn by those that don't know any better or by the aristocracy.' *The Times* was 'so calm and conservative, so typically British'. Reporting the reaction of the English press to such phenomena as the rise of nationalism was something he and his parents wished to reflect on in their correspondence. Mussolini had been in power in Italy for ten years and Hitler was poised to eliminate most of his opponents in Germany. He decried the Australian paper's mania for 'American sensationalism', without which they would become 'really useful public organs'. Australian papers took ten minutes to read, twenty was needed for the *Sydney Morning Herald*, but at least one and a half hours for *The Times*. He finished with a salutary message for any newspaper reader in the 1930s: 'So many opinions are given and questions viewed from so many different points of view that it is an education to read it.'

Whilst 'devouring' *The Times*, Jock read widely for his study of Modern Greats, and for pleasure. Often work and play were synonymous. Towards the end of term on 5 December he reported that he had also managed to read more of the Bible, finishing Acts, Romans and was 'well into Corinthians'. In late October he had written how he had been 'on a buster' at Blackwell's. That he managed to continue the family tradition of reading the Bible is all the more significant, because once term was in full swing Jock experienced a regime that might have been considered punishing at times. Meals in Hall were hardly a burden, but there were lectures to attend, political economic papers to read, rowing in the college clinker four after lunch, a read of Maurois' *Disraeli* and an OTC lecture after the evening meal. Friends were invited round for port or sherry, and good friends round for tea! Everything was new, and Jock frequently informed his parents that, although he was aware of his blessings, he was also aware of the great need to justify his good fortune. In early November ice-skating became yet another way to test and enjoy himself at the same time: 'I look forward to the time when I shall be able to glide so swiftly and gracefully over the ice, and dance too. I must learn to skate backwards soon.'

Jock found the time to buck up the spirits of his elder sister who was certainly suffering from the pressures of exams at Lady Margaret Hall. The Sunday cycling and picnicking had been therapeutic for both of them: Jock was adapting to his new life away from home and Elizabeth was in great need of distraction from an exam revision routine that sometimes seemed almost beyond her. Arthur and Elsie knew that studying would be tough but they had insisted that their daughter should have the same opportunities as her brothers. David considered that his parents were 'ahead of their time' in this respect. However, at one stage Elizabeth was beginning to develop an antipathy towards the whole academic merry-go-round; Jock would take her off to the Cotswolds and out of Oxford at exam time. His comment at the end of October was typical of the supporting role he took towards his siblings: 'It would take a worry indeed to oppress her now we are together.' By mid-December he was able to send them evidence of her own improved spirits, and finally enjoyed the pleasure of announcing 'Elizabeth gets through!' The Sauternes that the pair drank at Elizabeth's celebratory meal in Oxford at the 'Moorish' tasted all the sweeter.

Christmas 1933 was spent with Jock's Auntie Marjory in Jersey. Jock and Elizabeth were now back together with their cousins, Peggy and Mary, with whom they had spent much of their childhood in Australia. So a week before Christmas he wrote about his cousin Mary whom he nicknamed, 'Miggles':

> She seems a very responsible lass and capable of looking after her family – but the old Miggles is still very much there. When we were at length settled in the train I squeezed Mary's hand and said, 'This is very good; all being together again.' Across Mary's face came Miggles' s smile and Mary's eyes smiled too

and into Mary's eyes came Miggles's tears. Can you imagine her? I hope so. I find it difficult to tell others what I think of people we both know so well.

Jock enjoyed the company of younger relatives and he was usually very receptive to the playful behaviour of children. A month before, whilst advising his parents about their planned trip to England in 1935, he had suggested that his own voyage on the Bay ships had sometimes been marred by the lack of a quiet spot due to a multitude of children on board. However, entertaining amused young relatives was another matter altogether and a brief but welcome distraction from the responsibilities of taking his place in the adult world. Jock believed that he had 'sometimes shocked Elizabeth', for 'I enjoy playing with the children'. He had whooped with delight with the youngest of the family and noted on Christmas Eve that 'I am still a naughty boy and all erring brother – ably assisted by Mary. Mary was still Miggles.'

He managed to make a lock-up box for Mary's sister, Peggy: it was a treat for him to work again with good wood and good carpenter's tools. He enjoyed the sun in Jersey too, and sent off several weekly diaries to his parents. Their deep interest in his life and development, and the knowledge that they read his letters was for him 'a thrill'. It seems that the feeling was mutual for all correspondents. For on 2 January he wrote that he didn't know if his letters were worth filing 'as you suggest. Perhaps my sons will be grateful to know that their father went through the same mill when they are up at the House.' Jock thanked his parents for suggesting they keep his letters, 'let alone file them'.

After one term it was clear that Jock's writing had a resonance for at least his own generation:

It must be wonderful to watch one's children grow and take their shape beneath their parents' increasing care. For the wheel of life is much more subtle than the potter's clumsy tool, and a little soul in the hands of its parents far more delicate and difficult to handle than the finest clay spinning beneath a potter's thumbs . . . .Ah! How will it emerge from that exacting process in which so many beautiful vessels are marred? Yes How?

Will that final finishing (the glazing) procured at such sacrifice be burnt and cracked and worn? And the colours; will they have faded? Let's hope the fire gives to them a brighter lustre and a richer tone.

A fortnight before Jock tentatively supported the idea of disarmament in Europe that had been encouraged by the Versailles Treaty in 1919. He seriously questioned whether pacifism, advocated by the League of Nations, could bring about a 'brighter colour and a richer tone' to Europeans which the League purported to parent. It would take him several years to see that the threat to internationalism came from within Europe rather than outside it:

It has struck me since I have been in England that one is much nearer death than ever in Australia. The memorials . . . battlefields . . . tombs . . . the large number of invalids daily seen being wheeled about . . . In Australia I see all that speaks of life and the length of it, in England death is everywhere apparent. What a great and wonderful nation we are and in what a difficult position we now are. Having gained power will we use it wisely? If we eventually succeed in unifying Europe into a great community of nations, disarmed and at peace, what of the rest of the world? Will they wait till we have forgotten how to fight and then engulf us? Which raises the question, is unity stronger than diversity? I think not. Disarmament conferences are a step in the right direction but what is one step in so great a distance as still remains to be covered? The world will only be constrained to take another step after more fighting whether on battlefields or in trade. We progress by our mistakes; experience is such a hard school that progress is slow and very painful.

Jock built up to that pitch of student life during 1934 and 1935. It wasn't all activity. There was time to enjoy the increase in the college beer allowance from a pint to a quart during his first summer at Oxford. The college oarsmen, who included the future Commander-in Chief of the UK Forces, Basil Eugster, had been given orders to get to bed by 10.30 p.m. each night. They were also building up to their reward of sparkling wine or 'giggle water' for being 'early birds'. Jock took advantage of college largesse, but also noted that on 'dry nights' he would make Ovaltine for himself and two of the crew, 'the other two babies'. He went through alternate phases of temperance and indulgence and informed his parents that he would let them know 'if ever I decide to start drinking again'; he was interested in the way alcohol affected his mental and physical state, and this body-consciousness became a feature of his later experiments on his ability to endure a diversity of physical conditions. He was also informing his father of his alcoholic intake because the latter continued to offer suggestions to his son on a host of issues. Few of Arthur's letters have survived but in one Arthur suggested that Oxford 'will answer all your questions'; Jock replied and discussed his father's advice, and the significance of their correspondence to his own development. In his letter his ambitions to lead well and with detachment are high-lighted in his comparison of letter-writing with soldiering:

> You say my daily notes are a joy to you and I gladly believe it; they are also a help to me. I feel like an officer reviewing his recruits before dismissing them. A great many of them he will never see again, except as members of a homogeneous whole, his command. Some he will have to deal with personally as defaulters, some as meriting promotion. The recruits I review each night in company with you are my actions of the day, each one a new addition to my army of experience. As I pass by each one I look at it carefully up and down, trying to divine which I am likely to meet again either as hindrances or helpers,

and which are going to take their place in the unit and discharge their duties with efficiency and in silence. It is a joy watching this army grow and there is no pleasure in life to equal that which is given by the feeling of the power that the possession of this vast army confers. That power I feel is growing within me day by day, and its presence is disclosed in the confidence I have in all I think and say and write and do. Not that I mean to imply I have perfect confidence in myself, the unruly and rebellious faces that I see each day in the ranks of my recruits see that that does not occur, but as the number and variety, this latter most especially, of the men in any unit increases, so does the power I possess of thinking coherent and comprehensive thoughts.

It may have been with college champagne that Jock and Basil Eugster 'fixed' a local constabulary car. Both men were very practical and enjoyed taking machines apart and seeing how they worked. On the night that they interfered with the mechanisms of a police vehicle they may well have not seen clearly how the transport operated because it was apparently dark. Bow of his college crew, Major Sandy Gordon, remembers that when the car door was opened the lights flashed, and turning the ignition blew the horn to the great distress of the would-be driver. The incident was reported to the Senior Censor of Christ Church, since those responsible were believed to be rowing men in the college. The prank apparently was successful, but Jock was identified as the practical joker. His punishment matched his crime for sheer devilry and intrigue; he was required by his tutor, Gilbert Ryle, to hand over what was then considered to be a highly prized and sought after emblem belonging to the fascist leader, Sir Oswald Mosley. These were the days when it was possible for college pranks to be punished in the spirit as opposed to the letter of the law.

Philip Warner, the historian and fellow of Christ Church, remembers that the intrusion of the British Union of Fascists (BUF) could be very irritating. Mosley led the BUF in an attempt to solve what his widow recently recalled in *The Spectator* as the 'forgotten' 'misery of Britain in the early Thirties: mass unemployment, distressed areas, hunger marches, appalling slums and hopeless poverty.' Plenty of students like Warner, however, defended freedom of thought, in the street if necessary: chairs, bottles and knuckle-dusters flew in the violent struggles between the BUF and its opponents. Jock Lewes may or may not have been involved in the discord that met fascist gatherings; what is certain is that he did shin up the flagpole of the BUF Headquarters in Oxford and remove the symbol of 'Modern Dictatorship' in a mostly successful night raid. The reason it was not entirely successful was that Gilbert Ryle had discovered the details regarding Jock's latest acquisition, his head for heights and total contempt for Blackshirts.

Gilbert wanted his pound of flesh for the irritation of having a call from the 'blue shirts' at police headquarters: Jock reluctantly handed over the flag of the 'party of action' and no more was said of the incident. It is not possible to know whether he informed his parents of this affair, because fewer letters of Jock's weekly diary survive in this period. On paper he was becoming a constitutional vandal, for his most hurried essay that term was the best 'academical plan' to reform the House of Lords that had yet been put forward to his tutor: the gradual abolition of the hereditary nature of the titles of peers was advocated and their creation for life only on the nomination of the Crown, subject to approval by the people in referendum. His political persuasions were unlikely to be poles apart from Mosley's beliefs, for when he attended a recital of 'Russian music', he not only considered it 'ghastly modern stuff' but the audience 'seemed to consist of a mixture of communists and nitwits'.

Jock seemed to be taking up the mantle of responsibility when he had written to his father of the 'great and wonderful nation we are'; it was as if he was already aligning his destiny with the stars that still shone on his new home in England.

Wearing his 'For King and Country' badge was the part of the patriot's identity that he was seamlessly beginning to personify with every step that he took – for all his dislike of English tea parties! He was reworking all that he had ever learnt on the anvil of learning at university. Berlin beckoned, but he was not yet ready to say goodbye to Oxford. His letters that year sometimes alluded to the boat races of life that he knew he must row. For the moment those races were on the Isis, and they had to be won.

4

River Man

Great works are performed by perseverance and
not by strength – Dr Johnson.

Arthur Lewes had rowed for Christ Church until the early
1890s when a swimming test was introduced for oarsmen that
he either ignominiously failed or did not take at all; however,
his eldest son took up the oar with a vengeance. David Lewes
joined Jock at his college in late 1934 and he also took up
rowing. Where the brothers diverged as sportsmen was that
while the younger brother rowed to take his mind off the
pressure of study, the elder oar studied to take his mind
off the rowing. Studying Modern Greats under Hugh
Gaitskell, the Labour leader, and the philosophers Sir Freddie
Ayer and Gilbert Ryle fulfilled Jock; metaphysics and philosophy honed an already contemplative mind. John Garton,
a keen oarsman, rowed with Jock in the trial Varsity VIIIs at
Oxford and remembers Jock spending the lion's share of his
time on the Isis rather than in the library. For all that, Jock
still discussed his Philosophy, Politics and Economics in his
letters home nearly as much as he did his rowing. He was
'happy, very happy'. His philosophy seems to have put him
at ease in a busy academic week when he was also stroking
the Christ Church VIII and coaching the Keble College VIII for
Henley:

Failure is not a missing of the mark, as the Greeks thought,
for the mark is unattainable. Happiness is to be striven after,

not attained; it is ever ahead of the spot where our shaft falls, and complete success is not to be found in hitting what we aim at, but in hitting what we wished we had aimed at when we have come up with our shaft and seen where it has fallen . . . .

Jock was developing his experience in rowing as power-house of the Christ Church VIII rather than the OUBC trial VIIIs. By the end of 1934 he was training with the Varsity trial VIIIs but was fairly sure that 'whenever they want a boat to go slower they put me in it.' The training continued into 1935, and again he warned his parents that his studies were suffering and that 'VIIIs have been cutting into my time rather'. He had been elected a member of the Junior Common Room Committee, whose first task was to enable a large number of Christ Church clubs to regain solvency. Regattas at Henley and Marlow were helping to develop Jock's approach to college leadership of the crew, not only as stroke, but also later as Secretary of Christ Church First VIII in the autumn. On 5 July he wrote that 'I was losing my grip of the crew. I could not make them do what I wanted.' After two successful races in the Ladies' Plate at Henley, his insistence on keeping the rating of the boat down in order to win comfortably convinced the crew members that they did not have to 'give her ten' every time their opponents appeared to be winning the race. Jock's confidence in Christ Church's ability to beat opponents that were rowing at faster rates was paying off. He was driving the VIII as stroke, insisting that their temporary coach was, 'not there to command but to advise', and sometimes giving the sharper edge of his tongue to a doubting Thomas rowing behind him.

After reading some of Berkeley's philosophy he mused that, 'What a pity it would be that I stopped writing if ever I became as famous as Bishop Berkeley. A droll thought and which would occasion no little mirth if I gave voice to it among my friends.' He seemed blissfully unaware of how highly friends like Basil Eugster and Sandy Gordon actually rated him. For several weeks on Army camp after Henley he was not at all sure whether he could 'live my own life, reading and perhaps writing and still be an efficient soldier'. This attitude conflicted with his desire for wanting 'to learn to serve and command', he believed that whatever path he found 'I feel will be something great, something connected both with science and philosophy'. All this made him wonder whether to extend his study to a fourth year. On this question he received an answer soon enough.

By the end of 1934 the Dean had categorically said No. 'He had not one good word to say for me,' Jock wrote on 13 December. His uncertainty about his future may have partly stemmed from the fact that when he was studying Philosophy he was doing so to the detriment of his Economics. This was not helped by the fact that, although he respected his Economics tutor as a teacher of the intricacies of the subject, 'his advice on subjects touching one more closely as an individual I feel very unwilling to follow at all times, and this no less.' However, he admitted that he had approached his work by 'cudgelling an empty head to extract therefrom what I never attempted to put into it, namely some inkling of what I ought to do as distinct from what I should like to do.' However, the year had not been a dismal failure. The Dean, in his concern for Jock's academics, would understandably have omitted to mention the student's success at being elected a member of Vincent's Club for élite sportsmen.

Jock had not been very impressed with the organization of the trial VIIIs' training in September 1935. Writing from the Leander Club, he berated the time-wasting that went on during the trials when oarsmen were left 'waiting to row'. He wrote that he felt 'very selfish and uncharitable' because he had the impression that 'he was past hope and . . . merely a very useful means of helping freshmen and others get their Blues'. By 4 October he was difficult to please because, when he did receive more attention than an 'also ran', he considered that the coaches were trying 'rather too much to be pleasant at times'; Jock's standards were exacting. He became critical:

> In my opinion they made a big mistake last year having 'A' crew as the prospective varsity and 'B' and 'C' merely possible substitutes. I believe it is a good idea to have three trial VIIIs as long as one has been good enough to get three first class trials, but the whole idea of trials is taken away if the crews aren't made as equal as possible. Also I think it is a bad thing to get the crew together too early. However, I am not running the show, so it remains to be seen what will be done.

Rowing was beginning to leave little respite for anything else. Jock does not seem to have had as much time for socializing with the opposite sex as his nick-name 'Jock' might have implied; college friends insisted on paying tribute to his conspicuous good looks and generous helping of testosterone by christening him 'Jock' for jock-strap, with all the machismo that such a sobriquet suggested. 'Jock-strap!' was once shouted out loudly from the bank as he rowed on the Isis and stuck to John Steel Lewes on the insistence of all fellow bloods. However, he felt an affinity towards one of his crewman's sisters and agreed to attend a ball with her. Perhaps he was unaware of how a woman might become attached to him, even if on his part it was unrequited love or on hers only infatuation (certainly he was only fully aware of the power of attraction when he fell in love with Senta Adriano three years later). This was possibly the case when on the night of the ball the party consisted of eight men and seven women, and Jock, feeling somewhat enervated by a busy schedule, opted to drop out of the evening's entertainment, leaving his partner to pair with a mutual acquaintance. Jock had some misgivings afterwards, because he had not informed the lady of the change of plan in person and discovered to his surprise that she was 'rather cut up about it'. He mentions such attachments very rarely to his parents and this might be because he did not seek them. Now lodged with friends at No.1 Brewer Street he indicates that evening study was sometimes interrupted by the attentions of girls, who had to be 'shooed out' so that the fine training dinner that the crews received nightly could be justified and some reading achieved before Ovaltine was served.

Jock became restless at the end of 1935. The summer revealed doubts about a military career, the autumn was filled with club responsibilities, but Jock's disillusion with his attainment in 'schools' underlined a strange sensation of being adrift. Obtaining his Blue for rowing was hardly compensation for this uncertainty. By the last week of November he confided to his parents that 'I feel that I began my life's work a long time ago' and 'it would be wilful waste to stop my present work perhaps for good and turn my attention to some form of livelihood quite remote from it.' The trial VIII's race between 'A' and 'B' crew, as described by Jock, might have been a fitting description of the way he 'rowed' into his own finish of the Michelmas term: 'stolid, stylish, and unsatisfactory – no race, no fire, just the mechanical precision of an engine'. He was unable to contain his frustration at not being given the chance to stroke the 'A' crew. He admired the former president of the OUBC, Ralph Hope, who had once stroked it, but Jock, for all his investment in university rowing, may have felt that Hope was in no position to effect the sort of changes that the Oxford crew required. His academic achievements were superficial and the Trial VIIIs' Dinner was the occasion for pent-up frustrations to fly; caution was thrown to the wind.

Jock confessed that 'The most blameless and most law-abiding member of the college was found guilty of a complete outbreak of lawlessness.' A penchant for police cars and fire extinguishers had got the better of him and his rowdy companions after the majority of revellers had dispersed at the end of the dinner. Oxford men seemed to have a penchant for man-handling police cars: the 1935 dinner was not so drunken as the previous one, but 'unfortunately the evening was spoilt by a fool of a chap wilfully damaging a police car' after a student was nabbed for putting out a lamp in the same street. Jock saw the Chief Constable in the following week and 'persuaded' him to drop the case if Trial VIIIs would take responsibility and pay damages. The Chief of Police was good enough to agree; after the affray Jock had clearly lost none of his charm.

However, though on this occasion he was blameless, he seems to have taken it upon himself to take full responsibility for the revels when he was questioned by the university. The proctors invited a roomful of the oarsmen to leave their office if innocent, and 'they all did except me'. Jock had not tampered with this police car but evidently shielded the culprit. Perhaps he thought, with Lady Luck often sitting on his shoulder, that he might get away with it. He was discovering the limitations of his charisma; in fact he was fined and gated for several weeks into the spring term. That summer Jock had thoroughly enjoyed eluding the bulldogs, the university 'police', who had pursued his college crew down Merton Street. On that occasion he had requisitioned a bicycle and circumnavigated a pair of very breathless keepers of the peace. However, at the end of 1935 Jock's 'good fortune' appeared to be running out:

> The gating runs concurrently with another I had just received from the Junior Censor, going out of college after hours with a fire extinguisher; entering University after hours with a fire extinguisher; giving the wrong name to the Dean, disappearing into the depths of the College- still with the fire-extinguisher – climbing out of University – having first knocked on the first door I came to and asked the inmate to show me how to (without the fire extinguisher) enter Christ Church after 12.20 by an unrecognised route – still without the fire extinguisher; actually they amounted to only about half of my misdemeanours that night. I had visited all my friends there (New College).The climb back into the House (Christ Church) was

a long and perilous one starting at the high fence at the far end of Merton Street, through innumerable backyards . . . into the House garden, through a Canon's garden, the Cathedral graveyard and into another Canon's garden, into the Dean's garden and so into College by Kilcanon tunnel where the wall meets the library. It wasn't that I was tight – for in that case I couldn't have done that climb to say nothing of the others (escapades) that you must admit are not child's play.

Jock was chastened and decided that it was 'worth it the first time . . . but twice – No!' Having driven his old Vauxhall into London and purposely abandoned it on Vauxhall Bridge he decided to channel some of his daredevil spirit into racing Alice, a splendid 1926 Alvis sports car that enabled him to reach Henley from Magdalen in under twenty minutes. Bertie Eugster had purchased a 4.5 litre Bentley, Mike Ashley an Aston Martin and John Garton a Straight Eight Packard. These friends would vie in achieving the fastest racing times between the bridges of both places in order to reach Henley for the rowing; they also became a great source of support and friendship to Alice's driver. Jock's doubts would soon end and his strong sense of purpose return as his leadership and experience on the River Isis gained momentum.

After writing to his parents concerning the unorganized state of Trial VIIIs in September 1935, Jock continued to note down all his observations relating to Varsity rowing. He had watched the 'enemy' practise at Cookham Dean and enjoyed the champagne that the Ogilvie family generously laid on every night during the crew's stay at The Dolphin Inn at Thorpeness. Since the training had begun that September, Jock estimated that the oarsmen had rowed over 1,000 miles by the following March. In his weekly letter, he kept his parents up to date with everything that made him 'tick' and remarked that Oxford's chances were helped by 'having the finest President a crew could wish for' in Bernard Sciortino, who impressed him with his efficiency and the fact that 'in his dealings with the crew he is kind, humorous and very firm'. The only reservation in this thumbnail sketch was that 'he takes his games very seriously and is too easily provoked and at times provoking; for this reason one cannot call him a true sportsman.' Jock left cameos of most of the oarsmen, warts and all. He was beginning to develop detailed research on recruitment for the Varsity VIII, and his written meditations on the crew attest to his interest in attracting the best combination of men. After the Boat Race of 1936, when Cambridge led Oxford from over half way, crew dynamics would be important in order to end the string of thirteen Cambridge victories.

The choice of Jock as President was not at first popular. He had hardly received the news when in mid-May an anonymous letter appeared in the *Isis* casting a little cloud over the appointment with the title, 'Surprising OUBC Election' and signed, 'Charon'. This particular 'ferryman' conveyed an important omen across the pages of the *Isis* magazine, even if it was not to be the successful prophecy of another failed and 'dead' Oxford crew. For 'Charon' emphasized that 'the office of President of the OUBC, a position which gives almost unfettered discretion in the selecting of the University VIII, must necessarily become more responsible if Oxford rowing is to regain its old prestige', but J.S.Lewes was considered to be 'conscientious' and little else when compared with the Olympic oarsman, J.C.Cherry. What 'Charon' did not know was that the President, piqued by the letter, was determined, and in mid-June wrote that 'I shall be brilliant or nothing . . . but mediocre, never.' If selecting the crew was the key to 'Charon's' race then perhaps a keen and determined oar with a flair for assessing his men was as good if not better than an Olympic one.

If Jock's best was 'never mediocre', then it was just as well because he was preparing daily for the double sculls, the rowing pair's race which he eventually won with Sandy Gordon; at the same time he was coaching Pembroke College 1st VIII, Christ Church 2nd VIII, and covering the college rowing secretarial duties whilst its President. Jock relinquished both offices when they could be filled by mid-September 1936, because he evidently did not wish to spread himself too thinly as President of the OUBC. In early June he had admitted that he had found 'Charon's' letter 'a rather unpleasant surprise', but was rescued by the next issue of the *Isis*, a week later, by being chosen as the magazine's Isis Idol. An extract from the article hinted at the vacuum in Oxford rowing which he seemed to fill:

All this, however, is a description of Jock's character. And though this side is enough to make everyone who meets him like him, there is a more serious side to him than that. Perhaps the greatest testimony to this is the fact that, at a time when the OUBC needed unity more than ever before, and when innumerable theories about the Boat Race were likely to divide it into at least three camps, Jock was made President for the simple reason that everybody liked him, and everybody knew that he would give them a fair hearing and have his own mind firmly made up at the end. Oxford has been lucky in a series of Presidents of the OUBC who have been willing to give up everything to Oxford rowing, and who have been quite conspicuously brilliant at their job. Jock Lewes may very easily be the best of all. No one doubts that he has difficulties before him; but he has done difficult things before. And there is no one who will not give him help, if he needs help, and the praise that he will certainly deserve for the work he will do and is doing already.

Perhaps the *Isis* had not been guilty of 'Idolatry', for this view of the composition of 'at least three camps' in the OUBC is partly supported by the national press in early June, when a 'Special Correspondent' in the *Manchester Guardian* reported that in Jock:

Oxford have a man not only of great rowing ability but one whose character is such that Oxford has entrusted its leadership to him at a time when she is torn between different parties, so great is this dissension that neither can see the good points of the other. Nothing could be better than the example of a broadminded president in attempting to pick out the best points of both factions.

So not all Jock's contemporaries were surprised by his election. In his history, *The Oxford and Cambridge Boat Race 1829–1953*, R. D. Burnell writes that Jock was put up 'primarily as a non-controversial candidate'. The *Morning Post* on 9 May had reported that the 'surprise' lay in the fact that 'his name has not been seriously mentioned in this connection. It was expected that the presidency would lie between D.M. Winser, the retiring Secretary, J.C.Cherry, and M. Ashby.' Michael Ashby, the boat's bow, took over from Winser. Jock's letter home on 8 May tells how Oxford rowing had been fragmented into conservatives who wanted to row with fixed pins, radicals who supported swivel rowing, and others who wanted to try both as long as the Oxford boat travelled faster. Jock indicated why some commentators were surprised at his nomination and election:

> David Winser asked the parties if they would accept me as a coalition governor and they consented. When they asked me to stand for the office I said I would not stand against either Con Cherry or Mike (Ashby), but when I learnt that they would stand down if I stood, I agreed to stand on condition that if I were elected I would have a perfectly free hand as regards policy.

In his unpublished memoirs Ashby chivalrously recorded why he was glad that ex-President Hope's suggestion that he be President was overruled so that he took a supportive role to Jock as Secretary:

> Oxford had a narrow escape from further disasters. Hope put me up to be elected President. It is no false modesty to stress

how bad this would have been. I was a newcomer to rowing, and would not have had the grip of the experience of Jock, who had had years of tough rowing experience in Australia. For all the brash faults of some Australians, and Jock had none of these, they do have a tremendous drive and determination to succeed. Jock had unerring judgement and power of leadership: he was older, wiser and moreover he was a fine and persuasive President.

A few months later Jock confounded some of the 'old Blues" scepticism over his election and put his determination to the test after the OUBC's rowing 'jolly' and tour in Europe. Before walking in the Black Forest, Jock sought isolation and endurance tests in the Harz Mountains in Germany. He wanted to increase his stamina and be the fittest man on the river, even if he was not the most technical or powerful. His opportunity to shine on the Isis and the effects of his training came at the end of the year with the Silver Sculls Challenge Cup, the University's single rower's race. After the sculling races he considered that 'the reserves of determination upon which I could draw and which were in fact my real strength were built up in the solitude of the Harz Mountains'. On 6 November he wrote home and explained the significance of his part in the Silver Sculls, 'even if I should happen by some mischance to lose the final, I consider that I have accomplished all that I set out to do, and that is to demonstrate to the men who, against the advice of the coaches, elected me President that their confidence has not been misplaced.' The *Isis* reported that there were signs of a sculling revival with more than twice the number of entries since 1935 and that the magazine's 'prophet has been trying to drown his sorrows ever since his lamentable appearance in print' because the Silver Sculls competition 'serves to enhance rather than detract from the President's achievement'. On the day of the Silver Scull's race Jock wrote that 'the most satisfying and delightful feature of the whole incident, however, was that everybody, except my opponents for obvious reasons, wanted me to win'. The President's challenges were not over yet, but for the moment he had succeeded in restricting 'Charon' to ferrying the dead over the Styx rather than the Isis.

Three weeks before he won his sculling race Jock first began his 'own show' of Trial VIIIs on 19 October. He needed to improve on the Trial's organization as he had once suggested, and also to show himself capable of earning a seat in the two crew's boats. After the Silver Sculls he conceded that 'I had a sort of smug feeling that I could walk into the Oxford boat . . . I learnt that the standard of Oxford trials is higher than I had thought.' Perhaps the combination of better oars – as the entry of the sculling contest suggests – and Jock's determination to avoid wasting crew members' time all helped to make Mike Ashby's 1936 trials 'one of the most carefree of our lives'. A year before, Jock had written that 'a big mistake' had been made having 'A' crew as the prospective Varsity and 'B' and 'C' crews merely possible substitutes. Jock told his parents that 'I believe it is a good idea to have three trial VIIIs, as long as one has men good enough to get three first class trials', otherwise, 'the whole idea of trials is taken away.' This led him to keep what R. D. Burnell considered 'an Isis crew in training with the university crew throughout Boat Race practice': a member of the powerful Isis second VIII could be moved at any time into the Dark Blues' first crew without noticeably slowing the boat. Jock also considered it 'a bad thing to get the crew together too early' and he arranged to give a dinner to both Trial VIIIs the day before they went into training on 15 November. The President wrote of his plan:

> Collect all the men together where they can get to know each other, so that the whole of the trials will be carried on in the spirit of a jolly party and not become the grim ordeal which it so easily can be. The system of picking a crew by means of trial VIIIs is only really good if trial VIIIs realize how important a

part of boat race training they are. Trial VIIIs with the wrong spirit can lose a Boat Race much more easily than half the things to which Oxford's failures have been put down.

The meal used up much of Jock's remaining funds for the term but it had been worth everything, for the oarsmen 'want to row in trials as much for the fun of it as for the cap' and, despite a shorter row than planned, the actual Trial VIIIs' race 'could not be called stylish' but 'it was useful and very promising.' At the end of the year he made new resolutions. The Isis crew would not be 'abandoned as we were in 1935 or allowed as a sort of favour to enter for the Head of the River race a few days before the Boat Race, it will be turned over to properly selected coaches and carry out a well organized training.' The President envisaged that the Isis crew would be placed within the first dozen of 150 crews. Such optimism augured well and Jock could 'settle down to my rowing as an ordinary member of the crew'.

In one of Jock's last letters of 1936 he excitedly wrote that 'I have a new scheme afoot'. Potential divisions amongst the Oxford coaches were initially settled when Jock, Dr Patrick Mallam, Nono Rathbone and Gully Nickalls decided that each of the four men would coach the Varsity men respectively at each stage of the last training period. They all sat down to dinner in London in mid-December 1936 at Nono's invitation. Jock was very pleased with the meeting, where 'we brought out of our own respective cupboards all the skeletons and tame ghosts that might have broken loose halfway.' Perhaps Dr Mallam was less ambitious about covering the great mileage of training that the President envisaged but overall Jock had good reason to be optimistic. The Dark Blues had already sorted through a host of oarsmen and were more ready than Cambridge to prepare the new year's work; such a meeting of coaches, Jock wrote, had 'been conspicuous in Oxford rowing . . . only by its sad deficiency'. R. Hope, President of the crew in 1936, resigned over disagreements with the coaches, of whom two subsequently themselves resigned. It was a tribute to all the coaches of 1937 that they developed the right spirit of co-operation from the very beginning.

There was a plethora of theories as to why Oxford had lost the Boat Race for thirteen years in succession. Rowing style figured chiefly among them, but the excuses were legion: Cambridge positioned their exams more favourably in the calendar; Oxford men were more conscientious and dropped out to work harder on 'Schools'; the weights of coxes; the size of the Isis versus the Cam; the winning of the toss; negative press coverage; and the eternal controversy between those who had advocated fixed-pin or swivel rigging, to say nothing of the choice of President. 'Jesus Style', it was called after the Cambridge college which was being coached by the famous Steve Fairburn; Jesus College oarsmen were the most marked proponents of the new style: less body swing and more leg drive. A large number of Oxford crews had been using the fixed-pin and orthodox style where backs were not bent as they appeared in the Fairburn Style, which pioneered a stronger finish at the end of the stroke. With less swinging back and forth, the boat rides through the water more smoothly.

In mid-November Jock was evasive with the Press, as was his custom. He wanted to give little away so as to achieve maximum advantage in surprising the opposition. On 20 November he informed his parents that, 'I want to spring this crew onto Cambridge . . . to that end I am concealing our great strength even from Oxford itself as far as is wise.' Since childhood he had revelled in a good scheme, and was able to keep it secret, especially when he judged he would thereby be able to create maximum effect for his enterprise. As Jock wrote home, C. Venables reported in *The Times* that 'The President has not made up his mind whether the University crew will row with swivels or fixed pins, though two boats have been fitted with swivels for Trial VIIIs.' In the previous summer of

1936 Michael Ashby had observed Jock in Berlin noting 'that not a single crew used the fixed-pin oar mounting which the Phoenicians and Pharaoh's boatmen had found so useful, and determined that Oxford should change.'

Jock was aware that Cambridge managed more abreast rowing on the wider Cam than did Oxford, and it was partly that fact which encouraged him to tour the Continent with some of the future trial oars. The tradition of bumping crews in College races was not an ideal preparation for rowing alongside another crew for several miles from Putney to Mortlake. From Germany Jock wrote that 'we must have experience in side by side rowing' and observed all the Olympic rowing, where crews were used to rowing under the pressure of being in a seven-lane race. Michael Ashby considered that his President's assessment of the American crew also helped later to engender stability in the order of the Oxford crew; the Americans had changed their rowing order very little and were victorious in the final of the VIIIs at Berlin:

> Jock thereupon determined to pick the best set of men, and weld them unchanged into a strong winning crew, and this indeed is what he did. In 1935 Peter Haig Thomas was the principal coach, and I still remember seeing the Varsity Boat going out with almost daily changes in positions, and even worse, different members of the crew.

In addition to these 'vital decisions which were to have dramatic effects', the Oxford Secretary considers that 'Jock somehow persuaded' the powerful Jan Sturrock to stay on to do research, and also be Oxford's powerhouse at six. Many regarded him as the 'finest oar in England', and there is no doubt that the crew was built up around him and his Olympic partner, Con Cherry.

In September 1936 Jock purchased a calendar for 1937, in which the daily entries came with a quote for each day. The date for the race had been set for 20 March and he mistakenly wrote in 20 April whose quote was by Bagehot, 'The most benumbing thing to intellect is routine.' Though inappropriate to the day of the race in several senses, he tried his best to honour this maxim: perhaps that was why he told the Press that he would avoid Henley in February because, 'I don't want the men to get bored with one place', and 'we may change our minds during training.' Jock was learning to manage the Press and wanted seclusion for the crew away from the cameras.

For young and modern fans of sport it may be difficult to imagine how sensational the Boat Race had become in the eyes of the public, who without the benefit of television coverage were still able to follow often front-page headlines on the Varsity race in the fortnight leading up to it. For weeks the sport sections of the big daily papers tracked the very latest form of crews and individual oarsmen, presidents and coaches. In the end, fast river conditions forced Oxford to Henley rather than the secluded Sandford-Abingdon water. Jock disliked the sensationalism of 'papers full of war' and negative comments in the press about Oxford's performance.

He considered that some secrecy on his part might limit interest in the event, but by mid-November he had begun a healthy banter with some correspondents that seemed to be a genuine part of his unstoppable spirit to win. In the *News Chronicle*, Conrad Skinner remarked on both the President's humour and enthusiasm: 'If I say more I shall come under the lash of a witty remark that the Oxford President once tossed at rowing correspondents: "I love the Press just as I love my pipe – and the one is as bad for training as the other".' Behind the bravado Jock considered the match between the Universities to be an 'honour', but he also hoped that the public would 'highly deprecate the intrusion of privacy' to which he with M.P.Lonnon, President of Cambridge University Boat Club, considered their crews to be entitled 'as true amateurs'. In 'A Presidential Protest' to *The Times* later that April, the two Presidents also quoted Punch's satire of the Press before the Boat Race as:

In far better taste than we can hope to achieve, it seems always to have been the practice to criticize: the faults and peculiarities of individual members of the crews in terms which might be considered rude if applied to a favourite of the Derby, who presumably does not read the sporting papers, and which when used in speaking of gentlemen who may perhaps have feelings to be hurt, seems to the unprejudiced mind offensive.

Jock received fan mail during his Presidency that ranged from the zany to the banal. One anonymous letter from 'an old varsity man' informed Jock: 'Do get your crew to have their hair cut before the race; their photographs look so appalling.' J.M.Heath, an ex-coach of Thames Rowing Club, was violently anti-Fairbairn and wrote several times in early 1937; he was a little more helpful but also blunt: 'You are not going to win this year if these faults are not corrected, and I don't damn well care if you let your men know of my criticisms, but I would like to see orthodox (and the best) style win again.' Heath was 'not deceived by Oxford's fast row' in late January and enumerated the faults of each oarsman, reserving the harshest caveat for Jock himself: 'Swinging out of the boat, looking at his blade. How can a man row like that?' The most favourable comment went to David Mynors at No. 3, 'Good. Might keep his head from falling off.' 'Broadway Bum' from the Putney Mens' Institute preferred his assessment to be anonymous: 'I bet Cambridge will win if you don't larn it up quick.'

The soothsayers of the race were clearly passionate in their tales of woe because in the first half of February the President received another barrage of derision and gloom. Frederick Crowder, 'a very old Blue', hoped that Jock had seen 'the picture in the *Daily Mail* of your crew – it is good enough for *Punch*. How about "Eyes in the Boat" or "Swinging together with bodies upright"?' No solace came from the one letter of support to Jock from Noreen, who had written to the

President as a dare with the promise of £5 from her office colleagues, 'but if I receive a reply the stakes are doubled!!!!!!' With this offer she enclosed a photograph of herself in a swimsuit and a man clutching her tightly who may or may not have been her 'brother'.

Confidence was more important to Jock than zeal. In *The Field* on 23 January 1937 Haig Thomas suggested that Jock's success lay in his 'real fighting spirit and devilry'. Fighting spirit was more possible if the foundations of hard work and training had been achieved. Jock indicated its importance in a letter home in the last days of January: 'Only a few realize the difference between enthusiasm and confidence but those are towers of strength to me'. However, the President was not just suffering from a bout of flu in this period, he was beginning to become aware that he had been 'too Presidential and insufficiently one of them'. Perhaps it was merely a coincidence that 'the crew have been in better and brighter spirits' whilst Jock 'learnt a lesson from my enforced absence'. He considered that it was no accident that the crew was improving during his two days away.

It was Dr Johnson's words that were printed on the correct date of the Boat Race on Jock's calendar, and for his own part in the VIII they did not seem to be ringing true. 'Great works are performed by perseverance and not by strength' was a cold comfort to a determined President who was rowing on stroke-side, but whose boat was beginning to be rowed round by bow-side. Bow-side was so much more effective that the boat would eventually travel in circles or, if the cox tried to compensate, it would travel more slowly. At the end of November 1936 Jock had been ecstatic with happiness. 'With the President of the Boat Club,' he wrote, 'I know now, what I guessed before, that I can do it better than anyone else. But it seems too easy . . . I must be overlooking something.' It could be argued that he was a victim of his own success because the crew were progressing so well, that, though he might have pulled his own weight, he was unable to match the quick beginnings of his crew's strokes which all needed to be together for the boat to run smoothly.

After Nono Rathbone took over from Dr Mallam, some of the crew's weaknesses may for a time have been hidden partly by fast conditions on the river. The coaches were against Jock's plan to race against London Rowing Club which was a break from tradition, for 'they tried to dissuade me from going through with it'. Jock believed that, whatever the result, 'it will stand us in good stead on the day'. If he was concerned about his own rowing, he was certainly displaying plenty of confidence about his crew. George Drinkwater reported that the OUBC beat the LRC 'with great ease' at Henley on 25 February and regarded their rowing 'as having improved enormously since I saw them a fortnight ago'. 'The correspondent's sharp observations reflected upon mixed omens for the President, because he added that 'the five stern oars are now splendidly coupled up', whilst the rest of the crew's idiosyncracies were slowing up the boat in spite of the stern's sterling style. 'Gully' Nickalls took over the coaching and the OUBC moved to the Tideway where the bow oarsmen were increasingly exposed to what George Drinkwater identified as Nickall's main task: 'To get them quicker into the water, a part of oarsmanship which has been kept back intentionally until this stage of practice.'

Jock thought that Nickalls was being pressurized by the Press to make changes in the boat; he was aware of how a hostile Press could sap the confidence of even a confident crew. Champagne, hearty meals and golf had been a welcome respite at Thorpeness before leaving Henley; however, it was very much back to business as Jock had his first significant difference of opinion with a coach. Nickalls had requested that David Mynors at No.3 be replaced by Rynn Stewart. At first Jock refused:

> I told them (the crew) that I had told him (Nickalls) that I was
> staking my all on the crew as it is at present made up, and refuse

73

to make the changes that he, together with all the papers and most of the 'heavies', was urging. They responded grandly.

Jock's loyalty to keeping his original crew may have been extreme for a President intent upon ending Cambridge's succession of victories in the Boat Race. Time was running out. It was now 5 March and the race was less than three weeks away. Short of asking Gully Nickalls to stand down as coach, Jock, against his own wishes, replaced Mynors with Stewart. In early March he wrote from the Ranelagh Club, 'Gully Nickalls was really quite nice about it and did not press me; in fact he was only too pleased for me to take the responsibility of the change.' Five days later on 10 March Jock decided to keep his word again on the very last change to his crew. He planned to test why the bows were still significantly weaker than the stern. If Stewart was rowing well with the five stern oars, that only left a nagging doubt about the style of either the Secretary or the President. Michael Ashby modestly takes up the story:

> There was one sad drama for which I was unwittingly to blame. The bow oar in an VIII was supposed, for reasons which remain obscure to me, to have a 'quick beginning' in his stroke. This I had to a marked degree and was perhaps my only merit. Jock, who more than pulled his weight rowing at 2, had a slow beginning but more than made up for it in the more propulsive middle arc of the stroke. Danger breeds cunning, and I knew well that the best way I could show my propulsive powers, was to make the most mighty pull when we did our starts. On no account must I be rowed round by the President. Only Jock and the cox, Gordon Merrifield, later to be lost off Gibraltar, knew of my desperate efforts to survive.
>
> Cox reported that the VIII was being seriously 'rowed round' at our practice starts, which we were doing daily on the Tideway. It was then only two weeks before the race. The problem of a boat being rowed round arises from the drag

effect from the rudder, as Cox corrects it. Unknown to the rest of us, it was decided to make a test, by doing a start without the Cox guiding the rudder. The two bow oars were each doing their best but for tragically different reasons. As it was so close to the race I knew that I was safe, but my colossal heave at the start was my normal. I was not going to be rowed round!

After only ten strokes Cox called 'easy all', as we were heading dangerously towards the North shore. Cox then ordered us to turn, we headed back to the Boat House where David Winser was already standing ready. To our horror and astonishment, Jock our splendid President got out and Winser took his place. Now he could only watch the great victory for which he had done so much.

When the crew resumed practice that same day Jock was interviewed by *The Times* about the rowing order and replied, 'You can take it that the present order is permanent.' Giving up his seat in the boat to David Winser was a mixed blessing for Jock in more ways than one: David had become one of Jock's closest friends, and although he wrote that day that his standing down from the race was 'the greatest disappointment that I have ever suffered', nearly five weeks later he added that 'there was not a man in the University to whom I would have been more delighted to give up my place'. On the morning of the Boat Race the *Sporting Life* boasted that its rowing correspondent, Rennie Rodgers, 'has never tipped a loser' since 1884, and the paper's headlines confidently read, 'Cambridge to Win the Boat Race.' Four days before, E.E.D. Tomlin in *The Field* wrote that 'Oxford have potentialities far in excess of those of Cambridge, though it is doubtful whether they will be able to display them to advantage when the time comes.' Peter Haig Thomas agreed and wrote in the national press that 'Oxford Hopes Fade.' The tide was slack and the monotony of Cambridge's fourteenth successive win was predicted by many who also expected a slow time. However, the Oxford oarsmen were putting on weight and that never happened in a stale crew.

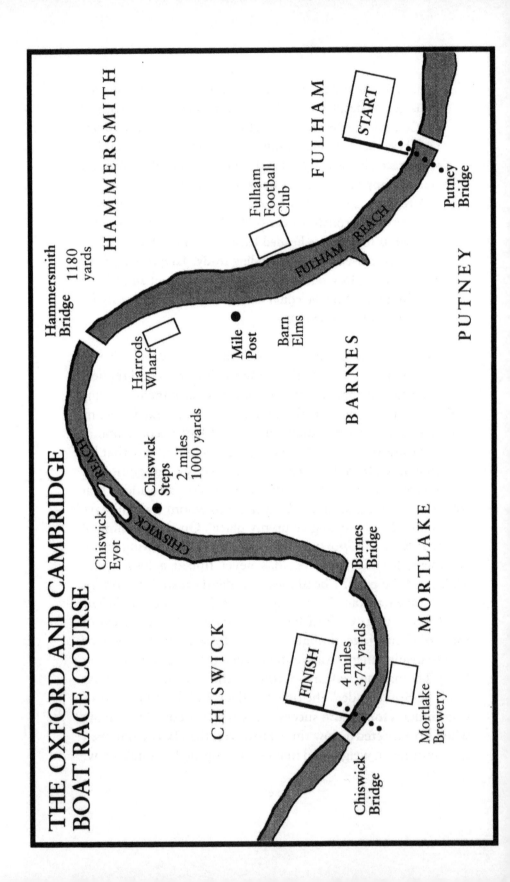

THE OXFORD AND CAMBRIDGE BOAT RACE COURSE

HAMMERSMITH

FULHAM

Hammersmith Bridge 1180 yards

Fulham Football Club

FULHAM REACH

START

Putney Bridge

PUTNEY

Harrods Wharf

Mile Post

Barn Elms

BARNES

CHISWICK REACH

Chiswick Eyot

Chiswick Steps

2 miles 1000 yards

CHISWICK

Barnes Bridge

MORTLAKE

FINISH

4 miles 374 yards

Mortlake Brewery

Chiswick Bridge

Cambridge won the toss and took the usual preference of the Surrey station, which gave their boat the great advantage of the Hammersmith and Chiswick bends as far as Chiswick Eyot. One of the first false starts in the history of the race seemed to ruffle Cambridge's feathers, but by 11.30 the two boats were away. Oxford's first few strokes looked sluggish in comparison with a lively burst from Cambridge whose nose was in front by the time the crews had reached the boathouses at Putney. As a result of a clever manoeuvre by Merrifield, the Oxford cox enabled the boat to take advantage of calmer waters and his oarsmen retrieved the lost ground at Fulham football ground. Oxford were now up a canvas, but at the Mile Post that lead was then cut as Cambridge spurted just before Harrods. The crews shot Hammersmith Bridge abreast; Cambridge gave a series of ten hard strokes and went slightly ahead by six feet, but R. D. Burnell writes, 'each time that Cambridge gained' Oxford 'made good the distance without raising the stroke'. Rennie Rodgers of the *Sporting Life* started to eat humble pie whilst the crews raced virtually level for three-quarters of the journey. With Brian Hodgson at stroke Dr Ashby remembers that 'we were pleased to find that for once we were not behind':

He [Brian Hodgson] was keeping at a steady and not too exhausting rate of striking . . . it would have more effect on the morale of both crews, if we could hold them without this extra effort. When we came out of the bend at Chiswick Eyot island, cox then called for 'ten', our first in the race. We did a good one and drew away about half a length. I was the first one to see their bow slipping behind, and we knew then that, barring some accident, victory was really within our grasp.

The blades of the crews were barely eighteen inches apart and at one point actually touched. Approaching Barnes Bridge Cambridge spurted again but the Dark Blues shot the bridge in 18 minutes 34 seconds, nearly a length ahead. The

Cambridge Stroke, Parfitt, drove his tiring crew at 34 strokes a minute. Oxford were still rowing at 32 but then jumped to 38. All this time the President's voice had been reported as being frequently heard above the cheers from Chiswick. One minute from the finish the Dark Blues were a length clear. 'After passing under Barnes Bridge we knew that we had won,' the Secretary concluded. Oxford won by three lengths in the slowest time for sixty years; many papers regarded the race as the 'greatest struggle in living memory'. In *The Boat Race*, Gordon Ross writes how 'Lewes was the first to greet them.'

Jock knew how to celebrate. A five-course luncheon was held at the OUBC headquarters at the Ranelagh Country Club. The first toast was 'To Cambridge', the second, 'To Us'. The sedate and gentle atmosphere of the Club took on a new ambience as great quantities of ale were consumed. The President hired an old-fashioned stage coach, 'Horse, Coachman and all'. As Michael Ashby remembers, 'He had a wonderful flair for style'. The United Universities Club received many telephone calls instructing staff to reserve tables with dark blue flowers on them. Jock left the Ranelagh Club for the West End sporting his silver coach horn; he gave a demonstration of the instrument from the roof of an OUBC vehicle in diverse locations, the most popular being Piccadilly Circus where thousands of additional revellers were gathering. Extra police were drafted in to monitor the swelling crowds, and at one stage twenty stalwart policemen formed a close cordon round Eros.

One national newspaper claimed that 'Undergraduettes outdid undergraduates in jollity. One party of girls clambered on to the top of a taxi and drove round and round the circus blowing toy trumpets and shouting.' Back in Oxford City the news of the OUBC's success resulted in a number of people performing a 'victory dance'. The Dark Blues visited a Kingsway cinema and saw the first showing of the film of the race in the afternoon, and after Cambridge finished their evening meal at the Junior Carlton Club, the two teams met up at the Hippodrome, Leicester Square, to see a play. It was the first time for nineteen years that both crews had been present at the same theatre and several papers reported that it was 'the noisiest Boat Race night in memory'. If there were minor tussles with officials during the festivities, incidents were reported as ending in good-humoured banter. Jock played the French horn with flair. Apparently Joe Loss once offered him an opportunity to play in his band. Just when is not known, but if the bandleader was in town that night he may well have heard or had report of the impressive blasts on Jock's post horn and offered him a first musical break based upon such fanfares.

It might be a cause for wonder at how the President, once at No.2, who claimed partial responsibility for 'the criticism of the bow oars' that 'was perfectly justified', could also write of his developing the then universally acclaimed top heavy-weight oarsman, Jan Sturrock. The answer partly lay in his having carefully thought through how the different personal-ities of the team would either gel or clash. Ronnie Rowe, at No.4, was poles apart from Sturrock in terms of rowing ability and temperament, and Jock reveals that it was for this reason that he was rowing:

> There were better oars than Ronnie rowing in the Isis crew. I chose Ronnie because of his tireless good nature, his complete naïvety and because he plays the piano extraordinarily well, he was a continual source of amusement, the butt of the crew . . . it really was he that kept Jan in such sweet temper during training.

Jock was entirely pragmatic in selecting his crew in order to ensure its success and R. D. Burnell considered that Jock was 'passionately convinced that the need was for men . . . who would be happy together'. Perhaps Ronnie also helped to bring out the strong light-hearted side of Jock himself.

Later Ronnie Rowe's naïve but charming ways attracted the opprobrium of his senior leaders during the war when, having returned to Cairo hungry after a mission, but with the prize of a captured German officer, he proceeded to give him dinner at the Officer's Mess there. Jock knew his men and indicates this in the same letter of 9 April: 'The race was ours because the morale of the crew was high, bad oars though the original four bow men were, it was mainly due to them that the morale was high.'

David Mynors had rowed at No.3 before the changes in the bows and Jock considered in late April that 'no man is better able to keep a crew in good humour and prevent them from taking themselves too seriously.' Jock's tribute to his old No.3 shows a little of why it had been so hard to let him go, 'He took the exclusion from the boat as nobly as he had rowed in it throughout practice, thereby setting me an example. I see in him myself, an ambitious youth with many faults.'

Jock had only just turned twenty-three, and yet he understood the men's strengths and weaknesses, but seemed only too pleased to marvel at their superiority over himself, and he talks of the crew's giant oar, Sturrock:

> Not once, however, did Jan find fault with our efforts after his experience in the Olympic crew, he was a fine example of keenness and a possession of the true racing spirit. I was delighted to hear he is to be elected Captain of Leander Club. I am sure you will not grudge him the position which I might have been asked to fill had I been good enough to row in the boat.

It was clear how big a part he had played in showing that Cambridge were no longer invincible. What a strange mixture of emotions must have coursed through him as he supported from the OUBC launch; after the race Jock wrote that 'I did cry like a great big baby . . . and was in among the gallant men who had done it: but I was not ashamed; I deserved to be happy.' One newspaper reported of Jock that 'it was he who imbued the Oxford crew with the confidence that carried them on to win. It was he who roared the loudest when Oxford were making their great effort to get ahead at Chiswick, and it was he who showed the greatest enthusiasm at the result.' His Secretary agreed with Skinner's assessment that 'Jock Lewes . . . is a favourite with all, but has done an immense amount for Oxford rowing, and for this year's crew in particular.'

5

Traveller

'Gather ye rosebuds while ye may'

Jock took the opportunity to travel in Europe while based at Oxford. By the Spring of 1934 he still entertained the possibility of returning to Australia after his Schools, or possibly seeking a commission in the Indian Army in spite of the prohibitive cost of being a polo-playing subaltern. Then such trips on the Continent would be far and few between unless he entered the Diplomatic Services of either Australia or England. These various careers were considered over the next three years.

In April, therefore, together with his sister Elizabeth and her friends Margaret Holmes and Joan Fitzhardinge, he set out on bicycle for a tour of Belgium. Joan remembers thinking that, 'To escort three young women, one of whom was your sister, on such an expedition requires courage of no small order.' Avoiding a wheel in a tramline that cut corners, keeping to the right and developing 'cobblestone co-ordination' became the first test of valour for the four cyclists. Jock wanted to see the battlefields. Observing the grounds of Ypres and the Menin Gate was a powerful antidote to the pains in the chest that the cyclists had endured after falling onto the cobblestones that had played havoc on the way there. Appalled at the numbers of British, French, Canadian and Australian dead, the group was impressed nonetheless by how beautifully maintained the graves were, with fresh-mown grass between the headstones.

Feelings of sadness were soon overwhelmed by more painful bruises; mirth was then the antidote. After racing dodgem cars in Courtrai, when the impact of Joan's machine onto Jock's 'carried away' his braces' buttons, the party engaged in a spectacular collision on two wheels. Joan recalled that:

All of a sudden for no reason I fell off. John fell on top of me and Margaret fell on top of John, there was a gendarme presumably on point duty . . . I expect he would have been happy to help us if he had not been totally incapacitated by laughter. He was still doubled up in paroxysms as we bicycled off.

The group reached Antwerp and visited the Cathedral the day after one of the panels of Van Eyck's triptych had been stolen. Jock later discovered that the theft had been a mark of German hostility towards the terms of the Treaty of Versailles which many Englishmen considered to smack of revenge rather than peace. The harsh execution of the treaty in the 1920s had continued to haunt Europe. As Hitler gained sympathy for his increasingly aggressive foreign policy time was running out for the holidaymakers, and Joan was grateful to Jock for ensuring that the end of the trip was a happy one:

The train conductor had torn out my boat ticket instead of my train ticket, and I was not able to embark until the conductor was summoned and the whole pile of tickets gone through. The faithful John stood by me while the minutes ticked away, until at last the ticket was found and we were able to return to England together. Jock was loyal to his sister's friends as he was to his family and continued to develop the sense of duty that he had often nurtured in childhood. He was predictable in that he always did what one expected of him, and if it was a grand gesture one expected, he did that too.

David Lewes spent his first Easter vacation with Jock on a tandem bicycle called 'Mulga-Bill', named after a character in a favourite Australian verse. The bike was truly inseparable from the brothers, not only as a mobile seat but as a friend affectionately referred to as one of 'we three'. Jock and David were not ready to swap their lives on ponies for the luxury of public transport, and cycling was a healthy way of enjoying the outdoor life that they had largely left behind in Bowral. Perhaps they were short of time, because they spent little of their Continental trip in Bruges and regretted missing its beauties. The two pressed on towards Liège, along the Rhine and onto Koblenz and Köln, where the rain was their greatest challenge. The journal of the holiday was dedicated 'to the two loving people who have made it possible for us to do such things as are herein recorded, Mother and Father', and most of the record was pencilled in Jock's hand.

At farmhouses on their route they began to discover more about the New Germany. Not possessing a bed and breakfast guide for 1935, the young men were resourceful and usually managed to obtain good rooms for a Reichsmark, often with breakfast thrown in. Britain had not yet allowed Germany to break the Versailles Treaty by signing an agreement to allow Hitler the right to increase his fleet to only 30% of the size of the British navy. That was two months away. German students discussed the unfairness of the treaty with the cyclists, and also the restrictions placed on their people. The brothers later learnt that 'more Germans would go to England but for the fact they are not allowed to take money out of Germany'. The Lewes's diary dedication must have seemed increasingly appropriate as Jock and David saw their situation in stark contrast to their hosts': the two were able to cable ahead for currency to be collected several day's ride away. They were also clearly able to gauge something of what ordinary German people were thinking: democracy in Germany had lasted little more than ten years and a significant number were celebrating that.

Germany was impressive to the outdoor men. It seemed a home from home in some respects; German youth celebrated the value of their environment in healthy pursuits. A few of the differences between the Lewes's freedom in Australia and the activities of the Hitler Youth was that the land around Sydney was more rugged and the two brothers lived by an entirely different philosophy. Yet, apart from swapping ponies for motorcycles, Jock and David would have enjoyed many of the same experiences as Hitler Youth activities: camp fires, shooting, hill walking and running, marching, and a gamut of games and recreation that engendered pleasure in fitness and self-sufficiency. It may not have occurred yet to Jock and David that with the currency restriction Hitler had killed two birds with one stone and kept his economy seemingly buoyant whilst depriving his own young men of the chance to travel and learn the ways of others. By the end of the trip Jock discovered the importance of travelling when a Belgian train official mistook him for a Nazi supporter and voiced his disgust. Jock wrote that 'Belgium is exceedingly fearful of Germany and she has every reason to be.' He had bought a knife, 'such as is worn by the German youths. The blade of which is inscribed in Goebbel's handwriting with the words, "Blut und Ehre", or "Blood and Honour!" And yet Hitler tries to tell Europe that he does not want war and that Germany loathes war and desires nothing but peace!!' It was an unpleasant presage in a wet but otherwise happy itinerary.

After the Boat Race Jock was asked to join a new University committee that monitored 'the true spirit of English Sport'; he had witnessed a deterioration of spirit in sport during the Olympic Games at Berlin. The Vice-Chancellor was to be the

85

chairman of this new think-tank, and delegates from Cambridge University were also approached, so that they too could help give a lead to the rest of the English amateur-sporting world. Several incidents at the Olympics had caused disquiet amongst the rowing fraternities of both England and Germany. However much he might have been disturbed by the aggressive attitude of Germany to her neighbours, and the conspicuous competitiveness of the German crews, Jock clearly admired the positive and hard-working approach that many Germans were taking towards regeneration. Gunther Maz, a former Rhodes scholar and Oxford graduate, returned the compliment to his old University crew in an Essen local paper when he likened the respect accorded to the oarsmen as being the same given to a soldier hero in Germany: 'it was not only a sport but a cult.' When Jock took his scratch VIII to Essen in 1936, he had the fortune to be the guest of von Bohlen und Holbach at the Krupp Armaments factory. At Bad Ems he wrote of 'the wonderful spirit of good fellowship and hospitality', but this evidently began to evaporate as the tour developed.

At first he sang the praises of the Germans, who were not liked by 'indolent men', and Jock was initially impressed by the industrious host oarsmen in the regattas leading up to the Olympics. His crew was on a rowing holiday to enjoy wine, women and song; how much Jock indulged himself is not known – he certainly both drank and sang well, but he was there to mull over the OUBC programme for the year ahead, and forget his studies until September. The Germans seemed much more involved in their sport than the Dark Blues; he admired his opposition's determination to win but was surprised by the nature of their zeal to succeed: 'they were more determined to beat us, which they achieved by starting before the word "Go!"'. Jock reflected on what appeared to be the rising corruption of the general ethos in Germany: 'It was a pity because the practice does not seem to be considered immoral in Germany.' This hardly confounded the

Oxford crew who were also spurred on when a spectator spat on them during one of the races.

It was with some satisfaction that his Oxford VIII beat the crew from Mainz, then rated as the host country's third best. Jock was tempted to sour his parting regatta speech: 'I should have liked to have got up and told them how bad we thought their boats and racing spirit, so angry was I.' Instead he lied through his teeth and discovered the virtues of making short and sweet remarks, which he considered was about all that his audience could digest: 'Of course, the Germans can take any amount of sententious declarations, just as they seem to be able to deal with any amount of roast pork and potatoes. "British diners" in both respects are more subtle.' He concluded that 'I can see a very considerable change in Germany since I first came.'

Yet within two years Jock claimed that half of all his friends were Berliners. He continued to have reservations about the dangers of German nationalism, but that did not prevent him from befriending newspaper barons, generals' widows, Foreign Office pariahs and a beautiful Nazi girlfriend who might have become his wife but for her political persuasions. Jock spent some of his time that summer preparing the ground for a longer stay than was planned after he came down from Schools. He was keen to improve his German and thus be more eligible for the Diplomatic Services in Australia, England or India. When Joan Fitzhardinge had asked him about his future plans in 1934, he had immediately answered her, 'Join the Indian Army and play polo', despite the fact that his father would have preferred him to join the Indian Civil Service. Since then he had correctly calculated that war was inevitable and that experience in other fields would first allow him to enjoy the freedoms of youth. Perhaps part of his proposed attachment to Berlin might have been one reason why he didn't join the Cambridge crew when they decided to end the visitor's regatta with a student prank that insulted the Olympiad's own orgy of celebration.

Berlin was draped with the insipid realism of Nazi idolatry: the narcotic for impressionable foreign visitors was complete with welcoming parties of girls dressed as peasants and Renaissance pages, parades of horses, and anthems to resurrected German power. 'Chips' Channon, who kept a diary of his stay in Germany, arrived there as the guest of one of Ribbentrop's most trusted agents, George von Wussow. By mid-August the climax of the Olympic celebrations escalated with fantastic entertainments held by Ribbentrop, Göring and Goebbels. 'Chips' Channon fell under the spell of what Harold Nicolson called 'the champagne-like influence' of the Nazis; however, Channon noted the effort the Germans were making to show off the world of grandeur, the permanency and respectability of the new regime. The shame of losing to the Americans in the Olympics was hidden in streets that were punctuated with tall crimson banners.

Every flagstaff crowned its swastika with an eagle, one of which was temporarily grounded by a tipsy Cambridge crew under the influence of beer rather than champagne: they had cut out the Nazi emblem and rehoisted the mutilated flag, before tottering home. Jock does not write of Nazi racialism at this time, and it was not unusual for tourists to be unaware of the extent of the apartheid that was steadily growing between the Germans and the Jews. During the Olympics the *Juden sind hier nicht erwünscht* signs, forbidding the presence of Jews, had been removed and stored in the basements of the local town halls. In July public condemnation of the Jews was suspended which helped to attract the 1.2 million visitors who visited Berlin that summer. The action of the Cambridge oarsmen seemed to be more than a prank inspired by alcohol; it was surely taken as disapproval of what lay beyond the Olympic pageants, ordained art, bannered horsemen and temporarily missing signs for the Jews. Mike Ashby, who with Jock and the Light Blues was then sharing the same accommodation at Krupp's factory, recalled that the perpetrators of the crime had difficulty concealing their booty because of its size; several huge men standing on the lid managed to squash the Nazi emblem into a large case:

> At last Berlin was aroused; the guilt was suspected to lie with some despised foreigner, probably of Jewish non-Aryan blood, and the order went out to close the frontiers! A Sunday morning is never the best for rapid instructions, and the Germans must always act through the proper chain of command. At last the frontier guards were alerted.

Fortunately the Cambridge crew had sped away, as had Ashby in his new Aston Martin. As he motored south to watch the motor racing at the Nurburgring, Jock settled down to watch the great concourse of oarsmen from all over the world. Two years later he was pleased that the OUBC kept up this tradition and continued to send scratch crews to Germany. His close friend, John Garton, rowed in that team and, like the Cambridge crew before him, piqued the pride of the Nazis, but this time it was achieved by winning the General Göring cup at Bad Ems regatta. John Garton recalled that the elaborate embossing of the blades was intended for a winning German crew, such was the overconfidence in the Master Race; Göring, ever renowned for his *élan*, in his white uniform that dripped with medals, had more difficulty than usual producing a charmed smile during the presentations to Garton's crew.

Jock's sojourn in Germany in 1936 was more than a rowing holiday: he took advantage of the opportunity to move from the active to the contemplative life; again this was well reflected in his letters home. He quickly distilled all he observed in Berlin and leavened it with his study of history and philosophy. He had been studying Wells's *The Outline of History* and regarded the writer's great failing as accepting without question 'the superiority of unity over diversity':

> He seems to assume that 'nationalism is a bad thing, merely because it leads to diversity in human affairs and that internationalism is a good thing, because it leads to unity. I don't want to set myself up as a champion of nationalism; in fact, living in Germany one would tend to lean in the opposite direction. Perhaps for the future unity will be right but not complete unity; that, I am persuaded, will only come with the consummation of the destiny of humanity . . . Wells is too German in outlook. I want the world to adopt, not ideas, but a way of thinking . . . that the English have been quite unconsciously using for centuries and which I believe is largely responsible for the success of this people in coping with the bigger problems of life. I am equally certain that there is something Eastern about this way of thinking. That word, I think, sums up the whole of our generation: shallow conservatism as contrasted with 'narrow conservatism'.

Jock's curiosity and openness to ideas would have certainly been of tremendous assistance to him if he had chosen a career in journalism; it explains why he had been on good terms with a variety of Germans, in spite of their Nazi sympathies. When he returned to Germany a year later in 1937 he set out 'to try my hand at a little amateur journalism . . . for pin money'; his weekly cycle of letter-writing developed as his own horizons widened. He had become a compulsive weekly diarist and it gave him the confidence to see that his own writing might one day be read. At the end of October he was only a little self-conscious about this realization: 'I must say that I had to admit to frequently wondering, when reading the letters of other people, whether some day people will be reading mine, and even to having this in mind sometimes when writing.'

In the summer of 1937 he had again stayed at the Krupp

estate and joined David Winser at short notice to row in a scratch Oriel college VIII. Jock may not have found the sober zeal of the German pageantry disturbing in 1936, but a year later he expressed regret for Holy German art which celebrated German nationalism as the new religion. He kept in touch with Continental artistic tastes or lack of them when he and David Winser visited the Exhibition of International 'Products and Pastimes'. There his favourite pavilions were the Rumanian and Czechoslovakian exhibits, 'with an air of humour and gaiety which was ominously lacking from the German and Russian efforts', which he regarded as all show and no substance. His second summer break in Germany had not changed his mind about German art, for the year before he had written how 'an artistic sense implies also its opposite, a sense of the ugly and unbeautiful, and this the Englishman in my mind does not possess in nearly such a high degree as the Germans, the French or Italians'.

In between his rowing trip and travels to Berlin, Jock returned to England to pack up his things at Oxford and do a bit of research on his impending need to earn himself a living during the next year. On the way to the Channel he rested at Fontainebleau with David Winser and basked in the Indian summer of his student days. He wrote how the two men played in the sun, 'huddling together in cool little caves we discovered, and seeing how far we could walk along felled tree trunks without touching the ground.' In exactly four years Jock would be posted to Tobruk to complete many missions inside the German-occupied territory. Those salad days of stepping on tree trunks may well have been remembered by him during his missions to locate and avoid German S-mines in August 1941; both activities were so far removed and yet strangely linked, for both men later needed to sharpen their wits in a war that was far from their minds in the forests of Fontainebleau that summer.

Once back in England Jock seemed to be at a loose end until going back to Berlin to improve his German. Before leaving

Oxford, when hearing someone approach his rooms, he confessed that 'I snatch up a book, and fumble it open; sometimes it is upside down when the person comes in, and still I never realized how ridiculous it all was'. He visited Australia House in order to gain a place in the Australian Department for External Affairs, but the department was no longer recruiting. There were few acquaintances in London, so he took himself off to Scotland and joined his friend and double-sculls partner, Sandy Gordon, at Kerrow. Here he coped with his discovery of the horrors of lassitude by composing a black comical piece that featured the death of a deer hunter. If he had settled on a definite career, he might have enjoyed his break much more; he admitted to his parents that 'I don't think I am cut out for a life of hunting and shooting. It doesn't leave me with much except tall stories and stuffed heads.' Before storing his vast quantity of books and goods, he did have time to organize a social calendar for the young son of his future friends in Berlin, and so letters were sent to Miss Macdonald of the Isles asking if she could dispense with tradition and place Herman Solf on her first list of invitations, 'though it was breaking the rules'.

Jock's social arrangements started to burst at the seams almost as soon as he arrived in Berlin. The city was the most powerful industrial centre in Europe and, the year before, 'Chips' Channon had observed 'the general gaiety of Berlin; the ugly city pulsates with life, and, it would seem, with money and prosperity!' Indulgent Nazis could enjoy a relaxation of their edicts in Berlin: the streets buzzed, cocktail parties were all the rage and clubs stayed open all night. Jock moved in different circles from Channon and his powerful hosts, but he was introduced to politicians, diplomats, businessmen and the fossils of the old regime, and also met the upstarts of the new. His lively calendar was also brightened by new acquaintances whom he met at the home of Frau Hannah Solf, the widow of the last Imperial German Foreign Minister to Tokyo and mother of Herman. Her other son,

Hans Heinrich, was one of Ribbentrop's acolytes who had already served with the Duke of Windsor's entourage during the latter's controversial visit earlier that October, which ended a few days before Jock arrived in Berlin on 20 October 1937. Hans Heinrich Solf offered to act as a *cicerone* for Jock, who was promised he would be shown around part of the Duke's itinerary that included a visit to the Nazi's model Stock factory. 'In between such distinguished visits they deal suitably with such small fry as yours truly'; nevertheless, he was pleased to be at the heart of Nazi tours even if they were 'all the things' foreign visitors 'ought to be shown' by the office of Herr von Ribbentrop, whom the English papers graced with the title 'Herr Hitler's ambassador at large'.

Jock was under no illusions that he was meant to leave Germany, 'duly impressed', yet he seemed well disposed to the 'spin' of the New Germany. In 1937 he had admired Dr Ley's Labour Front that 'has responsibilities to the men he employs almost greater than to the people whose capital he uses'. Jock's memories of his mother feeding Sydney's wandering jobless when they knocked on the door of the family home at Bowral were still vivid. The Duke of Windsor had every reason to be less enthusiastic about the boorish Dr Ley. In *King Edward VIII* Philip Ziegler shows how the Nazi leader, who had been the Duke of Windsor's own official guide in mid-October, had misquoted the Duke to such an extent that the fate of the Edward's visit was further sealed as a 'dangerous, semi-political move'.

Writing to his parents about the fair and supportive pay and conditions, Jock also sang the praises of the facilities and opportunities of another Nazi organization, the *Kraft Durch Freude* (KDF), which was open to members who benefited from the many sports and holidays that were freely provided. It may well have occurred to him that he had personally had most of those activities laid on by either Oxford or the friends he had met there, but in Germany young workers appeared to be gaining similar chances without the benefit of his privileged background. Yet he had the sense to note that this was KDF information that 'I am quoting, and one has no means of discovering how much is the ideal at which they aim and how much the reality they have achieved.' In his *Berlin Diary 1934–1941,* William Shirer, the North American reporter, also seemed bemused by the direction that Nazi policies were taking weeks before Jock arrived in the city. Shirer commented on them and on the writing of the German historicist, Oswald Spengler, who had unwittingly encouraged those policies:

> Somehow I feel that, despite our work as reporters, there is little understanding of the Third Reich, what it is, what it is up to, where it is going, either at home or elsewhere abroad. It is a complex picture. Certainly the British and French do not understand Hitler's Germany. Perhaps, as the Nazis say, the Western democracies have become sick, decadent, and have reached that stage of decline which Spengler predicted.

However, if initially Jock was hoodwinked by the socialism of the Nazis as many foreigners were, his naivety was unlikely to remain unchallenged in the increasingly politically incorrect circle of Frau Solf, which was, as Giles MacDonogh explains in his *A Good German:Adam von Trott zu Solz,* a 'political oasis' for those who vented their hatred against the new regime. The Ambassador's widow introduced Jock to Karl Silex, the Editor of *Deutsche Allgemeine Zeitung,* the Mayor of Hamburg and the Prince of Hanover in the first few days of his stay in Berlin. Squash matches were arranged with the Prince, and cocktails, which were all the rage, with the Editor, and a letter of introduction to Baron Munchhausen for Jock's forthcoming visit to Paris where the baron was based. Christian of Hanover would later be kicked out of the German army because he was a royal prince and related to the British royal family.

Jock seems to have befriended at least one general's widow whilst in Berlin and been rewarded for his pains with gossip and stories of both the English and German royal families. He accompanied the widow of General Seeckt to the unveiling of a statue dedicated to the General at the *Invalidenfriedhof* (the military cemetery attached to the pensioners' hospital*)*; he wrote that, 'I seemed to be the only person present who was not a general, a minister, a soldier or a press photographer.' A recently bereaved Frau Dorothee von Seeckt considered Hitler 'very weak over the issue of Polish-held Danzig' and she admired Edward VIIth, 'because he only meddled in international affairs when it was to England's benefit'. Jock regarded her views on the subject of the Duke of Windsor as 'strange', but she was, 'not the only German who holds them':

> She thinks Edward VIII a much too liberal king for our con-servative ministers who therefore considered that he would be best off the throne. They therefore arranged the whole of the Mrs Simpson affair, 'compromised him' . . . even down to the last detail – she mentioned the fact that Mrs Simpson rode to the final hearing of the divorce case in the King's car – can you imagine Baldwin hatching such a plot!? She [Frau von Seeckt] is now waiting quite calmly for the next war.

Through the Solfs Jock gained access to more relics of the Kaiser's regime. Old guard and Prussian views of the past were offered by von Bredow senior who had been the Kaiser's ADC during the First World War. He, like Frau von Seeckt, thought that England had 'backed the wrong horse in the war'. Jock felt this cynical attitude towards the British to be 'perfectly justified', but at the same time 'it displayed a funda-mental misunderstanding of the aims of British foreign policy that doesn't mind having bellicose neighbours or powerful neighbours'- 'but bellicose and powerful neighbours will always find Britain against them'. The Kaiser came off badly in these conversations, for von Bredow also considered 'that if the German nation had not had such a blind hero-worship of the Kaiser we should certainly have won the war; he was the biggest coward I ever knew. He was an actor, and a bad one.' Herr von Bredow referred to the Italians as 'half-niggers', and to the south Germans as 'little better'. Jock wondered 'where is the holy spirit of inspired German patriotism' that he had read about in his youth. He certainly began to despair at the cynicism of the generation that had fought the war and the questionable values of their children who were lining up to fight the next conflict. He later vented many of his frustrations on his father:

> Interesting isn't it? Yes, a damn sight too interesting! Man only makes himself ridiculous when he starts talking and fighting about Sovereignty, Freedom, Patriotism and National Honour. At any rate, when man is sitting half-naked in the sun minding his own sheep, he is not ridiculous, whatever else he may be. I often ask myself why I want to mix in this godless world of international relations; the answer is twofold: to prevent some fool greater than I mixing in it, and to try and bring Godliness into that world. What a hope!

Jock's social calendar prevented him from living the last flush of youth and idealism in a lugubrious state of confusion. Some of his disillusion was no doubt expected by Arthur and Elsie who had brought him up to serve an empire that was now unable to export England's liberal democracy even if it had tried. In his recent work, *Dark Continent: Europe's Twentieth Century*, Mark Mazower highlights how English MPs offered little alternative to Germany, and it was perhaps for this reason that three months later Jock still favoured some Nazi policies, having little regard for braying parliamentarians who won few supporters of their own. Business and politics took a back seat in late October when he had accepted an invitation to the *Jachtclub von*

Deutschland Ball on the same night as a big society ball that Frau Solf hoped that he might attend with her. Jock was sorry to miss the elegant social gathering, but he had already agreed to the first minutes before the second was offered. He mused that 'for pleasure I think I should prefer arrangements as they are . . . for the furtherance of my education they would best be the other way, so hurrah for having once to prefer pleasure to let us say lessons in deportment rather than business.'

After the Yacht Club Ball Jock went on to a select gathering that included the Führer and his propaganda minister, Goebbels; he clearly enjoyed his dance reception at *Kameradschaft der Deutschen Künstler* (a friendly society) and noted a few days later that 'after the great ones had gone, the evening was continued in the *keller* beneath: I got to bed at 5.30.' Before the ball Jock spent an afternoon in Dresden with Frau Solf, and wryly noted that 'it was almost sacrilege to go off so soon; I felt as if the spirits of the great masters were standing in the courts and, as they watched me go out, were nodding to each other and saying, "He has done Dresden."' Buoyant with wit and mirth, he was thoroughly enjoying his hectic social life in Berlin.

Jock noted that some German humour, like their modern art, was eggshell-thin, and perhaps certain young Nazis tried too hard to befriend him. Frau Solf introduced him to a Herr Schlottman of the SS, and on 1 November he wrote how the 'charming' Schlottman epitomized empty German humour. While cracking a walnut, the German officer had commented on its lack of contents, and like the nut his wit was no more than a quick 'Ersatz!' Schlottman had studied for three years at Edinburgh and been at great pains to cultivate an English sense of humour. Jock wrote how 'it does happen to be amusing . . . the funny part is their firm conviction that a sense of humour is essential to the make-up of a perfect man, without the slightest conception of the reason why. Such jokes as the above they make rather to show that they have a sense of humour than because it amuses them.' He observed with some astonishment, the ease with which the SS officer had 'left the Church'. He observed that 'To my mind it is impossible to leave the Church, but they seem to consider it quite simply a process in Germany, rather like resigning from a club or something.' Schlottman had made a swift conversion to the religion of National Socialism.

It is possible that Schlottman, who had looked after the Aga Khan when the latter visited Berlin, may have been monitoring Jock as the latter wrote several times that he happened 'by chance' to bump into the SS officer at the Wannsee (later the location of the fateful conference of 20 July 1942 that mapped the 'Final Solution' to the Jewish problem in German–occupied Europe). In the autumn of 1937 the newly created lake resort, with its proximity to Grünewald and the forests of Potsdam, was then a joyful place for Jock to paddle about in a Canadian canoe with his new girlfriend, Senta Adriano. Senta was a friend of the Solfs and a young woman with whom Jock was soon to fall desperately in love.

Plenty of visitors were then monitored by the Gestapo; in Jock's case it might have been pure coincidence that Schlottman kept crossing his path. He was learning German and studying grammar during the day in order to prepare himself for his Foreign Office exams the following year, after a brief stop in Paris that was planned for January 1938 so that he could also brush up on his French. Yet in the company of such illustrious Germans as the Mayor of Hamburg, Karl Silex and the Solfs, he may well have been perceived as already working for the Foreign Office and his story of earning 'pin-money' as a journalist may have appeared to be a 'cover' to the likes of Schlottman. However he was viewed, Jock's visit reflected the propaganda imperative of the Nazis; 'small fry' like him seemed to have brought considerable attention to the regime's ambitious young spin doctors. Jock's 'guides' in and around Berlin attest to the organization of the propaganda machine; the experiences of other Englishmen suggest that some propaganda might have started to spin out of control.

One unpublished diary written a few months before Jock's admission into the Solf circle reveals that it was pride in the appearance of Nazi planning, rather than the concealment of the inhuman aspects of their efficiency, that was propagated. The Hon. Hugh Lawson-Johnston as part of the International Chamber of Commerce delegation, recorded his experience of being shown both a Labour and a Concentration Camp; he describes Sachsenhausen Concentration Camp, 55 km from Berlin:

> As a finale to our visit, a bell was rung in the middle of the parade ground, and immediately every man in the camp formed up in his group in front of the living quarters. When all was ready, each group was marched forward to a set mark and formed a line – the Political prisoners on the left and the habitual criminals on the right, closed in at the far end by the overflow of the politicians. We were moved backwards towards the gate so that, should it be necessary to use the machine-gun, which was now manned by four men, it could fire safely over our heads. Thus positioned, the entire 2,300 prisoners sang us a song which was non-political, but, rather, highly sentimental.
>
> We had been shown a good deal. In fact, the only points upon which, so far as we could see, we had not been informed were the conditions under which the work was carried out, the propaganda produced in the hopes of reforming the political prisoners (and for that matter the criminals too), the methods employed to achieve these ends, and finally the proceedings taken to dispose of the bodies of those whose will was made of iron. The first question applied alike to the labour camp; for it was palpably noticeable that our presence in both camps seemed to have called for a half-holiday on each afternoon. It was admitted that prisoners did try quite often to escape, and that they never succeeded.

Extremely good-looking and sometimes mistaken for Douglas Fairbanks junior, Jock would have blended in well at the Adlon Hotel where he met friends of the Solfs. There, Giles MacDonogh notes, Heads of State, diplomats and film-stars rubbed shoulders. These were the days before *Eintopftag*, 'one dish day', the dish being a tasteless stew that restaurants were obliged to provide during the war. Inga Haag, who worked for Admiral Canaris at the Abwehr and was a cousin of the anti-Nazi conspirator Adam Von Trott zu Solz, recalled that such company were looked after by a staff that, acccording to Louis Adlon, were 'mostly in the pay of the Gestapo'. Inga expressed little surprise that Jock's apparent infatuation with a young Nazi and the new Socialism might have attracted the interest of the security forces. Unknowingly he had shaken hands with Nazis who almost certainly had blood under their fingernails. Before that blood and the ink on the sheets of the international Press were dry he was busy reporting back European news to his parents. With a little prudery Jock recounted to his father how, 'a very irreverent German told me a joke':

> 'I see a naked man, sitting in the middle of a meadow eating grass', she said.
> 'And what?' I said, 'does your vision mean?'
> She replied, 'It shows the end of the Four Year Plan.'
> There have been some particularly venomous ones lately about Czechoslovakia; of course the Jews come in for it – they have a whole paper devoted to vilifying them, 'Die Stürmer'- and Great Britain, in the Mediterranean and Palestine, less venomous and perhaps more deserved, but wanting in humour.

Jock was writing almost exactly one year before *Kristallnacht* (The Night of Broken Glass) when the Nazis felt sufficiently confident to create an unofficial curfew long enough to destroy Jewish businesses and confidence overnight, and make even window-shopping an impossibility for Germans who were finding it difficult to keep purchasing goods in what was an increasingly stagnant economy. The well-to-do appeared in no better spirits: after a week at the Congress of the International Chamber of Commerce, Hugh Lawson-Johnston wrote that 'everyone you see is depressed. No one dare smile nor talk above a whisper.' Perhaps Jock was near the truth when he wrote in early November 1937, of how 'the 100% Nazi is not so popular as formerly and the original Nazi programme has lately been very much toned down by the infusion of a little more common sense. Still, the average German's faith in the efficacy of the human reason is quite staggering.' Jock considered that a popular view was that what most Germans felt, and what most Englishmen failed to see was that Germany was no longer stagnating; the main thing was that something was afoot – 'and it was immaterial for the moment whether it was right or wrong'. Jock had put the Englishman's view to Germans 'that Englishmen will never understand this abandonment of accepted ethical and moral standards for the sake merely of something to do'. Something was 'afoot'; it was cloven, but he had still not yet seen the Nazi regime for what it was.

Jock seemed totally unprepared when he fell in love with the Solf's family friend, Senta Adriano, who, 'though very nearly a pagan as most Germans seem to be', impressed him with 'her determination to drink the cup of life dry'. Writing from Paris in February 1938 he provided his parents with answers to most of their questions about a young woman he had once thought could be 'no more than a clever little flirt', at the same time wondering 'whether I am no more than an innocent and unsuspecting schoolboy'. In her elegant sailor suit and with Jock's *savoir vivre*, perhaps there was a bit of the innocent schoolboy and muse – rather than flirt – in both Jock and Senta. John Garton, who knew Jock at that time, remembers that 'there was no "shop-window" about Jock', and with his wit, energy and charm he could have been every bit her muse as she was his. Senta had succeeded in 'upsetting my calculations', for Jock admitted to being at first 'unable to think of myself as a separate character': she was 'hammering at a door that I had long ago determined to keep locked. It is the first time that I have been unable to disregard the knocking.' Jock admired the natural beauty of his sister Elizabeth, and made a favourable comparison between her and Senta – no doubt making his new love that much more acceptable to parents hungry for news:

> She is a little taller than Elizabeth and very much the same build though she is slightly better covered than our wiry little Elizabeth and slightly longer in the limb. On the whole she resembles Elizabeth more closely than anyone else I know.
>
> She has the same hair, perhaps even a little more golden, the same teeth, eyes greeny blue and well spaced, fine delicate eyebrows – not plucked – full lips and a charming smile. I think I told you that she is her father's secretary, helping him with his translating work, and more important still planning all his work for him. She has excellent judgement in that respect and usually ends up doubling her father's rather sanguine estimates as to the number of hours of work a certain book or article will require. When she works, she works with an application that turns me green with envy, when she plays she does it equally whole-heartedly, and when she rests she does so with a completeness and tranquillity that few humans have remembered how to attain – perhaps I should say few Europeans. Your last question, 'Will she enjoy *Hollyman*?' I am in no position to answer. One of her own sayings is: 'You can't argue over matters of taste.' I should say she will enjoy it, but not as much as David Winser, for instance. She is sentimental in very many respects, but not about children. *Hollyman* will appeal to her imagination and to her sense of beauty, but not to her sentiment.

Jock seemed to have found his match. It was Senta's 'frankness and sincerity' that appealed most to him, and she possessed an attractive vulnerability; he was both gentle and sentimental and there is a suggestion that he might have been happy with her, especially if friends like David Winser had not been far away. He certainly needed close friends, because in mid-November he finished his letter to his parents conceding that the contents were, 'another fat wad of self-commiseration', and perhaps he should 'confine himself to facts about Germany, society gossip and the weather'. Jock had been attracted to at least three young women at Oxford, but admitted that it had been 'comparatively easy not to fall in love with Susan Davis, Daphne Smithers and France d'Auriol', all of whom he had made scant reference to in his letters. It seems that Jock felt he was undergoing a case of unrequited love, because, before he admitted exactly how he felt to Senta, he suffered a terrible bout of uncharacteristic alienation and self-pity:

On Saturday I went to a ball with Senta, she was not feeling at all well and could not dance. I was sullen and morose all evening, preoccupied with dear Johnnie [Jock] and his troubles. I became unreasonably angry that this should have happened to me now and Senta became the butt of my temper. Looking back on my behaviour I can hardly believe that it was I who acted thus. That it was I who was so unpardonably rude to a lady. Eventually I became so unbearable that she left me and went to look for her father. When she found him I hastily said goodnight and left. They came into the cloakroom just as I had finished putting on my cloak. I did not give them so much as a look and swept out of the door in fine style just as if it were I who were offended. I might have been dead drunk for all the control I had over myself that night. You can imagine what I felt like the next day. Senta would not see me and I felt quite lost and bewildered. I went to Church for the first time for some weeks.

This evening I saw Senta. She accepted my apology and then gave me some very sound advice for the future. She is a wise girl, much wiser than me, and I consider myself extraordinarily lucky, if lose my heart I must, to lose it to her. She is too kind to wish to hurt, too proud to stoop to conquer, too wise to lose her head in a crisis or her heart in six weeks' acquaintance. She will be a good friend to me, of that I am as sure as I am of your love, and for this I thank God.

Jock gathered his balance for the moment. He contented himself with the knowledge 'that there is something of [Kipling's] Kim in her – little friend of all the world – and I love her for it.' By the end of December Jock turned twenty-four and he celebrated his birthday with Senta who marked the occasion with a little book of poems 'and a souvenir of a time in my life that I know in retrospect will appear among the happiest because it is among the most difficult'. Jock continued to be stoical, without repressing his pain. As the New Year approached when he prepared to leave Germany, Senta asked him to send 'my very kindest regards to your mother and father, and tell them I am looking forward to meeting them very much, but,' she added, 'I am afraid I never shall.'

Senta did not allow herself to hope for things that seemed improbable, and he put that down to the fact that once she had been very unhappy, 'which is something that has never happened to me'. Jock's and Senta's physical separation was now dwarfed by the abyss of the political divide in Europe – however much Jock claimed that 'England is no democracy and Germany far from a totalitarian state.' Whilst staying at the 20,000-acre estate of his artist friend, Frau von Kahlreuth, he couldn't help wondering 'why individual men in their homes are so charming and so lovable, or alternately why nations are so hateful.' In his essay, 'A Tale of Childhood', which he wrote in about 1938 on the subject of his own upbringing, he observes how the cuckoo clock 'was not allowed to hang on the wall and "cuck", just because it was German'. How much he must have hoped for circumstances that would prevent similar prejudices in his own generation. In his tale he had written of the 1914–18 war that 'it was the last war of all, so it was even more wonderful that he had been born just then.' Yet now the threat of war haunted him and seemed to overshadow his and Senta's future together.

6

Propagandist

Be Something Great – Arthur Lewes

Perhaps Elsie's question as to whether Senta liked *Hollyman* was one of the few ways of helping her son from the other side of the world: *Hollyman* was again a lodestar to help Jock, this time so that he could find a like-minded partner. The New Year began ominously for Jock, who concluded that 'it makes me sad to think that it is possible for me to love someone very much, to admire them in every respect, and yet to differ so fundamentally on some of the most important points of belief as I do with Senta.' A quick visit to Paris in January 1938 may have only temporarily dispelled his disappointment and, after brushing up on his French, he returned to England. Perhaps Senta's Nazism consisted of too much nationalism and not enough socialism for his liking. Her likely reactions to reading *Hollyman* indicated that Senta was less sentimental than Jock, about children and perhaps life in general.

Senta visited him in England in the spring of 1938, by which time he was advocating that Britain and France, which purported to be democracies, should take a tougher stance with Germany and Italy, as this was the only 'democratic action they were likely to listen to.' He still supported elements of the Nazi programme but he was as doubtful about the motives of Britain and France as he was about the consequences of German intentions when Hitler broke the terms of the Treaty of Versailles by uniting with Austria. Listening in

Berlin to a speech by Herman Göring 'setting the seal of popular approval' for a new plebiscite confirming the popular appeal of Nazis in Austria, stimulated him to report back to his parents and consider what lay behind 'the seal' – 'a very waxy substance in these "progressive" days'. His letter on the international situation in early April remains an astute commentary on the growing disenchantment with appeasement and the discomfort of those who felt increasingly compelled to choose between 'democratic decay' and the New Order in Germany. He was twenty-four and was still formulating his views, but, in a modern world that had still to reject communism and fascism, he remained insightful, despite being dazzled by National Socialism:

> Who can deny that the British Empire is the result of actions no less evil than those that brought about the *Anschluss*? I would not dare to. No British statesman has ever stated his intentions as plainly as Hitler has done continuously, and still nobody believes that he will do what he says. In *Mein Kampf*, which I have been reading, he told the world years ago that he would build up Germany's army, that he would reoccupy the Rhineland, that he would effect the *Anschluss*; moreover, he has continually repeated that his policy is to be found written down in black and white in that book, but still nobody believes him. Perhaps they will when he has got his colonies, which he will very soon do, as soon in fact as the war in Spain is over; and then perhaps England will make a clear statement of her own intentions, instead of dishing up to the world meaningless talk about ideals and subtle evasions of anything that may commit her to a definite line of action. I always understood that the Englishman did not talk much about the ideals that he prized most highly but reserved talk for facts. Either this is not the case or else Englishmen don't set much store by their ideals of international goodwill. Britain has long ago lost the initiative in international affairs and with the initiative she has lost all opportunity of putting her ideals into practice. Germany

and Italy are now the pacemakers in the world, and it is hardly surprising that it is German and Italian ideals that are practised in that world. All that is left for England to do is to say how good are her own rules of the game and how bad those of Germany and Italy are, but that does not prevent her having to play the game according to the latter set. In the last nine weeks the House of Commons has had thirteen full-dress debates on foreign policy, most of which time has been spent maligning the leaders of various foreign powers. So far nothing has come of all this talk, and unless Lord Perth brings back something pretty substantial from Rome, I believe that even the democratic Englishmen will begin to believe what Hitler and Mussolini say about 'braying democracies'.

All this sounds horribly fascist and dictatorial but there is no doubt in my mind that strength is the only reply that will carry any weight with Germany and Italy, and that since we have allowed things to get this far we have no alternative. France is on the point of becoming either semi-fascist or entirely communist, and we in this country would do well to take her plight to heart and take the initiative both in foreign and home affairs before it is too late.

Perhaps Jock had listened to too much German propaganda, even if his arguments were sound. There was no logical reason why Germany should be forbidden to form a union with Austria. Yet only part of Spengler's view of the decadence of the Western democracies was being served up for public consumption, for, as William Shirer noted in Berlin in late September 1937, Spengler had included Germany in his view of the decline of the West. Jock turned his thoughts away from the rhetoric and inaction of the English Parliament to how to preserve peace. Senta had been staying with him in Oxford and at his flat at Holland Park. It was springtime and he had so much to hope for. He had so many German friends that it was difficult for him to think about the prospect of war, and being close to Senta meant that he couldn't agree with his

Arthur Lewes playing the piano at the Bengal Club in Calcutta, c.1904. (see p.10).

"A series of return trips from Calcutta to Southampton created his first meeting with Elsie Robertson" (p.9).

3. Arthur with his Khansamah in about 1916.

4. Jock at the age of eight months.

5. Arthur's nanny Fanny with Jock in about 1915.

6. The drive approaching the gardens at Fernside, the setting for *Hollyman* (see p.17).

The Lewes family in about 1918.

8. David and Jock at Fernside in about 1932.

Cadet Lieutenant Jock Lewes, King's
School, Parramatta, Sydney, 1931.

10. Cadet Corporal David Lewes, King's
School, 1931.

11. "David spent his first Easter vacation with Jock on a tandem bicycle called 'Mulga-Bill'" (p.84).

12. David and Jock in Germany, 1935.

13. The *Isis* Idol, 1936 (see p.63).

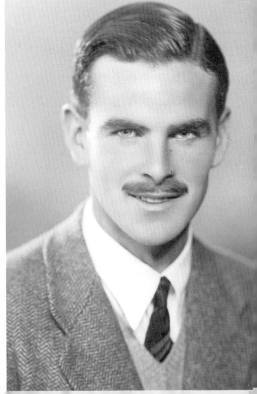

14. Jock winning the Silver Sculls, 1936.

15. "The Double Sculls, the rowing pair's race which he won with Sandy Gordon" (p.62).

16. Elizabeth Lewes, Jock's sister, while at Oxford.

17. Jock in 'Nancy Lea' with Donald Paton at Henley.

18. "A welcome respite at Thorpeness" (p.73). *Left to right:* Winser, Garside Lewes, Kirk, Cherry, Sciortino, Ashby, Wood, Ogilvie, Sturrock.

19. "To our horror and astonishment Jock our splendid President got out and Winser took his place" (p.75).

20. After the change, Jock talking to the Coach, Gully Nickalls.

21. "The most favourable comment went to David Mynors at No. 3" (p.71).

22. "The crew's giant oar, Sturrock" (p.80)

3. The winning crew, 1937.

4. "On Saturday I went to a ball with Senta [Adriano]" (p.103).

25. Jock, Senta and Ludeloff von Bredow outside the von Bredow's house, 1937.

26. Jock with Lady Mairi Stewart, daughter of the 7th Marquess of Londonderry, at the St Andrew's Eve Ball at Grosvenor House, November 1938. Photograph from *The Lady* (see p.125).

27. "Jock first met Mirren Barford at his sister's wedding in 1939" (p.132).

28. After parachute practice: Jock nursing an injured wrist as a result of jumping from a truck travelling at 30 mph.

29. David Stirling and Jock hatching a plot, 1941.

30. Jimmie Storie (*right,* see p.212) with Sergeant Rose.

31. Jock leading parachute jumps during General Auchinleck's visit to Kabrit (*Imperial War Museum*).

General Auchinleck with Major General Neil Ritchie at Middle East Headquarters Cairo *(Imperial War Museum)*.

33, 34. Paratroops practising jumping from the back of a lorry *(above)* and from a moving trolley *(below)*.   *(Imperial War Museum)*.

35. Corporal Sillitoe, one of a unit despatched to blow up a railway line to the rear of Alamein, walked 100 miles back to the British lines, carrying on the tradition of Lewes Marches (see p.209). *(Imperial War Museum)*.

36. Arthur Lewes in his garden at Little Fernside, Middlesex, in 1954.

37. Lord Jellicoe and Major Pat Riley at the SAS Originals' reunion at the Duke of York's Sergeants' Mess, London, 1994.

38. Paul McLaughlin (Stirling's doctor), Mike Sadler, Jim Almonds, Pat Riley, Douglas Arnold, 'Tubby' Trenfield, Bob Bennet and Alan Hoe in front of David Stirling's portrait, 1994.

father that a war between England and Germany was a 'possibility'. He perceptively wrote that 'it is just an attitude of mind which makes war possible'. He simply posited the problem and a solution to the human habit of war:

I am not going to treat all foreigners as potential enemies. If more people had foreign friends, the sort of propaganda that went on during the last war would not be possible, and the sort of frame of mind in which the Treaty of Versailles was made would be less likely to occur. I don't want to merge the whole population of the world into one homogeneous mass, any more than I wish to level out the classes and cliques in England. What I want to do, and what I am trying to do by example, is to bring to international relations the same sort of mutual respect which is the condition *sine qua non* of mutual understanding, that holds between individuals, classes and cliques of any nation. Not of course that I cultivated Senta's friendship for this purpose.

Jock had put his bohemian life behind him and fully realized that if he was to change the world he could only do so by first changing himself. Unlike most Germans, he had the freedom to travel and enough money to do so. Few of his Anglo-Saxon brethren had the privilege of his education and wealth to take advantage of Continental travel. Unlike most of the outside world, he was able to read *Mein Kampf*, the Bible of Hitler's Third Reich. No decent translation of it existed in English or French in late 1937 and Hitler did not allow one to be made. In spite of his susceptibility to some Nazi views, what certainly marked Jock out amongst his contemporaries was his vision for a better world. Part of his own success at encouraging links with foreigners was that he put his own philosophy into action, learnt several European tongues and many European customs. He was as ambitious about forging links with foreigners as the braying parliamentarians were inert with the paralysis that appeasement seemed to be bringing. He knew full well that 'circumstances were stronger than me and that one day I may be forced to fight for my country'. Until those 'circumstances' were brought to a head he continued to be a good ambassador for England and her Empire, and war was unlikely to change his ideals one jot.

Jock was ambitious. 'Father always said that one day he [Jock] would be Governor-General of India, but that wasn't really possible, only lords and people were that, but he would be something great when he was grown up.' In his semi-autobiographical essay, 'A Tale from Childhood', Jock was surely writing about Arthur, who, as 'Father' talking about young Jock, might very well have considered the viceroyalty of India no mean brief for such a son. Certainly Jock's letters to his parents suggest that if he had not set his heart on the higher echelons of colonial rule in India, he had at least, since early manhood, developed a very strong yearning to 'be something great'. Perhaps behind his throwaway comment to Joan Fitzhardinge during their cycling trip that he intended to 'join the Indian Army and play polo' lay an ambition to hold high office one day in India. That nonchalant remark seemed to guard a very serious side – like the scabbard of his youthful dreams that he appeared to wear loosely at his side when in fact it contained rapier ambition. He expected to do something great.

At University he had on several occasions written home explaining how expensive it would be to become a polo-playing subaltern. It was expensive in terms of time too: he had derived some benefit from Officer Training at Oxford but his letters also indicate his anticipation of experiencing more soldiering, and he felt it was better to receive other experience in the 'intermission' between wars. As early as March 1935 he admitted to his parents that 'I have very much altered in my outlook on life since I have been at Oxford', and he was then certainly questioning the life that he had once envisaged which would combine with 'interests and ideals which could never find expression and satisfaction on the frontiers of

India'. He had indeed changed his tune. For now he was no longer impressed with the army men of his age that he had met, 'for all they talked about was playing polo, pig-sticking, and going on shooting trips'. It seemed at twenty-four Jock would no longer be impressing his sister's friends with tales of conquest in India.

Whilst in Germany, Jock was having 'a very good time' and learning another language for the Foreign Office (FO) examination set for mid–1938. He wrote to his parents in November 1937 that he couldn't think of marrying Senta, even if he had wanted to:

> Suddenly I come back to my senses for a minute or two, realize what a complete fool I am being, that there can be no question of a proposal, not to Senta or anyone else, that I have no money, no.job, no immediate prospects, only insatiable ambition.

It had gradually dawned on him that his presidency of the OUBC in no way compensated for his third class honours degree in Modern Greats. The Chairman of the Civil Service Commission had also pointed out that a rowing Blue rather than a good degree was no recommendation for a job abroad. Only the outposts of the empire figured largely in his suggestions for Jock, since 'the colonies are notorious as places where Blacks are governed by Blues', Sudan being the most coveted of all. Jock had briefly visited England in early December 1937 to pick up his postbag from Australia and his Alvis sportscar, 'Alice', but mainly to talk with Davies the crammer, who was offering guidance and a place for Jock to cram for the Foreign Office exams. The FO had taken double the number of candidates the year before and Davies did not think Jock had the slightest chance, and even if he was lucky, he would need a fourth language including his mother tongue.

The plan was to aim for the FO as the best possible preparation for the Australian Service. This idea was scotched when the Commonwealth Public Service Inspector informed him that he was not eligible for diplomatic service in Australia because he had not been a graduate from a university there. He might have been justified in taking umbrage at a case of unrequited love had Senta not come over to visit in the spring, because he wrote how 'I owe Australia a great deal, and am also immodest enough to think that Australia, whether she likes it or not, needs men like me.' He dismissed the absence of a reciprocal relationship with his mother country by suggesting that work in England was more attractive 'partly because Australia now appears to me to be slightly barbaric ha! ha!' He must have been grateful to his old tutor, Gilbert Ryle, for following the 'golden rule' of writing references by praising with 'faint damns': for every institution to which Jock applied was informed that the President of the OUBC would have attained a good second as opposed to his third but for his rowing commitments, but on no account would he have managed a first. Eventually Ryle's reference and Jock's force of personality would bear fruit.

On his own admission Jock seemed to thrive only 'when I am working against personal opposition'. Both a balm and a fillip to his uncertain future was having the pleasure of Senta's company that spring. He was happily distracted by her, 'still here and still complete mistress of my heart'. Distractions in late May also included viewing the Oxford college crews, Gilbert and Sullivan in the evening and preparing for the Caledonian Ball. Whilst borrowing brother David's kilt for the ball, Jock checked that David was managing his intensive medical examinations at the London Hospital. He had been thrilled with David's first class honours degree the previous summer which the latter had gained despite answering only a third of the examination paper: on hearing the news at Henley Regatta, he had sent his boater 'sailing high in the air' to land on a rather bemused party in the Steward's Enclosure, where-upon he 'was excused'. He had expressed some surprise to his father when the latter greeted the same news in rather subdued tones; Jock may have wondered that his father's reaction was somewhat muted. Perhaps Jock was the favourite son after all. In his letter to David that May, Jock seems to fill a gap that Arthur was unable to meet had he wished to, for the older brother sensed the huge academic pressure he had himself avoided:

> Please do not hesitate to come to me for advice or encouragement: I take your confidence as a very great compliment, and strange to say in helping you over your fences, see my own way more clearly, and seem to gather strength for my own hurdles. My only advice to you now is to face the obvious details of your everyday life bravely and you will be surprised how conveniently the big issues will work themselves out as you go along.

Disarmed by this brotherly love, David did indeed respond to Jock, who was supporting the youngest sibling as he had the oldest when Elizabeth's academic life became too burdensome. Jock was full of the joys of spring and summer, but generosity came naturally to him – especially to kin. Joys continued, for friends in Godalming, had also become fond of Senta and asked her to stay for several weeks, thus making her trip longer and her proximity to Jock that much more close.

Still cramming for exams, Jock was consuming the bread of life with Senta and eating every last crumb before her return on 2 June. He, still jobless, wanted 'to get married as soon as possible'. When he did wave her goodbye at Waterloo, 'it was not at all a sad goodbye.' Yet the next day he wrote to his parents that he wondered 'Why did I ever fall in love and if I had to why can't I be reasonable about it?' Jock never saw Senta again. Sandy Gordon, his friend and Oxford double-sculls-partner, came to the rescue in 'Caviare', his new Bentley. The pair lunched at the Lansdowne Club and made their leisurely way to Eton College's Fourth of June celebrations that included cricket, rowing displays, and bacchanalian suppers to complete the occasion. He enjoyed strawberries and cream with Lady Harris, whom he had once impressed with photographic portraits of her that pleased. Perhaps he wasn't entirely relaxed, because he met a sea of old faces from Oxford and recalled very few of them, 'and it is all the worse because they all remember me either because I have a very old car, or blow a post horn, or in some other way disturb the peace.'

It might well have been a combination of all three reasons, for he had already appeared in court with John Garton, the President of the OUBC, that year. They had been driving a sports car and stopped at the lights next to an unfortunate driver who had had the temerity to signal to them that they were travelling too fast. Since the two cars were alone on the open road, John Garton's passenger had taken it upon himself to teach the cautious driver a lesson. At the lights a post horn was produced and blown several times into the ear of the driver. A few days later the local newsagent's bill-posters read, 'Oxford Rowing Man In Court'. The 'town versus gown' had their say, but the hefty fine of £5 was shouldered by John Garton. At Eton that June Jock was a passenger again as Sandy whisked him to the Leander Club for dinner and back again to view the second procession of boats and the fireworks at Eton. It was a happy day for the two of them, as they had enjoyed rowing in a pair again. Jock joked with his parents in his letter that he and Sandy Gordon had both decided that 'we were so good that we must win the Goblets in 1939 and then row for GB at Tokyo in 1940, weather and wars permitting.' These were happy carefree days that were fast disappearing. The fireworks were magnificent and nearly as grand as their names, 'Jupiter's Thunderbolt', 'The Huge Umbrella of Fire', 'Cluster of Coruscating Diamonds', to name a few; 'Flight of International Bombs' suggested storm clouds rather than fireworks and seemed to be tempting fate, but it was also part of the festivities.

Jock began his examinations for the FO in late June, and just before they began he was keenly aware of his teacher's pessimism about his chances in them; it was not the outcome of the exam which dogged him as much as his uncertainty as to 'the place' in which he was to work after those results were published. After a trip to Aberdovey to bask in the warmth of David Winser's family home by the estuary, Jock waited for his results and continued to make job applications. He contented himself with the fact that England, 'centre of the world' as opposed to Australia 'at the periphery', created most positions of employment for an overdeveloped society:

England has no more simple worlds to conquer: all her achievements must be complexes, for the most part of her own devising. Such a complex was perpetual peace and the League of Nations; I should be the first to enlist in that cause by any means whatever but for the latest developments in that sphere. Somehow my faith is shaken and my attempt at the Foreign Office is all I am willing to risk. Why she should struggle to maintain her existence as a great power is not readily answerable. There are indeed people who advocate the giving up by England of all that could be desirable in the eyes of other nations and becoming another Belgium. And yet one look at Belgium is enough to persuade us to be unreasonable, if reason cannot be found for trying to keep up our precious prestige. It will be a long time before Australia can come to the help of England in the battle for peace. Australia's Everest is simpler, to mix metaphors, and more earthy. It is indeed a strange and wonderful choice that is offered to me, and I know what I would choose were I to consult only my own desires and preferences – England. The big question for me to decide is would I be more useful in Australia or in England?

A diversity of opportunities seemed to open up for him. That Britain was 'overstocked with men of my type' was a reflection of his ebbing confidence: in mid-June he had admitted to his parents that he had had 'a sort of inferiority complex all my life', and perhaps his hope for a diplomatic post in Australia was a compensation for what seemed to be diminishing prospects elsewhere. Yet he also rallied with the optimism of a natural-born fighter when describing such a complex: 'I have always done my best work when it has been at its strongest.' So posts other than diplomatic appointments were considered: a clerkship at the House of Lords, posts at the Banks of Lloyd's and New South Wales, journalism with the *Sydney Morning Herald*; and Lord Addis, a retired director of the Bank of England, made generous offers of help. If the Australian Civil Service Commission overlooked him, a political career was not out of the question, for, as he had mused with some prescience in mid-June, 'If there is one great service that is waiting for someone to do it is the saving of Australian politics from building up a tradition such as one sees in America.' He was under few illusions as to the 'mud-throwing' profession it could be, and he did 'not relish the idea'.

Jock the idealist was bent upon service that he would aspire to make special, if he had anything to do with it. He viewed the challenge of maintaining his integrity in professional politics as requiring an early start; if the gauntlet was to be run; that 'was no reason for shirking it'. He was by nature a philanthropist, but this choice of career would, it seems, certainly have been a life of sacrifice for the young and idealistic Jock, who may have found it difficult to compromise. It was partly sharpening himself for these opportunities that led him to produce his 'Journal' for this period, in addition to his weekly diary to his parents. He seems to have been keen on the idea of returning to Australia, because by mid-September he began to write for newspapers and submitted an article to the *Sydney Morning Herald* on 'German Political Opinion' that dealt with propaganda and its limitations. He seemed to be at ease with his own brand of 'inferiority complex' and in good humour when he commented on the article, 'but it may be entitled, "Dairy Farming in Lapland" by the time it gets published.'

Globetrotting was preferable to the frustration of endless waiting. On 10 September he failed his FO exams and had still had no reply from his applications for employment; he took action. He was not prepared to wait forever while his potential British masters made up their minds, and typically decided to return to Australia 'by some unorthodox route': 'driving across Asia and India is well worth considering', he wrote to his parents. In his well-stocked Alvis, he prepared for an overland motor trip home that would be complete by Christmas 1938, when he could celebrate with his parents in Bowral. The itinerary was on an epic scale and compared favourably with the pilgrimages of the Wife of Bath for the diversity of proposed locations: London, Dunkirk, Rome, Syracuse, ship to Bengazi, Cairo, Jerusalem, Baghdad, Teheran, Kabul, Lahore, Calcutta, boat to Bali, Singapore, and boat to Darwin. The AA had recommended the route via North Africa, which was not only cheaper but quicker too, 'along Mussolini's new Libyan road'. The venture was 'a sweet to take away the nasty taste in leaving England'. While waiting for permission to enter Afghanistan, 'Alice', his car, was adapted for what had now become an expedition. A special running board was bolted to the side of the Alvis, upon which he stored provisions that might have earned others sponsorship in a television age. They included: 10 pounds of Bovril, six of Cadbury's chocolate, cakes of Lifebuoy Soap, an Army shovel, nine two-gallon cans, chains, pumps, wire, rope and a two-guinea medicine case. The trip would provide material for a career in journalism and an antidote to the 'nervous indigestion' which he had endured since July while waiting for his future to unfold.

Jock overreached himself with travel plans and interviews. Sponsorship for the enterprise materialized, but from his ever-generous father; interview dates started to pour in as he prepared to leave for Dover. Parental approval of the scheme was assured with the £125 that was lent for the enterprise, but the Civil Service Commission had handed Jock's details to Sir Henry Badeley, the Clerk to Parliament, with a view to Jock's appointment in the Parliament Office of the House of Lords. Personally Jock was 'in a dreadful position': before his planned departure he had one good suit and a few pairs of khaki shorts, his Holland Park flat was let and the insurance for 'Alice' had just run out. Sir Henry Badeley had frowned at Jock's third class degree and wondered why his interviewee had not passed the Home Civil Service examination. The interview may not have 'felt right', because Jock wondered if he could put his powers to full use in this 'pleasant backwater' of the Parliament Office, even if he could read for the bar in his spare time. He was glad that he had another application in the post for what was 'a fairly recent creation of the government for the purpose of minimising the evil effects of the most modern methods of mass-producing prejudice and ignorance being employed at the moment in Italy and Germany' – the British Council.

On 25 October, the day of his interview for the British Council, Jock spent the morning in 'leisurely fashion' in Oxford, coaching the Corpus IV from 10 to 11 a.m. He drove to London in Alice and his 'short and surprisingly pleasant' meeting with Lord Lloyd of Dolobran augured well. Lord Lloyd, of medium stature, dark complexion and close-cut moustache, seemed to be the right sort of mentor and employer for Jock whose vignette described the Chairman of the British Council as '"The Lion", an expert in gingering people up – brusque forceful manner, very direct, charming open smile'. Jock enjoyed Lord Lloyd's sympathetic disposition and his straightforward questioning; this was a man whom he could respect and work hard for. It also helped that they were both rowing men: the Chairman claimed to be 'the ignominious cox of the Cambridge crew for the two years when they broke Oxford's series of nine wins'. Jock had the 'impression that my general bearing and behaviour were considered satisfactory'; the fact that Lord Lloyd enjoyed working with dashing young men may also have been in his favour. He was informed that he would be given a recall interview with Lord Lloyd. He seemed confident about his chances to solve his endless waiting for employment and laughed at his being left 'high and dry' after his trip was cancelled. Since he had forwarded all his clothes to the carriers, Carter Pattersons, he left the British Council 'and returned home to spend a pleasant night in my underpants'.

He was interviewed by Mr Croom-Johnson, Secretary of the Lectures Committee, and after a few more questions a post was offered on the staff; it was not long before Jock started in earnest, but that day he wrote how he 'wanted to sing or honk the horn, and drive madly across the traffic.' His meticulous planning for inter-continental motoring to Australia was dashed, and a possible career in journalism with it. The only wild driving that was possible was in the teeming rain across the English countryside. He set out for Oxford, took down the windscreen, and after he was quite lashed by the weather, sat down in the George Hotel and ordered a dozen oysters and plenty of Guinness. The efforts to make something happen in his life had paid off for he now had a job that had meaning for him. It seemed timely that Jock, who clearly cared about his fellow men and women, should be determined to now take part in the propaganda war that grew apace. On 9 November, the day of *Kristallnacht*, he wrote to his parents of the rationale of the Council which he endorsed: 'We must be prepared to back to the limit our convictions that in the present war of ideas, it is essential that the British point of view shall prevail.'

So had Jock changed his tune over supporting the efficiency of the New Order in Germany? He had glimpsed the Nazi creature from its adolescence to the onset of grotesque maturity, and was not alone in his condemnation of the outrage that Martin Gilbert recently considered 'a turning point in how the Nazi Party were perceived abroad'. The leading article in his favourite newspaper, *The Times*, declared two days after *Kristallnacht*, that 'No foreign propagandist bent upon blackening Germany before the world could outdo the tale.' Was Jock's change of heart necessitated by the need to conform to his new British masters? It had been over six momentous months since he had hoped Hitler would 'purge his work of all that is evil'.

The international situation had worsened soon after Jock voiced his idealism, and those months of uncertain diplomacy had more far-reaching consequences for Europe than any at any other time during the previous quarter of a century. Several weeks after Jock wrote of his hope that Hitler would succeed by extirpating from his regime all its brutality, talks between Britain and France had ended on 29 April with a vague promise to defend Czechoslovakia against attack. Actions matched the diplomat's words almost exactly six months later, when Chamberlain's 'sweet reasonableness' was counterpoised by the first Lord of the Admiralty, Alfred Duff Cooper, who believed that Hitler 'was more open to the language of the mailed fist'. Chamberlain's agreement with Hitler at Munich may have confirmed to Jock that Hitler was intent on, and able to, pursue his evil. Duff Cooper, the would-be British Councillor, was writing of Hitler's 'ignorance and prejudice' only three weeks before *Kristallnacht*, although few then could have visualized the spectre of Jewish persecution.

What Jock might have appreciated now was the significance of his initial support for the socialism of the Nazis. Hitler had claimed to raise the workers' prestige in society ('Work ennobles') but this so-called respect for labourers was a sham; gradually it meant that inferior work was a political offence. In general, universal obedience was claimed by the Nazi party, agreement with its views was dedication to the nation, and disagreement was treason. The intentions of the Nazis became clearer as their policies became more extreme. In *The Third Reich*, Hans Bücheim concluded that the ostracism of the Jews was demanded and collaboration with their persecution was expected. Just before *Kristallnacht* Jock cancelled his exciting expedition across the four continents when he opted for indispensable service with the British Council against totalitarianism; it seemed that his job was in rhythm with his new grasp of the Fascist threat. He wrote of the Nazi's counter-propaganda in the wake of *Kristallnacht* and how he was unlikely to be a reluctant soldier in the event of war; the scales over his eyes had at last been lifted:

The last anti-Semite outbreaks in Germany are outrageous, and it is only because it touches us more closely that we in Britain tend to be even more outraged by the answer the German papers make to our revulsion of feeling against them. No doubt you have seen the German accusations against British colonial administration and how, in the comparison they draw between our treatment of our colonial subjects and their treatment of the Jews, we are made out bloodthirsty terrorists and they magnanimous administrators of inspired justice.

I have been struggling to believe or rather retain my belief in German sincerity, but only a fanatic faith could withstand the evidence they choose of their own free will to put before us.

I have great faith in Britain. I swear I will not live to see the day when Britain hauls down the colours of her beliefs before totalitarian aggression. If we are given peace, I know which set of principles will stand the test of time: if war, I shall willingly take up arms against Germany, almost gladly. I wonder how many Germans could say the same of fighting Britain.

Far from following British Council policy, it was as if Jock's disillusionment with Hitler's 'socialism' turned to bitterness at the realization of the false dawn of Nazi policies; it was as if he took the lie personally. It was surely a letdown to have invested such hope in the new Germany, and even if he had once admitted that 'I cannot love the British nation any more than I can love the German or French nations,' he had also conceded that 'I find it so easy to love individuals from all three, more particularly the first two.' His willingness to fight made the stock of his patriotism for the British Council and for his British friends high indeed.

Within two months he was handed responsibility for organizing the lectures sector of the British Council. In one of his last letters to Fernside before his parents settled in England, he wrote that he was 'at work in a calling' which he knew was 'the right and only one for me. God be praised!' The proclaimed aims and objectives of the British Council were essentially 'To co-operate with the self-governing Dominions in strengthening the common cultural traditions of the British Commonwealth'. However, as the propaganda of the totalitarian powers gathered momentum, it became apparent that 'in the present war of ideas, it is essential that the British point of view should prevail.' In *Ribbentrop*, Michael Bloch explains that eventually the work of the Council under the chairmanship of Lord Lloyd was to prove most helpful to Churchill who had in the chairman one of the most ardent supporters in opposing Nazism – in spite of Ribbentrop's belief to the contrary in 1937.

Jock started at the British Council a few weeks after its move to 3, Hanover Street from its old quarters in Belgrave Square, SW1, and he was pleased to find that he was to be given the organization of lectures in foreign universities, schools, and Anglophile institutions by 'eminent Englishmen'. In view of the increasing tensions within Europe, he was hardly plunging into the shallow end of British Council waters. In the previous two years William Wedgwood Benn, Kenneth Clark and Robert Bruce Lockhart had all sharpened their teeth as speakers for the British Council lectures. The experience of Jock's detailed preparation for his car trip across the world came in useful: one of his first assignments was to plan Lord Snell's lecture tour in the Near East and international timetables were no longer foreign to him.

Jock had more work than his immediate boss, Mr Croom-

Johnson, had suggested because one of his colleagues, Jennings, was often absent due to sickness. On Armistice Day Jock wrote that 'I am so glad Jennings is ill: it sounds very callous of me,' but in fact Jock thrived on using his initiative, and since childhood had often been 'able to shoulder the tasks others were unable to do'. As a child he had grown to love his father's insistence that he finish difficult labours in spite of mental and physical discomfort; cutting out blackberry bushes in Fernside had begun this acceptance of happily undertaking challenges that were burdensome to others. He was making mistakes as any junior might, but 'he was encouraged by the philosophy of his father's oft-repeated phrase, 'wait awhile'; and 'Well done dear boy', when the waiting was over. Jock's ability to be patient was to prove useful to him when he discovered that some of his superiors were inundated with 'such a mountain of over-work' that they were too often 'quite unapproachable'. He had the common sense to seek out helpful individuals from other departments who could guide him.

Jock collated reports on the Council's completed lecture tours and with the recommendations of his colleagues abroad concluded how best to amend future trips in the light of experience. This became increasingly important as the polarization of countries into different ideological camps intensified in the year before the war. Lectures were not undertaken only by 'eminent gentlemen'. Two years before, Rebecca West spoke on 'Contemporary English Literature' and Jock noted in early 1939 that Miss Jean Batten's lectures on 'Flying Experiences' was 'easily the most successful tour arranged this season'. He had certainly been impressed with Miss Batten's flight from England to Australia at the tender age of twenty-five, and in his file at the British Council he described her as 'prudently courageous'.

Not every tour was so successful. Jock was concerned about the popularity of some lectures, and also noted that the Council should be wary of sending staff who were sightseers

first and talkers second. 'English Gardens in Scandanavia'
'should not be repeated ', and the speaker on 'Eight Centuries
of British Songs' was one of those 'who will only go to those
countries where they have not been before: this is a fairly
sure sign that with them the tour comes first and the lecture
second.' Anglophile societies in several countries were
particularly aware of British Council policy and attitudes
after the Munich Crisis. With the controversy over appeasement the lecture tours were becoming that much more
significant and accordingly were now under the limelight.
Opinion in England was polarizing into those who advocated
appeasement towards Hitler's breaking of the terms of the
Versailles Treaty and those, like Churchill, who were vehe-
mently opposed to encouraging the German leader's
disregard of International agreements.

The tour in the Netherlands became controversial. Harold
Nicolson was given the task of talking on the subjects of 'The
British Empire and World Peace' and 'The British Heritage'
in the Netherlands in the New Year; the talks had already
been cancelled in October due to the crisis. Local reports of
the tour in Amsterdam were positive; however, at The
Hague the situation was very different. Harold Nicolson
talked on the perilously sensitive ground of 'Are the English
Hypocrites?' Humour was attempted during the talk about
England 'muddling through' the crisis of appeasement, and
the Council records indicate that 'the Dutch did not think it
was funny' and that public utterances abroad must not be
interpreted as 'defeatist'. Harold Nicolson had undertaken
the same lecture tours in the Balkans in April 1938, and in
his diaries writes of the trip in the Balkans rather than the
lectures in the Netherlands. In spring 1938 he was treated
more grandly than he thought his position justified, 'I was
Anthony Eden himself.' Then his lectures were used as pro-
Western demonstrations in three capitals. However, in the
Netherlands estimation of British Council lecturers by the
Dutch seems to have had a deleterious effect upon the impact

of the tours. Jock was keen to safeguard 'the British point of view' and proposed principles to govern senior lecturers. It might have been only the enthusiasm of a new recruit, albeit a bold one, but it was natural for Jock to exact standards upon others that he was prepared to follow himself, had he the same opportunities. This was his 'calling', as he had put it, and thus he offered guidelines for Council and lecturer alike:

> We should be at pains to select 'sympathetic' lecturers who are able and willing to take an intelligent interest in the culture of the country to be visited, be friendly with the people they meet without condescension and to be more ready to learn than to teach.

Before issuing caveats for superiors 'even of Mr Nicolson's greatness', Jock was fully enjoying a hectic social life that sporadically mushroomed with contacts that he made in his new career. His natural sensitivity was often in high demand at both formal and informal occasions. At the St Andrew's Eve Ball one of the organizers warned Jock that he was going to put him next to the Marchioness of Londonderry or '*the Derrière*,' because he could think of no one else to make talk to her.' Jock did what was expected of him and more: Lady Londonderry 'made it quite clear that she expected me to ask Lady Mairi [her daughter] to dance with me in the first reel, by saying very pointedly that she could not allow her to dance with her partner at dinner because he was not wearing a kilt: Simply could not be seen in the first reel with a man in tails. I must say I found it odd that I danced the sixteenthsome better than Lady Mairi, which, I regret to have to admit, is still not saying much.'

Soon he began to appear in what he called 'the snobbery bumphs'. The *Lady* magazine featured him on its front page in December and Jock noted that 'it is notable for the occasion the Steel in me has turned most conveniently to Stewart': the printing of his middle name was then incorrectly made more Scottish. With much amusement and not a little self-mockery, he wrote to his parents of his inability to detach himself from the voyeurism of this particular issue from the media:

> It is rather like coming suddenly upon a road accident, with its usual maggot-like crowd, and half of you wanting to see it while the other half wants to run away. I knew several pictures had been taken of me in the company of the mighty at the St Andrew's Ball, and I would look privily and furtively between the half-opened pages of the likely periodicals in the days immediately succeeding. I must admit, however, that I had lost interest by the time the worst of these photographs did eventually find its way onto the printed page, not that the surprise with which I greeted the news when regaled by John Jennings in the office was not thoroughly feigned, and not that I did not go out that very dinner hour and purchase two of these highly glazed scandal sheets, over which I gloated with smug delight during my solitary lunch.

Portugal was correctly considered to be an important target of the British Council's 'war of ideas', and Lord Lloyd was glad to invite Jock to smooth relations with that country at a luncheon held at the Chairman's home in December 1938. Jock had already sent pictures of the King and Queen and Neville Chamberlain to the Anglophile societies in Portugal and had commented as he did so that 'It all sounds slightly ridiculous, as indeed it would be were it not taken so terribly seriously by other nations.' He was enjoying having to take his work seriously and he was studying Spanish in earnest in order to make the most of his first job. He was fast becoming one of the bluest of Lord Lloyd's blue-eyed boys, and it was just as well that he appreciated the Portuguese point of view, because at Lord Lloyd's dining table at Portman Square he was placed between the wife of the Portuguese Ambassador and Lady Chamberlain, Austen Chamberlain's widow. Jock noted that the Ambassadress was 'a most acute conversationalist and we touched on many subjects'. One topic may have been the new cultural links with Portugal created by Lord Lloyd's recent opening of the new British Institute at Lisbon, and his visit to the dictator of Portugal, Salazar.

Delicious courses, including egg and mushroom soup, and pheasant with chestnuts, were conducive to relaxed conversation that turned to the subject of gossiping, and the Portuguese interjected as to how the English lagged behind other Europeans in this activity. It was an apposite subject for discussion, since it was gossips which the *Abwehr*, German military intelligence, were to rely upon particularly in the Portugal where neutrality made Lisbon the espionage centre of Europe. Any development of Anglo-Portuguese relations would later be highly significant for the Allied cause, when MI6's counter-espionage presented Salazar with a file on the *Abwehr's* intelligence networks that threatened to jeopardize Allied Atlantic convoys. The Lloyds' gathering may well have helped to nurture relations with the Portuguese; such cultivation of them may have encouraged Salazar to act quickly on MI6's information, so that the *Abwehr's* efforts were made null and void. The luncheon in Portman Square was to be part of one of the British Council's first significant battles in the war of ideas; Jock may have been a junior there, but whatever role he played this was his 'calling', and he was at the heart of the propaganda war.

PART 3

Maturity in the Middle East

7

Faith, Love and The Phoney War

'Will you, won't you, will you, won't you, won't you join the dance?

With war imminent in late 1938 Jock had joined the First Battalion of the Tower Hamlet Rifles as an Ensign and rejuvenated all the skills that he had learned in the Oxford University Officer Training Corps. The quest for high standards extended to healthy eating at his territorial base at Bow, London: he became acting President of the Mess Committee, improving the officers' meals 'not a little, showing cook how to make mashed potato and how to properly brown baked apples'. He and his sister Elizabeth had found their parents a new home in Middlesex; at last the Lewes home at Fernside, Bowral, had been sold and Little Fernside in Hanworth was now more suitable for Arthur and Elsie. Jock spent his weekends training or staying with his parents, and both his Journal and letters to them temporarily ceased, marking a happy time when the family was briefly together again. Arthur and Elsie encouraged Jock to keep an open house for his friends at their retirement home, and now he had the great pleasure of living life with his nearest and dearest, instead of simply recording it for them. As a result of his new domestic arrangements, little correspondence exists for most of 1939. However, the combination of Jock's meeting with Mirren Barford and the Declaration of War by Britain against Germany activated Jock's abeyant pen.

Jock first met Mirren (or Miriam) at his sister Elizabeth's wedding in August 1939. A Lecturer at Brasenose College, Oxford, had kindly lent his garden in Holywell Street as the venue for Elizabeth's reception party. Jock, who had been brought up on the mystical nature of gardens (in the story of *Hollyman*), said later that it was indeed an appropriate place to meet a lover. The nature of the meeting place seemed to lose some of its mystique for Jock when he realized that the nineteen-year-old Mirren had also caught the attentions of a potential rival. He interrogated David concerning a letter that he had sent to the young Somerville College student.

> Have you any news of Miriam? As I have had no reply to my delicately worded epistle, I can only presume that you foxed me with the wrong address, and that you are yourself already engaged to be married to her. I can find no other explanation for her misguided preference for your highly inferior person and her neglect of my well-bred advances.

In fact David had thought Mirren attractive but conceded that Jock 'was the older brother and had spotted her first'. The war was to interrupt Jock's romance with Mirren, and 'Joy Street' was the name they came to call their infrequent meetings in correspondence to one another, once Jock obtained Mirren's address! He had many reasons to be keen on her. The previous year he had been rather surprised at his inability to attract the right mate, after his relationship with Senta fizzled out with the prospect of war. The mutual attraction that he and Mirren enjoyed at his sister Elizabeth's wedding was a welcome break. He had made more contacts and acquaintances during his time at the British Council, but he was not so sure of his powers of attraction as his poem, 'She Wasn't Impressed', suggests:

> I went to school at Harrow and at Eton,
> I studied at Sorbonne and Budapest,

Then I got these dark blue socks for doing something up at
   Oxford,
But she wasn't impressed.

My calling list has all the élite on,
At palaces and castles I'm a guest,
I'm even on the roster of Henry Duke of Gloucester,
But she isn't impressed.

I've climbed where man has never set his feet on,
I've reached the summit of Mount Everest,
I've even shewn my mettle out on Popocatapetl,
But she wasn't impressed.

Jock need not have worried, because Mirren wrote and apologized for her belated reply on the same day as he sent his letter to David. Being fully occupied was another distraction. He had been busy in the previous autumn making new arrangements and training himself physically in preparation for his transfer to the Welsh Guards. He was first told of his move to the Welsh Guards by the British Council. Lord Lloyd wrote the day after war broke out and indicated his regret at losing Jock:

I was very much touched by your very specially kind letter, and I too was very sorry not to see you before you left. If you could possibly get away for lunch or dinner, would you come and have a meal with me? I should like it particularly.

It has been the greatest pleasure to me to have you as a colleague in the British Council, and I look forward to happier days when we can all continue the national work we have been doing in Hanover Street. I hope you will find time to write to me occasionally and let me know how I can keep in touch with you.

Ties with the British Council were far from cut, since another colleague, Kenneth Johnson, had joined Jock at the

Welsh Guards' Training Battalion at Corridor Camp in Colchester. This was one junior member of the British Council with whom Jock had an affinity. Whilst mixing with his colleagues there, he had preferred his company when they were in their cups – 'God be praised for the gift of wine', he wrote, since it was only after a drink that they began to relax. At weekends the two men would walk around the beauty spots of the Cotswolds and delight in taking their rest in either church or pub. Jock was keen to make use of any leave in the knowledge that he was likely to have fewer opportunities for further leave once he was posted abroad. It may have been the period of the Phoney War, but the momentum of training commitments gathered pace and corresponding with Mirren was the only contact he enjoyed with her by the spring of 1940. In early April he informed his parents that 'I am thoroughly happy with my work; hardly a moment to think of anything else much less do anything else.'

That February he had been posted to the Small Arms School in Hythe, Kent. He excelled at this weapons work, and after he did well at Bisley on the course run by Bill Stirling, brother of David Stirling, he had 'made himself rather too useful . . . and until a suitable successor has been found' was made Weapons Training Officer for the Welsh Guards at Roman Way Camp, Colchester. He now occupied 'a very definite position in the Battalion'. This was a small consolation for missing the draft for what was to be the Battle of Boulogne. He had also been unable to meet up with Mirren at Oxford, but did occasionally get back to Middlesex and entertain old friends like David Winser. He tried to persuade his brother to renew his acquaintance with Winser, perhaps hoping that another member of the family might be sustained by the warmth of a good friend, even if he himself was unable to, and so he gave him the latter's address 'in case you would like to beat him up any time'. Jock also let his brother know what he was missing: 'You would love it here – all manner of explosive toys to play with.' He was full of energy at a time when David was recuperating from illness, he finished his letter with characteristic irony and innuendo: 'I'm stopping. Don't bother to answer this: there's so little happening in bed I find.'

The previous autumn sandbags had been piled outside banks and offices, recruiting offices had been inundated with men aged eighteen to forty-one, and everyone including babies were sporting gas masks in streets made ready for war. Proponents of appeasement had warned that 1.8 million people would be killed by the *Luftwaffe's* bombers in the first sixty days of war. However, in early 1940 over a quarter of a million evacuated children had returned to London as the capital no longer seemed in danger of attack. The Nazi *Blitzkrieg* was very real to the Polish, but Great Britain appeared to be able to 'stand easy' in the Phoney War. Jock cautioned his brother about the pitfalls of believing their own British propaganda:

> Our uncontrollable desire to see everything that happens from as close as possible eventually leads to extreme shortness of sight, which is a tragedy because the distant views of events of this kind are always of greater value than the 'goebbled' reports of the time.
>
> There seems to be every likelihood that the war on land will start in real earnest before long, and then we shall have to learn to take our medicine from the curiosity box with a very much thinner coating of sugar. Casualty lists will not contain only the names of people run over by our own transport – otherwise what the hell am I doing here! As far as I myself am concerned, I should by rights be among the first to be drafted to a serving battalion, and I only hope I am, for then I shall stand a better chance of getting experience before experience gets me.

While others were initiated into the gentle art of killing, Jock had begun his own patrolling course for the Welsh Guards. His team of eight officers were 'pulling well':

I work them day and night, and further than that they know that a written exam faces them at the end of the course. In spite of the hardships, they paid me the compliment this afternoon of saying that they are all agreed that this is the most enjoyable course they have done since coming here.

He continued to use his initiative, and it was on his suggestion that a junior NCO went through the course with him as an assistant, so that he could be the 'greatest use to any successor I may have'. In charge of patrolling, Jock was responsible for fully recording his own course; this he did alone. The patrol programme didn't have the kudos and élan of Oxford rowing, far from it because 'this particular lot of officers are either my contemporaries or seniors here . . . and are not easy to make enthusiastic about anything entailing a good deal of physical exertion or discomfort' but 'they go through the most outrageous country without a murmur.' He felt the work had contributed 'its little to the general atmosphere of difference which I have noted'. He seemed to have found an antidote to the disappointment of missing the draft that would at best have landed him on the beaches of Dunkirk. Once his friends arrived back from France, his own battalion would endure the apathy of an extension to their own Phoney War. Both the Welsh Guards' First and Second Battalions suffered very heavy casualties. Friends arrived to take the places of those who had fallen: Gilbert Ryle, Jock's Philosophy Tutor, joined Jock at Colchester in early June, while his other tutor, Freddie Ayer, started his course at Sandhurst.

For some time Jock had no longer regarded himself as a 'new boy' at Roman Way Camp, and by mid-April he was confident about how the Army worked. He had made it his concern to know, because he wished to settle into Army life as soon as possible and get on with the business of soldiering. He echoed the eternal concerns of young innovators:

The most important thing which I have learnt is how to get things done in the Army. For anyone with ideas of his own and determination to put them into practice, the army is an absolute paradise, provided he knows how to go about it. Commanding Officers and chief instructors are thirsting for new and original ideas, provided that they do not appear to be either new or original.

Eventually Jock would confound all his senior officers with pioneer ideas that could never appear anything but original or new, but for the moment he was content to be mistaken for a man of some experience:

A rather odd thing happened last night after dinner. The Commanding Officer was talking to me about the patrolling course and then later about the training of the battalion generally. He kept referring to me and my contemporaries as 'you older people'; well my contemporaries certainly are older people, and at first I thought he was simply using the term to distinguish us from the latest drafts of officers from Sandhurst, who have for the most part been between the ages of twenty and twenty-five. But as he went on it became apparent that he thought me to be much older than I am, so I remarked casually that of course I was a good deal younger than most of my contemporaries:

He said, 'How old are you, thirty-four?'
'Goodness no. I'm only . . . '
'What, thirty-two?'
'No, no. I'm only twenty-six.'
'The devil you are! Twenty-six are you?' and he laughed.

One clue as to how the increasingly over-qualified Ensign was mistaken for a senior subaltern lies in the Welsh Guards' Weapon Training manual, which Jock also prepared at this time. In his recent book, *He Who Dares*, David Sutherland, who was led by Jock whilst patrolling German-held Tobruk, referred to him as 'a formidable man'. Perhaps part of Jock's strength lay in his own moral approach to life, as indicated by the introduction of his training manual:

Appreciation of the Situation
1. Object :

The object of this Battalion's Training Cadre must be to make and keep available to the service battalions the best trained reserve in the Brigade. Any endeavour falling short of this is unworthy of the sacrifices of those who are upholding the tradition of the Regiment in battle. This object is attainable only if pursued with complete singleness of purpose: to be the best in the Brigade is to simply be the best. It requires the organization of the whole strength of the Training Battalion to this one end, the inclination in each of its endeavours in the unswerving drive to the objective. Apart from this, the Training Battallion has no justification, and every consideration affecting its organization, its personnel and their positions must be subservient to this one end – the production of the best the nation can produce for the disposal of the Regiment.

Discharging one's duties was a matter of personal honour for Jock. He was vigilant about addressing the inadequacies of training undertaken before soldiers arrived in the Welsh Guards' camp. Officers coming straight to the Training Battalion without first passing through an Officer Commanding Training Unit should, according to Jock, 'be treated as recruits and passed through the training companies in the normal way', whereas he wrote of the high standard of training at Sandhurst and considered 'it a fatal mistake' to underestimate this standard and compel soldiers to repeat their training, and thus cause them to lose interest.

By early June he was ready for a move, but it was no posting abroad, just a temporary billet at Sandown Park at Esher. As

France had fallen to the Nazis that month, the possibility of the invasion of Britain increased and the need for a Special Service Brigade gathered pace. Churchill had been impressed with the *Kommando* raiders during the Boer War, and when it was suggested that an élite corps of soldiers be made up from the Guards regiments, inter-joined with the regular battallions, the Prime Minister decided to retain the original name of the raiding group. Evelyn Waugh, who later joined Jock in 8 Commando, wrote of the months of waiting for an unknown life in his *Sword of Honour* Trilogy, where the main character, Guy, endures the answer to all queries about his future with, 'When the brigade forms'. For the first two years of war many home forces experienced their own shocks, which consisted of counter-orders and disorders where they were suspended in a limbo of standing by for the consummation of their special service training that never seemed to materialize.

Jock used the time of his own waiting period well, for his parents were close by at Hanworth in Middlesex, and he made several visits to Little Fernside with his friend, Rex Whistler, who was to combine tank commanding with his skills as a war artist. Rex was some ten years Jock's senior but the pair evidently enjoyed each other's company. Rex sketched, inked, pencilled and painted the kaleidoscope of life in his Guards' new depot at Sandown Park. He did Jock the honour of painting one of his finest portraits of a colleague. Unusually Whistler worked from the base of the portrait upwards. Jock sits on the steps of the grandstand at Sandown Park with his Bren gun astride his knees pointing towards the racecourse. David Lewes, who watched its early stages, recalled the fine likeness that Whistler had conjured up. The portrait was generously given to Arthur and Elsie Lewes by the Whistler family after Rex tragically met his death in Normandy four years later. Rex Whistler leaves us in no doubt that Jock was in the Special Service Brigade for action rather than the pink gins.

By the time he arrived at Sandown Park Jock found that he had missed an opportunity of action and possible promotion in the Battle of Boulogne, another pinprick to add to the waiting, which clearly began to leave some soldiers past their peak. Rex Whistler had lost little time perfecting his unofficial role as a war artist; Jock had the time to sit for him and also dwell on Mirren and the memories which seven brief meetings had so far left him. The two lovers used to write in code to describe their meetings that mostly took place in Oxford, where Mirren was at college. Memories were all Jock had, until he had an opportunity to consummate what was now a very strong love affair. By August 1940 their passion escalated with every letter that told the story of their 'chaste absence'. The opportunities to meet were still rare, and when they did spend a weekend together in Oxford it was painfully too little time to catch up with each other's news. By mid-April Jock conceded that 'we would marry if we could', but lack of money seemed to be the stumbling block. By his own admission to his parents, Jock had spent money 'wildly and delightedly', but 'gathered knowledge and wisdom at the expense of security'. He had also run up such a debt to his patient brother that Jock estimated that, if he paid it back at the rate of £5 per month, it would not be cleared until early 1943. Unwittingly this was to be a great benefit to David, who, whilst serving with fellow Australians and Americans on the Azores, had lost far too much of his RAF pay on unsuccessful games of poker and thus was prevented from losing any more. An engagement of two years for Jock and Mirren was out of the question, and philosophy drew the poison of poverty:

> Our association must remain in colloidal suspension. If the ingredients separate, it were better thus than wedded; if they remain forever thus, it were better than that they had never mixed; and if in the end they unite, so much the stronger the union. In the interval we both have to prove ourselves.

Whilst away from Mirren, Jock was plagued by the lack of training facilities at Sandown Park and hated 'to feel my body so full of strength and endurance, at the height of its powers, yet remaining unused and untried'. In his war memoir, *When the Grass Stops Growing*, Carol Mather described the racecourse facilities as 'most unsuitable':

> Apart from a wooded knoll there was no green grass at all except that of the racecourse itself which was flat as a pancake. The 'lines' were a long row of loose boxes, occupied by the men (four to a box) with the company office in another. The officers' quarters in the grandstand were almost as disagreeable as the men's.

Carol Mather and Jock were temporarily billeted in a Victorian boathouse on the River Wey in Woking where they led a team of twenty men. The two went on to Burnham-on-Crouch in Essex and were formed into 8 Commando. Whilst waiting for the Brigade to form, Evelyn Waugh wrote in *Men at Arms* of 'the smooth revolutions of barracks life' where 'there had been accumulating tiny grits of envy which were now generating heat'. Jock, with high aspirations for Special Service, wrote less of envy but more of his immediate disappointment with being based at Burnham-on-Crouch and his mixed feelings for those senior officers who neglected the *ésprit de corps*, which was fast becoming a shell. If Jock was something of a martinet, he was also a maverick:

> It will be strenuous as the Army reckons, but even here, where it is least expected and least desirable, the workless tradition of our old armies still clings and clogs. So long as what is expected of you is accomplished, its relation to the ultimate purpose is no concern of yours: as this tradition is carried up through all ranks in the command, it follows that what should be the business of those whom it most vitally affects, namely the sub-unit commanders, is either the business of the man at

the very top, which is plainly impossible, or else the concern of nobody, which approaches close to tragedy. But lest you think that I have started my customary carping and criticizing before attaining even a nodding acquaintance with my subject, let me add in haste that these views are based simply upon observations of those of the officers of this commando whom I have already met. The men are an interesting lot. Most of them have the typical English aversion to sustained physical exertion, convincing me that this nation is indeed decadent, but they are all willing enough to encourage it in their men, and, it goes without saying, when put to the test they will endure more than was ever thought even remotely possible, but still not as much as they would have been able to do had they condescended to train and bring their bodies into subjection. This is the tragedy of a civilized people: their education gives them tremendous variety of interest and this, which is such a blessing in the humdrum days of peace, survives into war and dissipates the energies to many unrelated points which should be concentrated upon the single task in hand. All this is much less true of the men with whom I am here associated than of the general run of my acquaintances, and certainly to these men cannot be attached the stigma of personal cowardice so bravely borne and often subdued though fearlessly admitted by so many charming men of character and cultivation whom I have known.

Carol Mather remembered Jock as 'a man apart'. As a young 'individualistic war leader' he was usually aloof, and his contempt for decadence was often perceptible in his demeanour. Mather recalled more recently Jock's caveats about the dangers of 'playboy soldiering', the ending of profligacy which 'all would change after the war'. Jock had always absorbed the incredibly high expectations of his father which partly explained why he may well have seethed with frustration at the apparent lack of purpose in the frequent moves towards creating a Brigade that still had no identity, let alone ethos or camaraderie. He was too hard on some of his colleagues and he was strict on himself. He continued his letters to Arthur and Elsie, but Mirren was competing for his correspondence too, and he seemed mortified that his parents might view fewer letters to them as neglect: 'I write often to Mirren but just now at least I seem to have energy for letters home. Why should I so carelessly admit a priority in claim upon my effort? Why prior to you? Why not you first and others after as of old?' Jock may have been 'a man apart', but these questions to Arthur still seem the confession of a shy youth asking permission to break away from the strong mesmeric pull of his father's shadow.

In fact, Arthur Lewes supported Jock's choice of Mirren and absolved any guilt Jock felt at admitting Mirren's 'priority' in receiving the lion's share of his letters. Stern Arthur may have been, but earnest, thoughtful and encouraging were his words in one of the few letters from him to his eldest son that survives:

> First, do not think of us as saddened by a new 'priority of claim', for as you say it is really gain rather than loss. 'For that cause shall a man leave his mother and father'- it is so natural and right. Then as to the legacy and other money which you have spent ' deliberately and without regret', you have solid achievement to show for it. Then last and certainly not least, I think you have both made a wise decision not to become engaged until you are in a position to marry. The interval of quiet steadfast work and waiting will be a real touchstone of happiness. I do not say that lightly, as if it were an easy thing to do: nothing worthwhile ever is easy: but out of my own experience I do know its wisdom. Your mother and I only met for a few days and then were separated save for letter writing; and it was three years before I could go down to Australia to ask her to marry me. I was well over forty before I was in a position to marry. Far be from you such a long ordeal of writing. When that happy day comes that you bring to us a new

daughter in your wife, you know without the saying what a loving welcome always awaits you both. God bless you my dear boy, with much love from your loving Father.

The last time Jock had been passionately in love he had spent most of his hours with Senta Adriano, and his parents did not 'suffer' any competition with his writing of love letters. Arthur and Elsie were very glad of his loyal intentions to them and he had been aware of their hunger for his news whilst he was studying at Oxford. He still seemed beholden to them in this respect and in many others. His father had been himself such a hard exacting judge on most matters that it was almost impossible for Jock – even with his mother's gaiety – to not do exactly the same. He had almost admitted as much to Mirren in June, when he had written of 'the romance of unselfish service in the cause of impractical ideals: impractical only because we, or rather our fathers, have set them so high that we cannot hope ever to attain them'. Much of his correspondence with Mirren explored what they thought might occur at their next meeting, vivid memories of the times they had already spent together, and what might have happened at their last visit to 'Joy Street'. He also wrote long and detailed allegories about the purpose of life and their own lives in particular, and these, Isobel Colegate suggests in *The Spectator*, may sometimes have best been kept for 'the early hours of the morning in a London night club'. Mirren was overwhelmed by some of these letters, but Jock had little alternative but to send her his parables; even if he had saved such writing for male company, it was unlikely to be on the comfort of a metropolitan 'bum-warmer', which he'd have hardly used had he the opportunity of such luxuries given the type of war that he wanted to wage.

He revealed a trait of his character to Mirren that was to continue to haunt him and his relationship with her: the burden of carrying out 'our father's' ideals was so great a weight that Jock hesitated to concede that it was a responsibility that he accepted of his own volition. With his comment, 'or rather our father's', Jock suggested that those ideals had been foisted upon him. However, it seemed that he had chosen to bear the cross of his father's ambitions, in spite of this letter where he appeared to displace the burden of lofty responsibilities onto his father's shoulders. In truth, Jock was going to be everything his father and mother had ever wanted him to be: to 'Be something great' and much more, to take the whole concept of special service very seriously. He did this to such an extent that it was essential for him to avoid the company of decadent soldiers: 'in the Brigade of Guards I have learnt to hate and fear it' [decadence]. Mirren sensed what Jock's colleagues may at times have felt acutely, that his austerity could be simply too much for other mortals.

Perhaps some of the spartan upbringing at Fernside lightened Jock's own sense of foreboding; he could endure difficult tasks – he had been persuaded to. This, and the experience of seeing some of his colleagues going to seed, was to have a great influence on the way he worked with others and the circles in which he mixed. He already had experience of selecting men for arduous tasks in the OUBC and was confident about his judgement of character and the standards by which he would recruit, if the British Army gave him the opportunity to do so. It certainly gave Jock much more security to carry the Lewes baton of Puritanism than to be a playboy officer and an ungrateful son to boot. When he wrote to Mirren a month earlier from Esher, he had certainly done his best to give her that impression: 'We acquire more merit on this earth in doing gladly those tasks set us which are least attractive than by any amount of enjoyable labour.' It was possibly less forbidding to a young lover than it might have first seemed, because Jock, who wished for a mate as stoical as himself, nevertheless was self-effacing enough to finish by adding that 'I wish I could bring something warmer than philosophical platitudes!' He had an idea that he did 'rail on so' but sent the discourses anyway.

Jock borrowed from Christianity what was expedient for him to do so, in particular the important idea of self-renewal. How strongly was he motivated by his religious beliefs? Mirren later wrote and asked him 'to spare me that austerity of yours', yet it seems that his ability to be stern arose more from his absorption of Lewes philosophy at Fernside rather than from specific Christian beliefs. He was no orthodox Christian, as he suggested to his parents a year into his Oxford education:

> I may be very foolish, but somehow or other any service but the communion service annoys me; I dislike hymns, and sermons even more. One spends all the time in the services beseeching the Divinity to grant benefits, half of which I feel I don't want, and saying all sorts of things I can't bring myself to believe; all I desire in church services is an opportunity to give hearty thanks for all the blessings of the life which are showered upon us with such generosity that all I can bring myself to ask for further is strength to use them properly and to make the best of my life. Religion to me is a purely personal affair and this is the essence of the communion service.

For the moment Jock seemed not to engage in half the battles between sin and shame that had cast a shadow over Arthur, who found it very difficult to enjoy the earthy side to his nature. Rigid interpretation of the Bible had meant that when Elizabeth had received a make-up set in her late teens, she was requested not to use the gift (within the confines of this 'edict' Arthur retained an element of fairness by refunding the cost of the cosmetics). This was one code of behaviour that the Nazis with all their might failed to enforce in Hitler's Germany, once women followed the lead of Magda Goebbels who became patron of the German House of Fashion in Berlin. It has not been uncommon for parents to mete out such guidelines, but Elizabeth never wore make-up again! It was such adherence to discipline which Jock also learned, digested and applied to his soldiering. Jock's Christianity was steeped in the lessons of cause and effect; gratitude and compassion could only be forged on the anvil of a strong belief that 'what you do comes back to you'. His letters to Mirren and his parents indicate how much store he set by this principle and that mastering his own mind was the only course open to him in dealing with the rigours of staying alive in war. This was one reason why he worked hard at his career, and also why one of his Corporals later described his training methods of late 1941 as 'far more testing than anything the Germans could throw at us'. 'Jock's thorough preparation for action against the enemy nearly did me a mischief,' Douglas Arnold recalled, but 'supreme confidence in dealing with the enemy was the reward.'

Jock would need all his faith, passion and letter-writing skills to persuade Mirren Barford to remain in close touch with a soldier who was parcelled off from post to post with as yet no definable fighting role and frequent suspension of leave. By the end of the year, when he was being moved to the Middle East, he had to endure the fact that he had a girl-friend who was being persuaded by a fellow officer that Jock 'won't be back at Esher for a long, long while, if ever'. In the same letter Mirren may have loyally written that the admirer was 'preposterous' but this must have been a small consolation for Jock, who had no doubt that he should only be wedded to Mirren when he was solvent. He expressed his vulnerability and occasional despair at what he described as 'personally malicious about our separation, which as a result of my ineptitude, renders letter writing ineffectual and even possibly irritating'. There was always a danger that the separation would cause either of them to be merely 'an episode of the past'.

Mirren's admirers were usually neither 'preposterous' nor 'little' and Jock may have surprised Mirren by his refusal to be irritated by her frequent mention of them in her letters. In private he may well have been exasperated, despite the fact that he might not have fully understood Mirren's predicament. Isabel Colegate writes that 'not everyone saw life as a matter of falling in love, marrying and living happily ever after'. Mirren was described by her best friend, Angelika Guyon de St Prix, as 'a very lucky person, full of high spirits: She had a lot of men around her, while she was writing to Jock, she had plenty of admirers. Yet she would take her time, because Mirren was a very warm person.' Jock and Mirren played with their names as they explored their feelings for one another: Jock might sign his letters with honest 'John' or finish up with 'Jock' the 'gentleman rapist'. He would be 'Ulysses' to Mirren's 'Penelope', which she used when 'you matter a great deal', or plain 'Miriam' when she was feeling 'rather indifferent and formal'. Jock refused to be put off by Mirren's 'Helen' who was 'feeling privately faithless'; at times he may have wondered if Mirren was Lucy Ballantyne's 'fine literary ironist' who used 'I'm in the thick of life force' code when referring to two recent 'harsh and unkind months': 'I was, perhaps, prodigal with my rage and impotence, my laughter, living, desiring and all those other things whose violence made my stomach lean.'

Angelika Guyon de St Prix remembers that Mirren was 'very flirtatious' but also 'afraid of physical contact', and at least Jock could gain some reassurance in the knowledge that it was he who had helped her overcome her fears 'because she felt so strongly about Jock'. She had suffered from a father who was temperamental and she had found him frightening; her mother later divorced him. Mirren found her neurotic mother far too demanding and cared little for her stepfather. Jock certainly seemed to restore Mirren's faith in men. Nearly two years of writing and receiving letters, two 'harsh and unkind months', and barely ten meetings eventually convinced her that her fears could be quelled by Jock, to whom she finally gave requited love: 'Promise you'll teach me, because other people can't; it's in your power alone.'

Training exercises in Burnham-on-Crouch kept Jock

distracted from the affairs of love, and it seems that he was under an entirely different spell cast by young Randolph Churchill. Jock began to acquaint himself with young Churchill on a dawn raid on 'the enemy' in mid-August. With sixty minutes to spare before zero hour, the two set out on 'a breakfast reconnaissance'. Randolph procured a pound of steak and Jock purchased onions, and the pair persuaded a village blacksmith to lend them his forge and breakfast was served. Jock, keenly aware of Randolph's preference for politics rather than soldiering, seems nevertheless in awe of him:

> Randolph is a most refreshing personality to meet and to live with. He is much too outspoken and militant in his convictions to be popular; in fact, I have heard nothing but ill of him before he arrived, but he puts heart into me by his robust and healthy character; while even a few young men of his character remain, all is not up with Britain. In a few days' time he is standing for Preston, and I shall be thankful to see him at last safely returned to Parliament. His agile mind will be a source of discomfort to that complacent assembly, his disdain for the idle incompetence of those who assume the insignia of responsibility without bearing its weight will earn him much disfavour, but only wicked self-interest or class interest can fail now to appreciate the rightness of his views.

In October 1940 Jock was posted with 8 Commando and moved to Scotland for mountain and landing-craft training. For a time he was based at Inveraray and exercised day and night on the Duke of Argyll's steep hills and deep forests above Loch Fyne. Censorship prevented him from writing of his proficiency at using landing-craft, crossing beaches at speed, attacks and re-embarking under counter attack, and so he wrote to his parents about the news of his latest posting. He had not enjoyed 'the dour apathy of Inveraray' and was relieved to move on to Largs in spite of its 'human wreckage':

'dear old ladies who have come to die. They are surprisingly cheerful and the place is anything but depressing.' Jock also wrote of his belief that 'Germany does not intend to undertake the invasion of Britain', and his concerns in the wake of the Battle of Britain revealed a prescience regarding the course of the war:

I think of my Berlin days still with pleasure and often with wonder at the smallness of that life compared with this. But from many small experiences a little great wisdom may be won. It is as though I had by me now books of reference long since out of print with which to help me translate the German moves into the language of our own policy.

I see the present situation thus: Italy's move into Greece is at present no more than a feint whose purpose is to draw us into Greece. The Greeks will be given a few easy minor victories to encourage us and them. If we go in to the mainland, we will doubtless be further encouraged until we have heavy commitments there, when the moment will be ripe for the Axis powers to move: Germany through Yugoslavia or Bulgaria into Greece and Italy through Albania, Italy into Egypt and Germany through Spain to Gibraltar and the African coast. In Greece they will try to drive us into the sea, with Italian submarines to forestall a second Dunkirk. In Egypt they will aim at our naval and air bases and try to force a withdrawal through the canal, even if they can't surround our armies. They wish to make Greece the battlefield on which to fight our Waterloo, and, because we are not ready, it seems as though Greece must go the way of our other allies.

There are thin times ahead, but we have at least this consolation: the framework of the Axis powers is by their moves being slowly distended without being strengthened; indeed, so long as their subject nations need policing, the framework is being slightly weakened while the load grows greater. This renders them increasingly vulnerable to attack when the time comes to make it, provided that we can escape from check until that time arrives. Whatever we do about Greece at the moment, the immediate results are sure to be unpleasant.

The morale of 8 Commando was temporarily raised by the arrival of three large, specially adapted cargo ships, the *Glen Roy* and its sister ships, the *Glen Erne* and the *Glen Gyle*. The Glen ships were 10,000-ton 17-knot converted merchantmen, but raised hopes were short-lived: the vessels presented a large distinctive silhouette, their lowering gear was noisy, and they could be heard four miles offshore; in daylight they would need an anti-aircraft cruiser or fighter escort protection and at night they were unsuitable for beach assaults. The inadequacies of the 'raider' ships would be exposed, once the commandos made their few perilous assaults on the North African coastline; at the start, freedom of movement on the craft was the problem. By 10 December Jock had boarded the *Glen Roy,* but was disappointed at the troop decks and was concerned that the men 'are very crowded . . . there is practically no exercise space . . . so that they get very bored'. He became tired of his own colleagues and confided to Mirrren that 'I would rather have the inspiration of the anger and disappointment of one I love than the soul-destroying indifference of the few here whom I respect and the praise of those I despise.'

In his diary, Evelyn Waugh remarked upon the indolence of some of the officers, but in comparison with 3 Commando, No. 8 was 'boisterous, xenophobic, extravagant, imaginative, witty, with a proportion of noblemen, which the Navy found disconcerting'. Senior officers did not remain unscathed in Jock's record of life on the *Glen Roy*. On Christmas night 1940 he considered it his 'misfortune' to sit on the Captain's table for dinner; the Captain was drunk before dinner and Jock took umbrage that the officer was so incapable that, 'we were unable to move until he gave the sign to rise which he could not either give or himself obey.' Jock conceded that his Journal, often written in letters, was 'high-explosive in any hands but mine', and he was 'afraid to bring it into a public room'. Some of his colleagues may well have breathed a sigh of relief when he was later forced to consign it to the Ottoman Bank in Alexandria, which denied possession of the Journal after the war. Rarely enjoying the company of bluff males, he blatantly dismisses one colleague, Eddy, as a theatrical windbag:

> He has admitted with naïve frankness that he believes that undetected sin is no sin at all, that he has no use for friendship but always wants to be meeting new people, and that the principle that governs his actions is to have as interesting time as possible and to "sell his personality to the public". He has a sense of honourable behaviour which fits in with his amoral principles and which fits him into our society. I have nothing good to say of him, though I dearly wish I had: it would make my task so much easier. The amusing thing is that he will frank this letter for me: his duties of censorship, however, sit so lightly upon him that he will in all probability not read a word of it. And if he were to, there is very little that I have written with which he would not agree.

On 31 January Jock sailed from the island of Arran to the Middle East as part of Force 'Z' (later Layforce) under Lieutenant Colonel Robert Laycock. The 'Glen' ships avoided submarines and were protected by two destroyers and a cruiser. On board were men with whom Jock would soon work closely: David Sutherland (Black Watch), Tommy Langton (Irish Guards) and David Stirling (Scots Guards). Among the NCOs were Pat Riley and Jim Almonds, whom Jock would later lead in Tobruk and then recruit in order to build his own training programme for the SAS. Jock had been President when Oxford rowed against Tommy Langton in the 1937 Boat Race, and he was glad that Tommy had been included in 8 Commando at the last moment. Randolph Churchill had not won his seat at Preston and was on board probably as a link between Robert Laycock and the Prime Minister. Not long after sailing, Jock noted that young Churchill had been appointed Administrative Officer and had obtained permission 'from Number One' to press-gang the services of a cat: 'to protect him from the depravations of the rats . . . a large tabby was shanghaied and brought aboard in the mail bag.' A fortnight later Jock added the Layforce Commander to his gallery of pen-portraits:

Colonel Bob is how we speak of him among ourselves. I suppose he is between thirty and thirty-five years of age – a regular soldier who has done much besides soldiering in his regiment – the Royal Horse Guards – including sailing on a Finnish grain ship to and from Australia. He is short compared with most of us but not by normal standards. He is beautifully built and mighty strong. He has a good open face, clean shaven with a firm chin, determined mouth, an undistinguished nose, very big eyes set wide apart and very blue resemble strongly those of Randolph, and above well-marked brows a straight broad forehead. He is a very positive character with a deep empathetic voice. He is able to combine affability and good humour with the maintenance of that respect for his person and position which is so essential to leadership. He lacks in my opinion the highest degree of that other essential to leadership, judgement of character, though even this he has in a higher degree than most men. It is easy for me to say this when I think him deceived by some of his officers, but I would only be too glad to retract and admit myself deceived instead should even the occasion occur to convince me. He is certainly not deceived by Eddie, but then only a fool or a film fan would be. He has imagination, initiative and tremendous courage to bring to bear on any military problem that may be set him, he has application to perfect his plans and the mechanical and physical ability to do anything he may demand of us. I have the greatest confidence in him and am sorry that he is no longer our personal leader, having taken command of the whole military force in this convoy.

By February 1941 'The Army of the Nile' under Lieutenant General Richard O'Connor, General Wavell's tactical commander in the Middle East, had taken over four hundred miles of land, over one hundred and thirty thousand prisoners and protected Egypt by eliminating the Italian Tenth Army. This lightning campaign had taken two months; by 21 January O'Connor had captured the port of Tobruk, which had provided the logistical support for his advance. Churchill later decided to switch O'Connor's armies away from their consolidation of this remarkable first victory of the war to help in the defence of Greece, which British Intelligence claimed could not be saved. There were other considerations for Whitehall; Churchill had made a commitment to the Greeks. However, this decision allowed Rommel to take back positions that were supported by insufficient numbers of men and equipment; a fillip that, over the next eighteen months, encouraged Rommel to cripple the British Eighth Army, re-taking two hundred and sixty miles of land and eighty thousand prisoners. The Prime Minister then replaced General Wavell and pressed his new Commander-in-Chief, Sir Claude Auchinleck, to begin a hasty campaign, for which the army was not fully prepared.

However, North Africa was strategically essential as a bulwark against attack from Italian Libya. The Middle East provided the three services with crucial oil supplies, and the area was vital in any action involving Italy, the Mediterranean, Turkey, Russia and India. Yet the way to wage war in North Africa seemed to elude Whitehall. Auchinleck sometimes depended on Major General Dorman-Smith, whose suggestions could be imaginative and daring at a time when there had never been so great a need for them. Inflicting losses on the enemy with as little cost as possible to the allies was a top priority for Middle East Headquarters (MEHQ).

Whitehall planners and GHQ Middle East aimed to establish control of the Aegean in early 1941 and the original task of Layforce was to capture the island of Rhodes. The Commandos that formed Layforce were interviewed for Special Service in June 1940, as the British faced the danger of attack in Egypt by the Italians, who had then declared war. Their large army in Cyrenaica heavily outnumbered the British, and Cairo, the operational base from the Balkans to Iran whose oilfields were essential to Britain's lonely stand against the totalitarian powers, was placed in jeopardy. On 6 April the Germans invaded Greece and, as Jock had predicted, the British made heavy commitments there, and the invasion of Rhodes was cancelled. The role of Laycock's Force 'Z' radically changed as Rommel occupied Cyrenaica and encircled Tobruk. It then became Layforce, of four battalions with former 8 Commando, now 'B' Battalion, under Lieutenant Colonel Dermot Daly. Some abortive raids were staged on the Western Desert coast-line, while 'B' Battalion stayed at Mersa Matruh as the Layforce Reserve. Jock had arrived on the *Glen Roy* at Suez on 7 March and wrote a fortnight later that 'I am sure that I was the fittest officer that came off that ship'. There was plenty of sickness amongst his fellow officers, but Jock seemed to travel well. He again questioned the reasons behind the Commando programme. In late December 1940 the Chief of Combined Operations, Admiral Sir Roger Keyes, had addressed all the Commandos and informed them that they would 'embark on an enterprise that would stir the world'; Jock wasn't so sure:

> We are still waiting about in the old old way, but still we believe people when they tell us with bated breath and a great air of mystery that very soon we will be performing a feat of arms which will astonish the world. When this does come easily the most astonished will be ourselves.

Action was promised to 'A' and 'C' Battalions in mid-April after Colonel Laycock attended a conference on HMS

Warspite; it was decided to raid Bardia and the 'B' Battalion 8 Commando War Diary indicates that the operation was postponed several times due to bad weather. HMS *Glen Gyle* sailed at 0230 hours on 19 April, but the Signal Section picked up an enemy source that indicated that the raid had not been a success, claiming that 'raids on Bardia had been easily repulsed and all taking part made prisoner'. The exaggerated report made good Axis propaganda, but Colonel Laycock's own critical analysis based on reports by officers and men clearly indicated his anxiety about the future of Layforce's fighting role:

> Point 10.(iii) Inexperience of active operations: The first few live rounds, fired by the detachment at 51863976, caused the majority of the troops (at least near me) to halt and lie down. The impropriety of this procedure has been explained.

> Point 11. Formations: Training in England was originally devoted to situations envisaging raids on the Northern Coast of France on very dark nights when the danger of losing touch necessitated moving in close formations.
> The inadvisability of adopting such formations in the Western Desert on a Mediterranean night when it is nearly always possible to see from 50 to 100 yards has now been pointed out.

> Point 12. Wayfinding: In the excitement of their first operation junior leaders were inclined to forget the precautions necessary to aid them back to the beaches.

> Point 15. Difficulty of landing craft in locating parent ship on return from beaches.

After this abortive raid Jock disembarked from HMS *Glen Roy* and went into camp at Amariya with the rest of 'B' and 'C' Battalion. On 28 April Colonel Laycock attended another conference in Alexandria, and this time it was decided that any Layforce troops at Sidi Bishr should take part in the defence of Alexandria. Half of 'B' Battalion would be made ready for raiding action at Tobruk, whilst the other half were to be based at Mersa Matruh 'to rehearse raids on beaches now in the possession of our own forces'. Jock's posting to Tobruk came later in the year, but for now he grappled with the prospect of rehearsing raids. Major General Arthur Smith, Chief of Staff to General Auchinleck, who was due to inspect 'B' Battalion on 10 May, wrote to the Middle Eastern Commander-in-Chief to register his own concerns about the men who had volunteered for Special Service. Extracts from his letter of 6 May highlight his unease:

My dear General,
Our situation is now becoming desperate . . . .

Since our arrival here, however, we have pursued the same heartbreaking course of working the men up to the concert pitch for projects which have eventually been cancelled.

The effect on the troops may be summed up by an inscription found written on the partition in the mess docks of one of the Glen ships (the culprit was never apprehended) which read: 'Never in the history of human endeavour have so few been b——-ed about by so many.'

Frivolous as this may seem I cannot but sympathize with the sentiments expressed.

I admit that one of the Battalions recently carried out an unopposed raid behind enemy lines and that it was not skilfully executed.

We did however learn many valuable lessons, and I am convinced that there is tremendous scope for our activities against the enemy's left of centre where, if we are lucky, we might create considerable havoc. I am sure that all ranks share this view, and I most earnestly entreat that employment may be found for us soon, if only in the form of small but frequent raids carried out by say 50 to 100 men.

However, 7 Commando and a small detachment of the Royal Tank Regiment's raid on Bardia on 19–20 April had appeared to show that considerable advantage could be gained by following a programme of small-scale attacks on the enemy's lines of communication, which ran for many miles near the coast. The enemy would thus be kept in a state of apprehension. The Germans diverted the greater part of a German armoured brigade from Sollum, where it was beginning to exert heavy pressure, and kept it for some time in the neighbourhood of Bardia. Three factors, however, prevented the use of Commandos for this purpose. Two weeks before the Bardia raid, the Axis powers had begun their advance through Yugoslavia and Greece, as Jock had warned his parents six months before, and the whole situation in the Eastern Mediterranean changed. Many of the best British troops in North Africa were sent to the help of the hard-pressed Greeks, and together the Allied force, which faced numerous and more heavily armed Germans, had to be withdrawn. Shipping to take them off was the main problem, and everything that would float was pressed into service. Infantry landing ships were therefore diverted from their original role, sent to Greece, and suffered considerable damage from enemy fire. They were not, therefore, available for transporting the Commandos to the scene of action; Force 'Z' was redundant.

In his letter of November 1942 to Arthur Lewes, David Stirling, later co-founder of the SAS with Jock, wrote that Jock 'became impatient at the poor training arrangements' and the hiatus Layforce now found itself in. In mid–1941 Layforce lacked the heavy weapons and transport of an ordinary infantry battalion, and enemy reconnaissance aircraft and rough weather had rendered 8 Commando's raids on enemy coastline abortive. Without the element of surprise, the scale of the Commando raids with 200 officers and men had little advantage, despite the defensive and aggressive striking power afforded. The Navy had lost the warships HMS *Diamond* and *Wryneck*, the transports *Ulster Prince, Pennland, Slamat* and *Costa Rica*; the Royal Air Force had lost 209 aircraft during the evacuation of the British Forces from Greece. In Stirling's letter to Arthur Lewes, he identified how Lewes quickly recognized the need to effectively adapt Layforce troops to provide successful raids on enemy coastline and aerodromes. Like Major General Arthur Smith, Jock believed in using fewer commandos in raids behind enemy lines. However, he devised a force of men, numbering only six to ten, and David Stirling's letter suggests that, unlike the Major General, Jock's own scope for operating did not involve trusting in 'if we are lucky':

In June of 1941, after a series of abortive operations . . . . He realized that the facilities for operating the large clumsily organized Commando was insufficient in the Middle East at this time, so he applied and got permission to detach a section from the unit and to train it on the lines required to enable it to cover an operation which he himself planned. Although this operation was never executed owing to lack of decision at the top, there was never any doubt that it would have been successful. The whole conception, the thoroughness with which he trained the men and the beautiful simplicity of his plan seemed to eliminate the chance of failure.

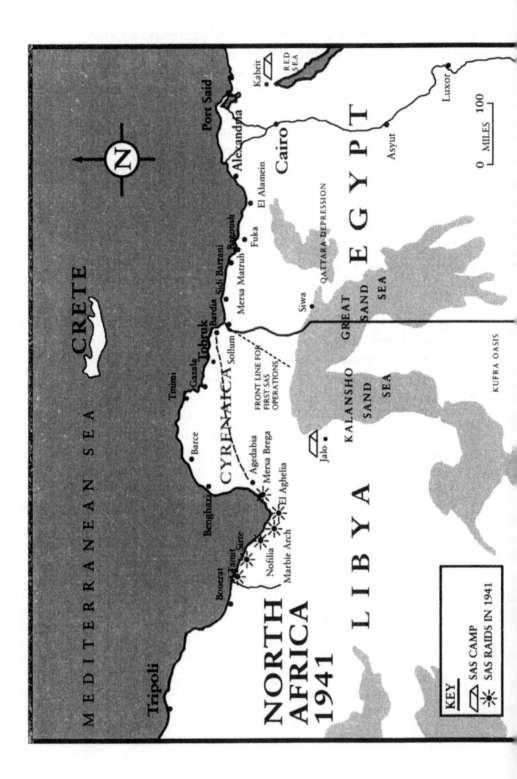

8

Pioneer

The tale must wait until the censor graciously condescends to release it from suppression. In the meantime you will be able to make up all sorts of stories about me and think them true until you know otherwise – J.S.Lewes

By 1943 the Middle Eastern theatre absorbed nearly half of the operational formations belonging to Britain and her Dominions. Until the autumn of 1942 the Army's most striking successes had been over the Italian army in Africa, 'and yet', Robin Higham writes, 'until 1942 training was very inadequate and a major cause of early setbacks.' So much so that the General Staff established a Directorate of Research to apply operational methods, but 'even so, training remained largely in the hands of the divisional commanders and, especially in view of the presence of so many Dominion and Imperial troops, who always tended to go their own way, was very difficult to standardise.'

It was ironic that the very chaos in the Middle East in early 1941, which frustrated Commandos like Jock Lewes and David Stirling, was fertile ground for anyone with the expertise and single-mindedness to mould Special Service, not just let it become another purposeless 'halfway house' like 'Burnham, Inveraray or Largs' where too many Commandos went to seed. Jock Lewes had bigger fish to fry, and in April 1941 had requested the permission of Robert Laycock to create his own small parachuting force to operate behind enemy lines. As Robin Higham indicates, there was a need for training methods that met the demands of soldiers fighting in North Africa and Jock sensed that he had begun to meet some of those needs. He shared his excitement with Mirren and also his parents:

> I have been preoccupied lately with a special task allotted to me: it is frighteningly exciting in preparation, but gives me just that which I have longed for all my soldier days – a team of men, however small, and complete freedom to train and use them as I think best.

Jock's determination to gain Colonel Laycock's agreement and support of a small unit along the lines of the future SAS was due to the 'frighteningly exciting' knowledge that complete freedom to experiment in training with his men might well create a totally new and powerful tradition of his own within the Army. In May 1941 he received the news of the invasion of Crete with a mixture of dismay and great interest. He had already attempted to raid a German airfield near Gazala using motorized gunboats, but one of the vessels, the *Aphis* (for a full account of the operations of the *Aphis*, see *When the Grass Stops Growing*, Chapter Six), was detected early by enemy air forces. It has sometimes been suggested that Jock 'had nothing better to do' and therefore decided to begin the first parachuting in the Middle East; the implication is that he was merely keeping fit with no other pursuit to channel his energies. However, it is unlikely that a deep thinker like Jock would have requested Colonel Laycock to allow him to pioneer the first parachuting in the Middle East simply because he was bored; if German paratroopers had succeeded in Crete, then Jock was convinced he could make it work with a small-scale operation against Axis air bases and installations in the desert. This was not simply to vent his frustrations at Layforce's lack of role, now that the invasion of Rhodes had been cancelled and troops diverted from the desert to support the invasion of Greece. It was to give Special Service a meaning when little of it remained at this time, but it did also offer Jock the opportunity to combine his disciplined drive with channelled wildness; it appealed both to the puritan and rebel within him. The training of his parachutists in May and June 1941 showed his ability quickly to adapt to a different mode of transport behind enemy lines. The element of surprise in assaults on the enemy was his priority, and parachuting would be another important string to the collective bow of his improvement on Commando training.

A few Commandos, like Carol Mather and George Jellicoe, were trying to make their own small-scale raids on German airfields, but without success. In June Jock had carefully prepared three parachute assaults, but, as David Stirling suggested in his letter to Arthur Lewes, they were cancelled due to indecisiveness at MEHQ. Jock had clearly been one officer in the Special Service Brigade to identify the clumsy Commando tactics and provide a foolproof plan to rectify the impossibility of amphibious operations, now that the Royal Navy was unable to justify further losses of ships in mid–1941. In July, when Jock was posted to Tobruk, Stirling personally presented a proposal in the form of a memorandum to senior officers at MEHQ which secured the founding of an embryo raiding force to be called 'L' Detachment, Special Air Service Brigade. Stirling had had time to reflect upon his own ability to promote Jock's ideas with his own contacts at MEHQ who really counted, notably Major General Ritchie, Auchinleck's deputy. David Stirling hatched a plot to give another opportunity to realize special service in the desert, when it appeared to have been temporarily lost after Jock's three plans were aborted. He wrote to Jock's father in 1942 to confirm that 'This proposal was largely based on Jock's ideas and was merely an application of them on a unit basis. Later MEHQ instructed me to go ahead and form a unit on the lines of the proposal.'

Brigadier Dudley Clarke, in charge of creating plans to

hoodwink the enemy, had dreamed up the title of such a brigade to persuade the Italians that there was a large airborne force in the Middle East. He had already been using fake gliders and also dropped dummy parachutes near Italian prisoner of war camps, and the presence of Jock's sixty trained parachutists – far less than a brigade – lent credence to the deception. The ruse clearly worked, for Field Marshal Erwin Rommel recorded in *The Rommel Papers* that the SAS attacks deep inside enemy territory 'seriously disquieted the Italians'. Jock's concept of the parachute force in May 1941 came at a time when the British were confined to Egypt and almost unable to mount any serious counter-attacks. With few men and little equipment the British needed to be effective at psychological warfare and use any ability to strike back at the Germans.

General Auchinleck and Major-General Ritchie, who had received the proposals for an SAS unit, favoured the idea of 'L' Detachment because it meant that if the SAS raids were successful they would assist any offensives that the war leaders planned. The main points of the original memorandum included many of Jock's observations on the use of small-scale raids behind enemy lines which would operate the 'fullest exploitation of surprise' along the coastal strip of North Africa where aerodromes were vulnerable to attack particularly from clandestine raiders operating south of the coast.

Few vehicles and troops ventured more than twenty or thirty miles inland, since no roads or maps existed for terrain that Axis troops considered unsuitable for campaigning. Just as parachutists were not expected to raid Crete, so Jock considered the Germans' relatively unguarded airfields easy prey. For the first six months after the inception of the SAS in August 1941, the Axis aerodromes away from the coast often had no fences around them; those by the sea were fenced in but lightly guarded. This allowed easy access for the SAS whose khaki uniform looked little different from those worn by the Italians and Germans. Sergeant Pat Riley, in one SAS raid, was unable to leave through the wire of an airfield he had entered by, and so with a parachutist who spoke some German, left through the aerodrome's main gates telling the enemy guards that they were both going to town for the evening. There was much to recommend the proposals Stirling had put forward: the SAS unit placed meagre demands on the British Army's own supplies, and there was little opposition to the unit recruiting from Layforce, which it had for all intents and purposes superceded. Auchinleck and Ritchie's support of the SAS would later yield fruit, and no accolade for the unit's success was greater than Rommel's own remark that it had 'caused considerable havoc'.

The very nature of the desert war meant that it was a war of supply. The SAS memorandum highlighted that the coastal road was punctuated with the occasional encampment where convoys could stop at night. Rommel's front line was so far east that his lines of communication were extremely stretched and most vulnerable to attack. *The Rommel Papers* continually make reference to the subject of provisions and petrol that were particularly important to the German *Afrika Korps*. The Germans needed 1,500 tons of supplies, including rations and water, daily. The Italians sent the supplies from Tripoli, which was 1000 miles from the front; from there they were less vulnerable to attack than they had been when compared with operating from Benghazi, which was much closer. Hence it was necessary for the SAS to gather intelligence. Siwa was well behind German lines and soon became the 'Clapham Junction' of all behind-the-line traffic. There the SAS established a temporary base where they could frequently patrol deserted coastal roads and reconnoitre aeroplanes or transports heading to the front or retreating westwards. In his *Born of the Desert* Malcolm James referred to the battlefield as almost limitless, 'a tactician's paradise and a quartermaster's nightmare'.

Good health and the highest levels of fitness were essential to a pioneering and self-reliant soldier. In May and June 1941, using a small group of men, Jock avoided all the problems of requiring air cover and naval support in any operation that his parachute detachment staged; parachuting behind enemy lines and marching back to base after missions would make his force more independent. Earlier in the spring of 1941 he prepared his parachute detachment upon which the first SAS unit was later based and he developed the fitness that he had maintained during his voyage to the Middle East. His own small unit would have to be fitter and more disciplined than the Commandos. His ability to cope with the temperatures in Alexandria was certainly helped by being accustomed to the heat in Australia; however, he was also able to react positively to the lack of operational work in the desert by experimenting, whilst off-duty, with long marches and rationing his liquid diet to one bottle of fluid a day:

> There has been a good deal of sickness in the Battalion chiefly among the officers, sometimes taking the form of bronchial and sometimes gastric trouble. I put it down to one or more of three causes: carelessness, ignorance and unwise drinking. I myself am neither drinking nor smoking and am sure that I benefit by it. I have been practising rationing myself all liquid just to see how my consumption works out. I can keep going almost indefinitely on light work and on one cup of tea at breakfast and tea and one glass of water at lunch and dinner supplemented by two or three oranges but I find this rather dry for long marches.

Jock achieved what became known as 'Lewes Marches' on his own initiative without vehicle, medical, or radio support so that soldiers could be independent of transport deep inside enemy lines. He did not inform his superiors of his experiments with marching, because he did not want to be hampered by unnecessary interference; parachuting into enemy territory to attack targets would entail a long walk and a difficult return journey. As soon as he arrived in North Africa, he continued to build up his physical and mental stamina and strength, keenly aware of the importance of being familiar with the new terrain. His early work in the desert paid dividends when he began parachuting. After Jock invited David Stirling to take part in his parachute detachment, Stirling developed his own creative approach to his Commandos' inactivity later in the year, and his career blossomed when he presented the SAS memorandum to MEHQ.

General Richard O'Connor, who had overwhelmed the Italians with his lightning victories at the end of 1940, had often written that 'you can't spend too much time on training', and Jock adhered to the General's maxim to a fault. In his letters to his father in the spring of 1941 he writes that:

> I have been exercising my section in the 'attack' by concealing myself with my little sporting rifle which I have with me in the line of their advance; when they appear I fire into some sand drift near them and they have to locate me and attack my position with as little delay as possible. They enjoy this and it improves their fieldcraft out of all recognition. The first time I did it I was a little disappointed to see how bad they were, but they will improve especially as I can with perfect safety kick the sand up uncomfortably close to any bad offender against the rules of concealment with my little rifle [a Mannlicher hunting rifle].

Jock took care to expose the less experienced soldiers to simulations of enemy fire and the *Sunday Times* recently reported that the SAS today use similar exercises when training Police bodyguards to 'stand in the path of a 7.62 bullet to experience the distinctive sound of a rifle being fired at them'.

Jock had expressed concern about the lack of vision in some quarters of the Army, writing: 'the typical regular officer' underestimates the ordinary recruit, content with catch phrases like 'we must never expect the soldier to think'. Jock had learned not to depend on the spirit of the Army, which, though 'fundamentally good', could not fire the imagination, awaken enthusiasm 'or inspire confidence in leadership'. Major General Dorman-Smith suggested that the root cause of its problems was that the leaders there 'lacked moral courage'. Within a fortnight of arriving in North Africa, Jock, with Mannlicher rifle slung over his shoulder, encouraged his men to get on with the business of soldiering, and in navigation exercises they would steer a course and bring a party to an exact point at an appointed time:

> The other day I marched my men about six miles into the desert hills about here on three consecutive compass bearings and, having got them there, set them the problem of finding the exact bearing and time of marching back to camp. Most of the intelligent ones got reasonably near the correct answer by a freehand rough-scale sketch. I had walked by myself over this compass traverse the Sunday before, so I knew the answer, but I was surprised and delighted at the accuracy of a simple method of solving my problem that I had thought out that morning. I simply surveyed by means of my compass (the one you gave me) a scale model of the morning's march. I stuck a bayonet into the ground to represent our starting point, then using the scale of one pace to a minute's marching I paced out our time of marching on each bearing, placing a bayonet to mark the end of each traverse. On taking the bearing of the bayonet representing our starting point from that representing our present position and pacing out the distance, I found that the answer was within ½ degree and two minutes marching of the figures that I arrived at on my walk the previous Sunday.

In March 1941 Jock didn't wait to have his spirit kindled by his peers and senior officers; he wanted the men that he commanded to be able to think, and do so quickly on their feet. In peacetime British troops had never trained for a desert war because war with Italy was never seriously expected. The empty solitude of endless sands made the Libyan desert an ocean, which the Long Range Desert Group were then learning to chart but which few Army officers were researching; hitherto, it had not been considered that forces could penetrate inland because of problems of supply. When Laycock permitted Jock to detach his 'band of cut-throats' in May that year, Jock was already well drilled in the necessity of leading navigators who had the potential to be first-class, finely trained and utterly reliable. He trained his men in order to frustrate Rommel's mastery of logistics, but first he needed to prepare them for parachuting. At the end of May 1941 Private D'Arcy, Irish Guards, who served in Jock's detachment, wrote one of the few early documents on the inception of the SAS concept:

Having been frustrated in his plans for a seaborne operation, Lt J.S.Lewes, Welsh Guards, decided to try it by parachute. He and his party first went to an RAF HQ located somewhere near Fuka, there he discussed the details with an RAF officer, who, although none of the party had jumped before, was most helpful. He showed us the parachutes we were to use. From the log books we saw that the periodical examination had been omitted, but Lt Lewes decided that they were OK. Next day, along with Lt Stirling and Sgt Storie who were hoping to do a job in Syria, we made a trial flight. The plane used was a Vickers Valentia. We threw out a dummy made from sandbags and tent poles. The parachute opened OK but the tent poles were smashed on landing. Afterwards we tried a 10-ft jump from the top of the plane and then a little parachute control.

The following afternoon we flew inland in the Valentia, which was used to deliver mail. We reached the landing field towards dusk, landed, fitted in our parachutes, and decided to jump in the failing light. We were told to jump in pairs, Lt Lewes and his servant, Guardsman Davies [were the] first the RAF officer was to despatch. The instructions were to dive out

169

as though going into water. We hooked ourselves up, circled the field, and on a signal from the RAF officer, Lt Lewes and Davies dived out. Next time around, I dived out, and was surprised to see Lt Stirling pass me in the air. Lt Lewes made a perfect landing, next came Davies a little shaken. Lt Stirling injured his spine and also lost his sight for about an hour, next, myself, a little shaken and a few scratches, and lastly Sgt Storie who seemed OK. Guardsman Evans was unable to jump as the pilot decided to land owing to the approaching darkness. We slept on the landing field. Next morning we jumped again, this time a stick [formation for jumping from a plane] of four, preceded by a bundle to represent a container. The previous night we had worn khaki dress shirts and shorts, but from experience we decided to put on pullovers. We wore no hats. We pushed the bundle out first and Guardsman Evans, myself Davies and Lt Lewes followed as quickly as possible. The first three landed quite close to each other and doubled forward to the container, but Lt Lewes, in trying to avoid some oil barrels, rather badly damaged his spine, Guardsman Evans also hurt his ankle. Sgt Storie who jumped after us, landed OK.

The intended operation was eventually cancelled.

With the permission of Laycock to train a small group of men 'as I think best', Jock was naturally on the lookout for anything that would release his detachment from the humdrum training practices that had frequently sent David Stirling off to sleep in lectures at Pirbright in 1939. A consignment of fifty silk static-line parachutes bound for India caught Jock's eye near Fuka in May, and he was prepared to find out how to use them. Although there had been plans to use the parachutes in India, there had been none for parachuting in the Middle East. Jock, as Guardsman D'Arcy reported, was determined to end his frustration at being thwarted from fighting behind enemy lines; parachuting appeared to offer excellent opportunities for slipping into hostile territory, invisibly and quietly. Lewes Marches would assist the parachutist to target-spot, destroy enemy installations and report back. In England the RAF used parachutes to bail out of planes, and researchers at Ringway, Manchester, were developing their own techniques in evolving parachuting. However, there were no military parachutes in the Middle East and neither was there any knowledge of the parachute training and techniques that had been developed at RAF Ringway.

It was to be a year before the RAF set up their Parachute Training School at Ramat David in Palestine. The RAF may well have advised Jock with their knowledge of diving out of aircraft. They may have seen photographs of the German parachutists, the *Fallschirmjäger,* in the Battle of Crete. However, Jock led alone, and his first jumps were almost certainly achieved with RAF emergency ripcord chutes – there could have been no others available. This may well partly explain why David Stirling came to grief in his first jump. If ripcord chutes were in fact used for that first jump the parachutist had only about forty-five seconds in the air in an 800-foot jump, and if you pulled the ripcord too late you were likely to hit the ground before the canopy opened up. It is possible that Stirling had pulled his ripcord too late after he passed D'Arcy in the air. Jock needed the parachutes to land him near a target; practice jumps would be necessary so that he could perfect his objective. Most of his men were able to avoid pulling the ripcord too early, tangling with the plane, or too late which would leave little height to make a safe landing.

Jock had no contacts with MEHQ who provided little support for him in June 1941, yet when the innovator showed that it was possible to be transported in a novel way behind enemy lines in the desert, senior officers insisted his planned operations were not safe enough to stage. It was true that the old Valentia, which Jock had borrowed from the RAF, had never been used for parachuting and the static lines had to be attached to the legs of the aircraft seats. Safety was further jeopardized by the design of the plane that meant there was a chance the parachute might snag on its tail. If you could avoid these snares, the impact of hitting the ground was likely to be the same as jumping off a 15-foot wall. Yet this was the best equipment that Jock could obtain at this stage of the war, and without much assistance from the Army. The Public Record Office holds the official report that MEHQ sent to a Captain Schott, who may well have been Jock's contact with MEHQ; it concluded that 'on the first parachute jump done in the Middle East' the operation was cancelled, 'chiefly because the parties were too badly shaken by the practice jumps'. Yet these were capable pioneers; Jock had made a 'perfect landing' and most of his men, except Stirling, had come through without more than a few scratches. Stirling's canopy had opened but had caught on the tailplane, and after he landed both his legs were temporarily paralysed.

Private D'Arcy, who parachuted in the same drop, reported a very different account to the official line taken by MEHQ: he in no way indicated that Jock's parachutists 'were too badly shaken'; Sgt Storie had achieved two good landings out of two. Jock had made one perfect landing. With practice the team might become expert; with better equipment they could eliminate mistakes. They were all determined to take the war to the enemy. Stirling was undaunted despite his serious injuries. In his letter to Arthur Lewes, it is his version of events of why Jock's plans were cancelled by senior leaders at MEHQ that seems plausible: although Jock's operation 'was never executed owing to lack of decision at the top, there was never any doubt that it would have been successful.' This gives credence to Major General Dorman-Smith's view about the need for 'skill and vision' in MEHQ and for those who were of the breed that 'unless you look as if you are 100% at home on a London bum-warmer, there is no hope for you'. Jock's poem, 'Parachute', which he wrote in the Middle East, suggests he was stirred rather than 'shaken' by experimenting with this novel form of transport:

Parachute

All your life's been waiting for this moment
And here it is upon you and won't go,
But sits and stares and wonders at the torment
Of its presence and Time's apostasy
Who promised a short passage of the agony
That's dread, and gave it and departed in the tumult,
Leaving your life waiting down below.

And there you see it all in that slow moment,
Spread out in space and telescoped in time.
A baby born and bred for this sick ferment
Of apprehension, led to this precipice of fear
From true instants of happiness, and dear
Minutes and seconds of remembrance,
Whose faculty for ending was sublime.

To stand and shrink from earth below and wonder
Why ever you confide in Time's word
That moments end and one is like another
Then suddenly to see the face of dread.
Stand by to jump, staring in signal red
Grimly determining whatever waits down under
To squeeze what remains of life dry of what's seen and heard.

Green for Go! Now! God, how slow it is!
The air doesn't rush and earth doesn't rise
Till you swoop into harness and know it is
Over, look up and love the white canopy
Steadfast above you, an angel in panoply
Guarding the skies.

Parachuting into enemy territory was the means by which
the SAS became noticed and established as a novel effective
force. In the stories of how the SAS developed these methods,

Jock is often portrayed as 'accidentally' and 'mysteriously' acquiring the parachutes and, more importantly, the implication often is that the methods were also accidental or that they were not of much significance for the formation of the SAS until David Stirling was invited to join him. Parachuting for the first time in North Africa, marching techniques in the desert and the invention of the Lewes Bomb were a corollary of Jock's experiments to activate his vision of fighting behind enemy lines rather than a 'one-off' accident or trial by an 'SAS expert', as Jock is sometimes mistakenly depicted.

By June 1941 he had suffered disillusionment when MEHQ cancelled his three plans, in which, as Stirling later recalled, he 'seemed to eliminate the chance of failure'. Anyone who had been working as long and hard as Lewes might have occasionally despaired at the opposition from MEHQ, whom Dorman-Smith described as these 'Bears of little Brain' or 'Solid red-faced people'. Yet MEHQ were under pressure from their lack of resources, and at that stage of the war private armies or independent 'bands of cut-throats' could be viewed as an unnecessary irritant and burden to the paper war that already existed. However, Lewes was not the only one who suffered disillusionment with Middle Eastern operations. The Chief of Staff at MEHQ, General Arthur Smith, considered that the men of Layforce 'had a terribly raw deal' and on 20 June 1941 Stirling wrote home, 'I shall probably apply to be returned to England, depending on how things shape out here.'

Stirling remembers the invitation to parachute with Jock Lewes in mid −1941 as 'the real trigger' for his own ideas on fighting behind enemy lines. In his letter to Arthur Lewes he argues as much, saying Jock's ideas on the use of a special force were the blueprint for 1st SAS. That Jock's parachuting was just a way of relieving boredom during the waits between operations is not supported by the wartime correspondence of either Stirling, Lewes or Private D'Arcy. Although Stirling and Lewes later became interdependent friends in war with a deep mutual respect, Jock was at first wary of allowing anyone to unsettle the work of his detachment. So when Stirling persuaded the parachute leader to let him in on the experiment, Lewes aired his doubts that: 'he was interfering with my task in hand' and that he was let 'in on it in the last days when all arrangements were made'.

Jock had had enough trouble getting as far as he did, what with persuading Layforce to let him form the force in May 1941 and then seeing carefully planned operations cancelled. Later he would see Stirling's exploitation of his ideas as essential, but in June 1941 he was justified in his reservations about his fellow officer. Carol Mather, who had trained with Lewes and Stirling since 1940, wrote how he and his peers 'thought we knew David too well' for such a scheme to work. Stirling's biographer, Alan Hoe, wrote how Stirling 'could be vague and seemingly uninterested in the business of soldiering when not actually engaged in training. Without the stimulus of testing situations he would either lapse into his private world or play some sort of prank on a comrade.' After Stirling miraculously survived his parachute jump, Jock had been requested in late June to leave for Tobruk; Stirling promptly went into hospital in Alexandria to recover from his injured back and there he reviewed the significance of Jock Lewes' work in the desert.

9

Tobruk

Getting experience before experience gets me
– J.S.Lewes

Jock at last found an opportunity to face the enemy and start 'getting experience before experience gets me'. The shortage of manpower in the Middle East meant that General Auchinleck decided to disband Layforce; it was too expensive, so amphibious operations by the Commandos were suspended. The depressing news for members of the Laycock's Special Service Brigade came through by the last week of June. Before this time Jock had been told that he would be posted to Tobruk and that the rest of the 'B' Battalion would follow later. As far as he was concerned he had not finished the work of his parachute detachment, as his letter to his mother in July 1941 indicates:

> I am very well, but most unhappy on account of our past record and anxious for our future; we have not weathered the storm which I saw approaching, nor have I succeeded in bringing my special task to any conclusion. But surely some great thing must be born of all this patience and high aspiration: our schooling has been stern and protracted, but then you will have been able to judge from what I have told you of the unit [Layforce] that both as a unit and as individuals we badly needed such ruthless discipline. Even so, we have not taken many lessons to our hearts which are hardened against the lowering of their pride. But now the storm is breaking upon us

and, if I am not mistaken, it will cleanse our oak of all its rotten wood and cankerous growth.

Jock had maintained his prolific output of letters home and to Mirren, whose own correspondence had usually been a constant source of inspiration to him. He was glad of the many letters that she wrote and which arrived in bundles every three weeks; he had 'not found friends here' and his source of optimism for his parachuting enterprise, that 'some great thing that must be born of all this patience', was rooted in his deep love for her. It was a love developed during their writing, or rather a vision of how great a love it could be. Secrecy was a theme from the days of his childhood when he absorbed the mores and mysteries of *Hollyman* and here his most intimate thoughts on love and lust are embellished discreetly and vividly; he shares them with Mirren, hidden in metaphor:

> We stepped out of our clothes and slid together into the lake. It was as though we had entered a secret door in the bank below the surface, for there was no splash and no lapping of waves as we went, the water just folded around us with a warm caress, touching every part of us to the roots of the hair, where the eyelid wrinkles, around each convolution of each ear, pouring in at the laughing mouth, swirling softly full-bodied down inside, making the chest heave and glow to its depths with the inspiration of its new element.

In *The Spectator* Isabel Colegate writes that Jock's letters, towards the end of 1941, sometimes became 'terse' and 'remote' as 'he comes to recognize a task he can do'. However, Jock also held little back, just as he had done so a year before; he openly adored Mirren and he could tell her anything: 'one thing remains constant through every day and through any change, however cataclysmic: my love for you.' He apologized for boring her with some of his news, and was undeterred by her striking lack of curiosity about the war. At these moments, Lucinda Ballantyne writes in the *Boston Sunday Globe*, Jock 'can seem so alone', but he nevertheless writes about the war 'beautifully': 'Here, the finest moments are the saddest, a man who's killing well or dying well or stamping out his mind and heart to do his duty.' Fired by his belief that the Axis powers had already lost the war, he wrote to his parents that 'he was happier than most'. Mirren had some justification for her reservations about marrying Jock, which she maintained until October 1941, for the business of Jock's war came before marriage. He was convinced that the time spent on leave to perform the wedding rite would weigh heavily on his heart, for he had 'no desire to return before the appointed hour'.

On 6 July he left Cairo and arrived at the docks in Alexandria in the dead of night aboard a Royal Naval vessel, one of several 'dark forms, sliding to their perilous anchorages', as a member of a sixty-strong advance party of the Battalion. Aboard the Australian naval vessel *Vendetta* he set sail for Tobruk; the destroyer that had set sail the day before had been gutted by dive-bombers. He allowed himself to become sentimental and even a little romantic as he loaded up his conscious mind with the vivid images before him: the defence of Tobruk, fortresses besieged, heroic defences, and the Navy's gallant support: 'When thought of thus, the whole atmosphere of the place is legendary to one of my generation; it is the last war come back to earth – a sector of the "front" being re-enacted with all the grim realism of the incident and romance of character that stories and poems of the war have handed down.' For Jock the romance was killed the moment he was told the remainder of the Battalion was not coming 'and that we were not supposed to be there at all'. Captain Michael Kealy (Devonshire Regiment) was in command; Captain Philip Dunne (RHG), Gordon Alston (Royal Artillery), Jock and his friend, Tommy Langton, were later joined by David Sutherland; the six officers led a force of sixty men.

By April 1941 Rommel had recovered many of the gains made by General O'Connor at the beginning of the year. However, after retaking Benghazi, he failed to capture Tobruk on 11 April. Since early January Tobruk, with its high ground enclosing the harbour, became the main fortress in Libya and vital to the British as a channel through which to supply the British forces who formed up as the British Eighth Army in September. The port of Tobruk is considered one of the very best on the coast of North Africa, being well sheltered all round. Situated seventy miles west of the Egyptian-Libyan border, its defended perimeter stretched for thirty miles in a wide arc from the coast into the desert about nine miles from the harbour. The possession of Tobruk would help prevent enemy troops advancing east and west or moving through the desert to the south. More protection could be given for Allied shipping on the dangerous run from Malta to Alexandria, and its good harbour would reduce the long haul for Allied forces travelling westwards. Churchill was determined to relieve Tobruk, but Auchinleck did not have enough men in the Middle East for such a venture.

Jock was assured that General Morshead would not easily let the Layforce men go now they were in Tobruk, so the philosophical amongst them resigned themselves to a long stay, and 'to like it if we could'. Not far from the men's camp was a beautiful bay in which the wadi, where they were based, ended. Jim Almonds, who was one of Jock's stalwart sergeants there, described it:

Date palms, fig trees with two freshwater wells; before the war this must have been a prosperous little valley. Everywhere, however, is visible the ravages of war, the ground is strewn with smashed up lorries, Italian equipment of all kinds, cigars of which our sector had a good share and now walk about like a lot of budding Churchills. Two golden eagles soared above their home in the wadi; it appeared to be a peaceful place of immense calm and grandeur which only wild rugged nature can give, until sudden bursts of gunfire goes crashing and rolling down the wadi and echoing up the side of the canyon.

Brackish chlorinated tea and ascorbic acid tablets accompanied meal times, 'Infuriator' Italian cognac for the fearless and French letters (condoms) – 'millions of them, a mockery and a laughter now in "defeminated" Tobruk, and used only for proofing watches and torches against the sea and sand' – were all small things that later came to symbolize the place.

That July Jock had moved into the line in the NW sector of Ras el Madauar and reinforced the 18th Indian Cavalry that had been there from the beginning of the siege of Tobruk. The Indians were on the sector by the western seaboard, where the wadis run deep and precipitous into the first escarpment. Italians were 2000 yards away from Jock's front line and the Indians maintained forward posts 800 yards in front, on the other side of the defended wadi, Wadi Sihel. Jock lived in the sangars, little rings of loose stone wall holding four or five men at most; he shared one with Tommy Langton and christened the spot 'Stonehenge'. There were subterranean passages and chambers twenty feet into the rock that had been used by the Italians, but they were filthy and full of fleas. Like David Sutherland, Jock could not speak too highly of the 18th Indian Cavalry:

They watched, and harassed and patrolled with all the efficiency of keen professional soldiers. They had established and maintained, in the face of enormous superiority of numbers and support weapons, complete superiority on that front. At night No Man's Land belonged to them, and Wopsie never ventured out in bands of less than forty. By day they hit out whenever he got careless or took liberties with cover; there was no question here of 'you keep your mortars quiet and I won't look while you walk across that open bit between point 84 and 86.' There was in consequence a lot of mortar bombing and shelling of the forward posts, their approaches, and the line itself.

With a new compass from Mirren hung about his neck, Jock commanded his first raid on a position known as the 'Twin Pimples'. He made light of the pressures of fighting in Tobruk and confided in his parents, 'I don't like being shelled much, it is just like waiting for the dentist to hurt.' Yet the forthcoming assault was to be some compensation for the disappointments and cessation of his plans after the intransigence of MEHQ before his posting to Tobruk. General Morshead, despite the opposition of the Commanding Officer of the Indian regiment, insisted that the Layforce men had come to Tobruk 'to do a show' and 'he would give us one worth doing'. The 'Twin Pimples' were two little mounds of rubble which often mark the position of Arab cisterns, in the making of which the stuff was excavated; they stood out clearly on the level plain and covered the whole area with observation. The CO of the Indian Regiment considered that the position that Jock was to raid was not an isolated forward post but part of a continuous line, heavily defended with mutual covering fire and the invariable defensive fire plan from the flanks and rear; it was strongly held and heavily fortified. The objection at the decision was that 'the raid was a bigger undertaking than we could handle alone and would be more costly than a hit and run raid should be'. The Viceroy Commissioned Officer also wanted to have more control of his sector and 'not have his affairs of honour dispatched for by hired assassins'.

The General had his way, and Indian guides led. The plan was to attack the left rear where the Italian line fell back a little into a shallow salient, and to withdraw to the left straight across the Italians' front. Diversionary raids were set to the right a few minutes before zero hour, counter-battery work to ease the process of withdrawal, a mortar platoon and a section of machine guns were pointed on the line to the right of the objective. Jock led with two officers and each man commanded a troop of fifteen. Six Australian Sappers brought ten pounds of gelignite each. Jock also had plenty of support in the form of Sgts Pat Riley and Jim Almonds, both giants of men and brave as lions. The men wondered what exactly they might find up the 'Twin Pimples': 'Indian patrols had heard a concrete-mixer going there for weeks – the Italians worship concrete, they set their idol and build his temples wherever they go.' The irony of these symbolic totems of Mussolini's African Empire didn't escape Jock, who added, 'Having made one set of concrete posts to keep us out of Tobruk they are now building another to keep us in. I wonder if they see the joke or even the implication.'

Everything went like clockwork. Jock arrived 200 yards south of the post and heard uproar from the Italian lines; before zero hour he heard 'laughing and singing, political arguments, a truck being unloaded like a Covent Garden lorry, the concrete mixer and a stiff breeze were all in our favour.' Dressed in tin hat, shirt, shorts, stocking tops, puttees and rubber-soled boots, he was given the job of silently 'bumping first' the outer defensive line on his right as he approached from the rear. Extracts from his Tobruk diary that was sent to MEHQ seem unedited, highlighting both the grotesque and banal in the heat of battle:

A hundred yards to go and up went the diversion, plum to time; the moonless night covered us, but the stars here are always bright enough to show you all you want to see without being seen. We came on faster and crouched lower, still there was talking and laughing in the lines; suddenly the pimple loomed up ahead, a single shot was fired, we were too far to the left but had to go on, I signalled the final rush, and as I reached the foot of the mound, firing into the embrasures with which it was honeycombed, there rose behind me the pitiful wail of the great Italian soldier *in extremis*. The head of my troop 'arrow' had actually passed through the outer line without seeing it and unnoticed; as the arms swept on they bumped it, and were now busy winkling out the wretched screaming Wop from his sangars and entrenchments with the bayonet, or rolling in grenades when he lay low. The place was like a disturbed ant heap; Italians, for the most part dressed only in trousers, ran grimly for their lives, silent and scuttling, fell screaming when brought down with fire, knelt with raised hands before bayonets, crying pitifully, or just whimpered as they grovelled underfoot. The top of the pimple we had bumped was chaos. Some of the Italians as they ran threw their absurd grenades at us, they flashed and filled the air with smoke and dust; the shots from our own men were crackling past from behind, and more and more men were climbing up the mound. Men from all troops were there, mad with excitement, shouting obscene profanities at the fallen and departing enemy. Prisoners taken by one man, and left in his eagerness for more, were bayonetted by those folding in from the left and centre. Soon the whole force was dancing a mad war dance on and around the pimple.

To get the troops off the pimple was the only way to restore control. I ordered my troop back. This was taken as the signal for a general withdrawal, the sappers lit their fuses and shouted their prearranged warning to get clear. The withdrawal had begun, the enemy were quick to sense it, and at once before we were clear of the outer lines an LMG opened up and got two men with its first burst. It was very gallantly attacked and silenced, and no more short-range fire troubled us. By now the troops were properly sorted out, the defensive fire was screaming over. Our plan worked perfectly; the long march southward with two wounded men, one unable to walk, was slow, hazardous and nerve-racking; the noise was terrific, and the coloured fire in the sky most awe-inspiring. The very lights seemed to go up every five minutes, not at the quarter hours, and we seemed hardly to have moved between its appearances, but at last we reached the safety of our wadi, climbed the other side, which was being mortared relentlessly, swallowed our tea and rum at the cookhouse, and so to our cave and sangar to sleep, while the Italian continued to roar defiance from a distance in the pleasant impersonal manner that he prefers.

Jock reported the two casualties and tended the pair, removing his pullover to warm the cooling body of a man shot in the neck; the soldier was fatally wounded, but the other escaped with a broken arm. The official estimate of the enemy casualties was one hundred, but Jock regarded that as 'an exaggeration, fifty would be closer'. Most of the guns on the 'Twin Pimple' went up with a 'lovely roar'. Jock was disappointed that he had been unable to 'exploit our extraordinary good fortune' while the objective lay for a while completely at the men's mercy 'instead of dancing our war dance on top of the pimple' – 'but there it is, that's how it happened, and I suppose, being inexperienced soldiers, almost without exception, it could hardly be expected to have happened any otherwise.'

The attack took place in the early morning of 18 July and the following day Jock wrote to his father that he was 'able to lift up my head in the presence of those who have been in battle and stood the test of action':

Last night I led an attack which has been universally proclaimed a success, but what pleases me more than praise of those higher up is the fact that the men of my troop are satisfied with me, and in knowing that with the help and strength which I needed on that night I can do much better. But the

Italian is no soldier and fighting him is a hateful business, so let's talk no more of it.

On 20 July David Sutherland arrived when Jock's senior officers decided that the 'Twin Pimples' raid had not after all been a complete success; they now demanded a much-needed prisoner. David Sutherland noted the nature of his raid leader:

> It was then I got to know and much admire Jock Lewes. He had an easy, powerful, long-ranging stride of an Australian grazier. Immediately I noticed how supremely intelligent he was, a rare conceptual thinker, a highly geared brain with practical application for everyday operational needs, and fearless too – a formidable man. We began to plan the prisoner snatch in which Jock took the lead and I, younger and far less experienced, followed. I remember him giving out his orders in a clear, confident voice, with Mike Kealy, the three men to give covering fire and help get the prisoner back and myself listening: 'We will start at midnight. We will move silently and directly to the enemy positions we already know. David Sutherland and I will carry pistols, the rest sub-machine-guns. I will go down the first dugout and search for and grab a prisoner. If there is no enemy there, I will come out and go into the next dugout and so on till we have a prisoner.

On a quarter moonlit night Jock controlled his group with visual signals. One diversionary attack on an Italian post was to allow his party to get through the wire and a supposed minefield in order to cut off the retreat of the occupants. After three-quarters of an hour he went into his first dugout and soon emerged whispering, 'Hell, there's no one there.' The diversionary attack never came but then Jock raced towards an unfortunate man with diarrhoea, whom he was soon to christen, 'Umberto'. Jock takes up the end of the mission when he caught the enemy 'literally with his pants down in true Smollett vein':

> We snapped him up, and tried to get out undetected, but his hob-nailed boots sounded like a smithy, as he shuffled along with his trousers around his knees, trying to hold them up and his hands as well. When we got him safely back to our lines he shook us warmly by the hand, and said delighted, that he was V for Victory: I wonder, I think he was just U for Umberto, or perhaps simpler still plain W for Wop. Poor miserable men!

After one month of fighting the Italians, Jock and his group moved twelve kilometres south-west to the area known as Pilastrino, the toughest sector of the perimeter about three kilometres west of the fort of Tobruk. Here the positions were reversed for the Layforce men: an active German Motor Battalion had complete patrolling, sniping, fire and observation superiority. Mortar fire by day and fixed line fire by night dissuaded the Australians on either side from patrolling where Jock was working and took a regular toll of ration parties, linesmen 'and plain careless people who didn't keep their head down like the rest of them all the time'. In the hard school of experience Jock was learning the art of war all the time, constantly being forced to outwit the ferocity of the opposition. In preparation for a big combined show with the Australians, he located a listening post in a derelict tank; the next night he took a patrol to 'clean it up, foolishly using the same route as before'. One hundred and fifty yards from his own lines, he walked straight into a minefield that had been laid since his previous visit. Sgt Bob Lilley tripped what seemed then to be the first of many S-Mines. He was the last man in the patrol. Everyone fell flat and 400 steel balls were sent whirring round at chest-height like ' a swarm of angry buzzing bees' before finally exploding:

How we got out of the field without tripping another, and through 'Spandau Sammy's' fixed line that was now hammering away like an *Idée fixe*, how we are here at all, and we all are, is a mystery and a marvel, and an occasion for continual thanksgiving. The big show was a 1917 effort from start to finish, forming-up place, starting line, tapes to follow, artillery preparation, counter barrage, attack, defensive fire repulse, withdrawal. We never functioned as we were only there to exploit success, which was not forthcoming. And so we sat in our holes and listened with awe to our barrage going over, and were shocked, when Hun defensive fire came down, at the thought that we should have to walk through it. The success signal never came, we were spared. We sighed with relief.

Towards the end of August Jock moved and patrolled north of the salient where the German and Italian sectors met; all were feeling the strain of nightly patrols for the past month. David Sutherland recalled the unpleasant side of this work that had rendered most of the other officers sick, impeded as they were by the poor conditions under which they lived. It was at this time that Sutherland generously recalled, 'Jock Lewes being far and away the most daring of us all'. The beleaguered group were to prepare a raid in order to support a large operation, which Jock noted 'still twanged with the same tired harp-string, "squeeze out the salient"'. Jock occasionally despaired at being 'nobody's baby', a hired hand with little identity or sense of being part of a well-organized team. The opportunity to change that would come two weeks later when Jock decided to 'throw in his lot with David Stirling', who had left the hospital in Alexandria to present Jock's plans and his own ideas to MEHQ for the enlargement of Jock's parachute detachment on a unit basis. Jock's experience on the Tobruk perimeter partly explains why he would want to implement his own ideas for such a force, even if he was still not sure that David Stirling was the officer with whom he might achieve that aim:

The Australians haven't got the art of accumulating local intelligence in the front-line posts, and so, as in the show before, we had to rely on what our reconnaissance patrols could discover in the short time available. It was not encouraging. I did most of the patrolling here, as desert sores, dysentery and the unspeakable squalor in which we lived rendered most of the other officers temporarily unserviceable; also I seemed to have luck in my patrols. We found out a lot, locating wire and minefields – this time without first walking into them – Italian working parties laying more mines, and strengthening a new established forward post. But not once did we get behind the Italians, or find a way for sixty men behind through their outer defences to the defended localities that we were supposed to attack. The large operation was suddenly cancelled, but ours was retained, and a night appointed. We shifted our objective to the newly established forward post, and I tried to learn something about it in the two remaining nights. We thought we knew enough, but when the night came, and I tried to repeat the tactics of the Twin Pimples raid, unexpected wire and a field of S-mines turned us back with nothing accomplished. It was an inglorious affair and I blush for my willingness to turn aside and run out of the jump, but there was much that militated against true courage. We were tired of being hawked about the perimeter like professional pugs at a fair. Since coming to the salient we had patrolled continuously – every night someone was out – and there were only four subalterns, one of whom was sick. It was two months since we came, and we had the news that the remainder of the Battalion had been disbanded, and of course rumour said that many were going home. We had fought a losing battle with Divisional HQ to get back to Alexandria ever since arriving: it didn't seem to be important in their eyes that we were no longer a unit, proud to use our name, but just

a bunch of Guardsmen and others. We were without immediate inspiration to the battle, especially since leaving the
Indians, who certainly took trouble for us and made us feel
useful, and our work worthwhile. But in the salient we were
nobody's baby – attached for rations here, then there, and
then onto the next fair in the covered wagon. It was being like
a tramp, going from home to home, given a meal and a hole
in the ground at each, and some work to do because we were
there, and they had something to show for the food we ate;
not because the work was of any importance, or the doing of
it well a thing to take pride in. And so we refused our last high
jump – for this was the last, we all knew, though it wasn't
official.

Jock may have felt like a menial and underdog, but he was
poised to perform better than some of the commanders whom
a generation before Rudyard Kipling had described as the
'brainy men languishing under an effete system'. The imperi-
alist's estimate of the British army was still relevant for those
who were blind to the needs of soldiers fighting a very
different conflict compared to the First World War. Six
months before leaving Tobruk, Jock's training and plans to
overcome or at least stalemate the mechanized forces of the
enemy for which he had initially received official backing
were dashed by uncertainty and indecision at the highest level,
despite the fact that the enemy's numerical and material superiority demanded the utmost daring if the British were to
push Rommel back to Tripoli. Jock was still convinced that
his ideas could succeed, and he wanted to be sure that they
would work. On 25 August he boarded HMS *Hastings* and
as he made for Alexandria there was no time, 'nor any inclination for imagery or sentiment'. An air raid started as the
vessel left Tobruk; the day before HMS *Vendetta* had
attempted the same journey and been sunk.

Any doubts about having to depend on others to achieve
success would have to be put aside. Jock, though emotionally

robust, was naturally tired after raiding the enemy every other night of his six-week posting; it meant he was vulnerable to the persuasive powers of David Stirling. The timing of when to find the opportunity again to execute his ideas was in rhythm with his determination to no longer be 'nobody's baby' – Stirling's help 'was a means to a very proximate end' and Jock had more chance of controlling his concepts of fighting in the desert than ever before.

10

The Special Air Servant

Together we have fashioned this unit. David has
established it without, and I think I may say I
have established it within – J.S.Lewes

After his troglodyte existence in Tobruk, Jock arrived in
Alexandria on 26 August and cleaned up in style at the Cecil
Hotel. For drinks he started with John Collins and relished
the smooth sandless fresh food. He spent the last weekend in
August in the luxury of Cairo's Shepheard's Hotel, living 'like
a nabob and eating like a discriminating cormorant'; this was
just as well, since that year he would pass over most of his
forthcoming leave and return only a few more times from the
desert to enjoy such pleasures again.

In July and August 1941 David Stirling had travelled
several times to Tobruk on the *Aphis* in order to persuade
Jock to join the new parachute unit backed by Auchinleck.
The boat made three trips there each week. The number of
Stirling's visits suggest that Jock had initially refused to take
up the offer of Stirling who had achieved the networking
that most young officers only dream of. The unit 'without'
required very skilful handling, and David Stirling's contacts
and knowledge of senior officers at MEHQ, and his ability in
dealing with them, was enabling Jock's plans to have the kind
of support they deserved. Since Jock's letters to his parents
have come to light, his reasons for joining David Stirling after
initially refusing to do so have become clearer. Recent biographies of David Stirling have suggested that Jock was unsure
of the feasibility of the ideas in the memorandum that Stirling

gave to Major General Ritchie: Jock had visited Stirling in hospital in Alexandria, and he supposedly expressed his 'doubts' about the memorandum by Stirling's bedside.

This is unlikely to be the case because those 'uncertainties' revolved around the plans in the memorandum, for it has now been established, on Stirling's own admission, that most of the memorandum was none other than Jock's own plans. Later writing on the SAS has often suggested that Jock needed persuading to join the force, because the Welsh Guardsman did not have enough faith in the plans for the new detachment. Yet why would Jock doubt his own blueprint for Special Service? He had been working on his own detachment for months, and he did not need any persuasion to fight behind enemy lines using his leadership in parachuting and marching. That was not the issue. He could not allow another officer to be involved in his enterprise unless that soldier could be totally reliable, a watchword of the SAS then and now. Quelling such doubts was as much a reason as any other for the conversations that took place at Stirling's bedside in the Scottish Military Hospital.

Apparently Stirling visited Jock three times in Tobruk to persuade him to join. The picture of both men and their meetings is incomplete and Stirling's descriptions of the meetings may have been taken at face value. Why did Lewes need such persuasion? Why did Stirling regard it as so essential that Jock be his second in command now that he himself had been promoted by the top brass to Captain? Stirling knew plenty of officers in the Scots Guards with whom he had more affinity. He needed Jock with his training methods and technical skills to implement the memorandum that had been presented to Major-General Ritchie. This whole enterprise gave Stirling a direction that, without Jock, would not have been possible for him to follow.

It is almost certain that Jock was questioning Stirling's suitability for a project that had already been carefully prepared by himself. This attitude is in keeping with Stirling's own view of why Lewes was at first reluctant to work with him:

> I think Jock wanted to be sure that if we got the thing working, I was going to stay with it and also tackle the enormous problems at MEHQ which he possibly foresaw more clearly than me . . . he just didn't want to get involved if it was going to be a short-term flight of fancy . . . I suppose I'd come across to him in the past as a bit of a good time Charlie.

Jock's 'doubts', which have been interpreted as representing uncertainty over the establishment of the SAS, were none other than his stringent concern to recruit the best team. That he thought Stirling 'was interfering in my task in hand' during the parachuting earlier that year suggests his very legitimate concern about the need to team up with a sharp operator. Later, the two men would be firm friends with a great respect for one another; however, Jock had some misgivings towards the Scotsman. The bitter experience of having his own detachment's operations cancelled in June 1941 meant that he was almost certainly wary of anyone else's intervention, however much they might thrive on his ideas. Jock only agreed to help his fellow officer when he was fairly certain that his own ideas would be successfully implemented. The abrogation of his operations was caused by vacillation at MEHQ, and if extraordinary projects like this were renewed, only to fail, senior officers rarely gave them a second chance. Jock's frustration explains why he needed to be sure Stirling would not jeopardize his ideas in the future. When Stirling went to Tobruk to ask Jock to join a bigger unit under the auspices of the Commander-in-Chief instead of resuscitating his abeyant parachute detachment from the remnants of Layforce, Jock may well have insisted on important conditions for his involvement: a free hand in organizing and planning the entire SAS training, which would also include Stirling's as well.

Later on it would be seen that David Stirling's genius lay in his recognition of Lewes's ideas and his determination to exploit them at all costs. Stirling, though still on crutches, forced his way into the heart of MEHQ to present the concept of the SAS on a unit basis. It was the only way a junior officer in his position might be listened to. The war had not been going well for Stirling before he made his sortie into MEHQ to gain authority for the SAS unit. He almost certainly found inactivity harder to cope with than his more professional fellow officer; just as Jock had the qualities to test out his training by himself, so David went less by the book. Having the capacity to be bold and ill-disciplined were attributes required for getting you past the guard at MEHQ, through the wire and into General Ritchie's office. Ritchie was an acquaintance of Stirling's father, with whom he had shot grouse on the Stirling estate at Keir before the war broke out. Another advantage of Stirling gaining an 'audience' with Ritchie was having grown up in the presence of very senior officers: Stirling's father was a General. The prospect of a court-martial was an extra incentive in Stirling's first of many bold acts to join with Lewes, in order to fashion the parachutists into the SAS Regiment.

Fortunately, Stirling had glimpsed an alternative method of waging war, whilst reviewing the significance of Jock's detachment of pioneers. Lewes was busy in Tobruk, when Stirling got permission from MEHQ to go ahead with what became known as 'Stirling's Rest Camp'. In due course Jock agreed to bring all his experience and ideas with him, and he recruited NCOs from Tobruk who were of outstanding quality and the vital backbone of the unit in the early days of the SAS. It is not difficult to see why Stirling made those trips to Tobruk in the summer of 1941; he was proving that he was not going to fail the undertaking – that he was not going to fail Lewes or himself. The latest biography of Stirling confirms this view: 'Stirling always felt that it was he who was being tested for persistence and faith rather than the idea.'

David Stirling admitted that when Jock returned from Tobruk he was 'an absolute wreck'. He was suffering from acute desert sores, and this was the moment when Jock 'was rather trapped by me'. In his interview with Television South Stirling also paid tribute to Jock and highlighted the importance of winning him over when he was so vulnerable to persuasion:

> He was lying in bed and I could really get at him, and persuaded him to join . . . I think he was the greatest training officer of the last war. The men had a huge respect for him. You can see how important he was for me, how I had to persuade him to join me.

This was a vital moment in the history of the Special Forces: in the late summer of 1941 Stirling was impatient to justify the pips on his own shoulders. He would gain fulfilment by implementing Jock's ideas, and if that meant walking down the corridors that led to General Auchinleck, Commander-in-Chief of MEHQ, so be it. It was to be fortunate for Stirling, Lewes and the SAS. While Stirling pondered his un-fulfilled career, he could not have met Jock Lewes again at a better time. Lewes's hard-won detachment was only open to the dedicated; and even if Stirling was 'a bit of a good time Charlie', he was also quick to pick up the training. Jock didn't want any risk of further interference, but then he was generous as well as being tough and Stirling was a good talker. At one masterstroke the latter could leave behind him a recent bleak report on his conduct, dispense with those senior officers he did not respect and guarantee his exclusive superi-ority in a mode of warfare which he instinctively knew he could wage.

Stirling was of a breed that didn't prosper well in an unin-spiring environment and Jock Lewes provided him with a method of fighting the enemy, which Stirling knew he wanted to excel in. This helps to explain some of his ingenuity required in preventing the 'fossilized shit' in MEHQ from sitting on the unit's progress. While Lewes was in Tobruk this was the first battle that Stirling waged on his own.

Jock met David again as he returned from Tobruk. After Jock left his rooms at the Cecil in Cairo, he talked with Stirling at Shepheard's Hotel. There he decided that it was no longer possible to pick and choose how he could execute his plans himself; he needed Stirling's help. He conceded as much to his parents on 2 September:

> I have joined up with David Stirling in a very modest but deter-mined attempt to give the lead in the rejuvenation of Special Service. When I consider my decision quite dispassionately, I am each time compelled to admit that I have been and gone and done the very thing which I promised myself in ———— [Tobruk, which he later referred to as the 'Monster of Tobruk'], that I would never let myself in for again. The only difference between this and that from which I am most happy so recently to have escaped is that now it appears that success does depend in a very large measure on what I do, whereas before it seemed that whatever I may do the result was bound to be the same dismal failure and bitter disappointment in the end. I am acting as chief instructor to this detachment and supervising, and to a large extent undertaking the training of the men and the officers.

Jock was then based with 'L' Detachment, SAS Brigade. The camp was at Kabrit, a headland situated on the western shore of the Great Bitter Lake near its junction with Suez Canal, about 100 miles east of Cairo and a similar distance south of Port Said where a large airfield was situated close enough to assist in the parachute training of its members. In September 1941 Jock immediately rejuvenated his parachute programme that was held in abeyance whilst in Tobruk. Jim Almond's diary shows that the first recruits, built around Jock's NCOs which he had commanded in July and August – the 'Tobruk Four', Pat Riley, Privates Lilley and Blakeney, and 'Gentleman Jim' Almonds himself – learned the parachute techniques that Jock had pioneered in May and June. Jock took a scholarly approach to the training and examined the new recruits after only a week's work. Reg Seekings, later Stirling's bodyguard and a highly decorated NCO, remembered how they were each given an exercise book and regularly tested and marked on everything they learned. Seekings was dyslexic and used to copy up the correct spellings of terminology and concepts at the end of the day when everyone had gone to bed – dyslexia then still being misunderstood, not least by Reg Seekings himself. He recalled how encouraging Jock had been when the men achieved a variety of levels of success, Jock reiterating that progress was in the grasp of all the recruits. Seekings was top in a group of what Jock called 'outstanding results', the others were told 'not to worry if they were not in the top ten, theirs were also good'; in this systematic way he communicated his eagerness and pleasure in the men's progress. These commandos were being carefully 'supervised' and motivated.

However, Reg Seekings also discovered a more abrupt side of his training officer. In the first week's lecture on parachuting, Seekings asked Jock about a point on a detail about which the latter clearly had little knowledge. The question was hastily dismissed and smacked of a petulance that belied the promise of the new SAS being a Brigade where all soldiers learned from each other's technical capability and skills. Seekings recently commented that 'Jock was naturally under a pressure that was unfair to him; a hell of a lot of that must have been his ideas that had never been carried out in our army. Nowhere else were we aware of such ideas.' Reg Seekings himself made the point that his training officer was pioneering and simply may not have known all the answers to some of the many problems that the detachment faced in those early days in September 1941.

Throughout Jock's brief experience of soldiering, he had been constantly mindful of the need to gain the respect of his own men before attempting to seek laurels from his superiors, and this want weighed heavily upon him as he began the establishment of a fully operational SAS unit. Strongly influenced by his father, he had very high expectations of the heights that he was prepared to climb in order to be a deserving role model. In this incident with Seekings, he fell between the two stools of embarrassment that his expertise did not match with the 'story' of leadership that he told to his men, and the crushing weight of living up to his idealistic self-image, the light of that image so strongly projected onto him by his father.

The new recruits, like Jock himself, had not been impressed with their 'usage' over the past year, and it seems that, before Jock's organized programme of lectures and tests, a significant number were not at all convinced whether 'L' Detachment was not just another 'Inveraray, Burnham or Largs'. Their doubts were such that Jock experienced a baptism of fire as far as his own control of the force was concerned. In the first week of September 1941, when he imposed a regime that appeared to consist of more mindless routines of digging the Libyan Desert to soften up the ground for the detachment's tent posts, he nearly witnessed a mutiny that might have resulted in his dismemberment by a lynch mob of hitherto leaderless soldiers.

Sergeant Major Yates was in charge of a very basic SAS camp that caused tensions when Seekings and Jock first arrived in Kabrit. Yates had little in the way of food except bully beef, biscuits, herrings and porridge, let alone equipment. Reg Seekings recalled, 'The food was terrible and there was no organization.' The Commandos who joined the SAS had opted for special service but were in a sense on probation. Once failed, they were informed that SAS servicemen would be permanently returned to their original unit which was anathema to most soldiers who would then suffer the indignity of being branded unsatisfactory for the fledgling SAS. Clearly a number of men at first considered their move to the

SAS as a bit of gamble. They must at first have wondered why they had made further sacrifices after the many disappointments in the Commandos. Seekings remembers that the final straw came when 'the men were asked to put up their own tents'.

Stirling remembers that at the beginning 'it boded well for 'L' Detachment that there was no moaning about the camp', but he was extremely busy away from it, gathering support, and clearly was not there for what was nearly a minor mutiny. The tents and equipment had not yet arrived, but the men started to dig holes in the sand anyway; then they decided to stop and refused to continue what appeared to be mindless training. Seekings continued: 'We then had a meeting in the marquee for lectures; *we* decided that we were going back to our own units.' The explosive situation seemed to be defused when Jock climbed onto the top of a table in the one tent that had been assembled and issued a declaration to all the men. He told the new recruits that there was method in the apparent 'madness' of backbreaking routine and he questioned their courage. There were very brave men in that tent, who had also been at Jock's side in action against the enemy. In spite of this, there was incredulity amongst the sea of faces that surrounded him. Reg Seekings recalled:

> Jock stood up on the lecture room table and told the men that they had to prove they were not cowards: 'Prove it!' he told them. 'Prove it! The trouble with you people is you've all got a bloody yellow streak a yard wide down your backs! You just can't take it! That's your problem! Unless you can prove otherwise.'

Some men present would soon be recommended Victoria Crosses, and later be highly decorated for those brave operations in the SAS that could be witnessed by senior officers. That time had not yet arrived for most of those there that day in early September 1941. The men were dumbfounded and momentarily stung into a very unpleasant silence, until someone chirped up:

> 'Prove what?'
> 'You will do anything I do,' Jock retorted.
> 'Yes, and you'll do everything we do.'
> 'That's a bet,' replied Jock.

Reg Seekings could not believe 'how on earth Jock got away with that', but he added, 'this was a test wasn't it? This was exactly what Jock wanted, to see if we'd stand up to it – to everything that we'd been bolshy about in the Commandos.' It was not long before he and most of the men understood that Jock had already undertaken plenty of training exercises with which he was more than willing to induct the new recruits. They saw him refine some of his concepts on his own and in his precious little time off, irrespective of the danger it posed to his own life. The rest of the training the men witnessed when Jock tested methods out in front of them. He was very determined to succeed in the eyes of his men and in the eyes of those sceptics at MEHQ, some of whom were christened the SRDG – the Short Range Desert Group – after their insistence on working in close proximity to the areas in or around the Cairo bars and watering holes. With such men in mind he may have composed bold declarations to his fiancée, Mirren, at the Shepheard's Hotel; Jock still loved her in letters and knew that 'I have power in you to create beauty which passes into bloodstreams of time on the adrenaline of happiness':

> I walk upright now and hold my head because I feel my strength, and fear is far away. I see how well dressed I am and look boldly at the passengers, when they are soldiers, compelling their reluctant salutes by meeting and keeping their looks. For I have said I will not seek to save my life but will choose the most difficult and dangerous work that is to be done. I shall not scheme to return to England because it is

against the order of things; it is ordered that I serve in Egypt. If I am to return home I surely will in God's good time, and if I am to die it matters only to those who live on and whom by living I might have helped, whether I die in Egypt or in England some time later. And yet I am proud in spirit and believe that in life is my release, that I have a mission and must seek fulfilment here – remember the spirit of the Guest.

Jock kept the men occupied in training with great purpose; it was tailored to suit the needs of anyone who could stay the course. Old factories were blown up, there was plenty of PT in the mornings, night schemes with navigation by the stars, and intelligence-gathering by lying out in the hills to observe enemy patrols and air observation. Reg Seekings considered Jock's instruction on medical care in the desert as the best the detachment were offered until Dr Pleydell worked with the SAS in 1942, and Pat Riley remembers that Jock even explained the importance of operating a plane on land in case any of the men required an emergency exit from an aerodrome. Jock created treasure hunts to develop navigation and used Kim's Game to sharpen wits; blindman's bluff in the tent developed sensitivity in the dark and made work a pleasure rather than humdrum routine.

He had promised that the men of the SAS Brigade would be ten times tougher than the Commandos. The men might get a beer in the early evening, but they were often back on duty for 10 p.m. for night marching in order to realize the super-awareness they were honing in Jock's games. It was the only time to train the all-important method of escape from a target area that would often be attacked in darkness. By Saturday 28 September the recruits were engaged in a thirty-mile night scheme and spent Sunday recovering; the first intensive training must have been backbreaking work. They would eventually build up to a ninety-five mile march over three days and four nights in the possible event of their needing that mobility. Little was left to chance as it had been for some of these men in the Commandos. Early in September Jim Almonds had gathered that 'this job is going to be in the front line'.

The men knew little of why Stirling was frequently absent in Cairo, where he steadily developed the contacts necessary to win the support of the middle managers at MEHQ, who were not 'with him or Lewes' and therefore 'against them'. Peter Stirling, David's brother, was attached to the British Embassy in Cairo and his flat was a useful base from which to gather the latest information before a host of double agents that appeared to infest Cairo got there first. In late 1941 Stirling managed to have dinner several times with the Countess of Ranfurly, who was secretary to both Generals Wilson and Alexander during the war. The Countess was one of the few English women in the Middle East who obtained access to sensitive information that could be invaluable when advising young ambitious officers. She was a model of discretion, but it is possible that she may have been able to help Stirling with the necessary contacts in order to help launch the conflict in the Middle East from the First World War into the Second.

Perhaps the need to prove that this was a *bona fide* fighting force and Stirling's absence was part of the cause of a loneliness that Jock felt but which few knew of. Reg Seekings knew only too well that Jock 'was in a difficult and isolated position'. He had thrown down the gauntlet to his men, and many in his position would have felt the strain of initially being constantly watched by the new recruits, when much of the responsibility for developing the unit fell to him alone. Yet he had an ability to keep his distance with all men; it could sometimes be interpreted as unsociability. However, what the men at Kabrit needed most was a strict training officer, who was going to enable them to look on their preparation as the best way to endure combat with superior forces behind the lines of the Italians and Germans. Jock's emotional resilience in all his planning for the unit would achieve his and Stirling's objectives, rather than being the heart and soul of the party in the canteen with the rest of the men after training was over.

There were four other officers to assist Jock. Lt Fraser helped out with map-reading, Lt Eion MacGonigal was a first-class weapons instructor and Lt Blair Mayne was PT instructor and also responsible for any punishments that needed meting out – which in effect meant doing several rounds in the ring with him. It may have been less daunting for the likes of highly professional soldiers such as Seekings and Riley, who had also boxed each other at Wisbech before the war, but Paddy Mayne was seventeen stone and usually 'a few quiet words' from him was enough to persuade any recalcitrant soldier that discretion was the better part of valour where training was concerned. Ernie Bond, David Stirling's Platoon Sergeant, recalled that Jock was largely responsible for all the ideas and schemes that developed the SAS in 1941 and enabled the men to hit targets and escape largely undetected:

> Jock was the thinker, he used to think the 'whys and where-fores'. Everyone thought, 'We'll do this, get there and do the other,' but little attention was paid as to how we were going to get out. David Stirling wanted the action without the preparation and training. I wonder whether David would have ever survived without Jock. None of the other officers were of Jock's calibre to take on the roles he did and all the preparation for operations that he took on.

Reg Seekings confirmed that 'Jock had a bit of help' from the others, but the onus of planning depended upon him and explains why his lantern burned late on into the lonely nights. His task with the men in such conditions was possibly the fillip for his appeals to his family in mid-October. In his letter to his brother David he fantasizes about having a brother-companion in arms, but actually learns to defend himself against his loneliness in letters. He had written in this way to

Mirren for most of the war, despite her lack of knowledge about the sort of conflict he was involved in:

> It's no good knowing that death is only a beginning, you've got to believe it, and you can do that more easily without metaphysics or knowledge. It's no good knowing that there is a creator of the world supervising this muddle. What one needs is a personal friend and companion who under no circumstances will desert you. That's the main reason why I delude myself with visions of you being here – I don't think God would mind you taking his place in that capacity for a while; after all you'd do it so much better than he can, and being a very fair-minded person God would be the first to admit your superiority and step down.

During the first few months of the unit's inception he was almost entirely responsible for the development of that unit 'within', while Stirling developed more contacts and assistance 'without', in Cairo particularly. This work of Stirling's was crucial to the successful execution of Jock's concepts and training: in the first few weeks of the SAS's foundation the equipment available amounted to no more than three tents and a three-ton lorry. Dr James Pleydell, who joined the detachment soon after its establishment as its doctor, wrote his own account of events in that first year; *Born of the Desert* was published in 1945. Dr Pleydell missed the opportunity to work with Jock, but his writing confirms the oral history of diverse original SAS veterans and Jock's own letters. He had this to say of Jock's work 'within' 'L' Detachment:

> Schemes were turned to actualities chiefly by the enthusiasm of Jock Lewes. Although I had never met Lewes, I had not been in the SAS for long before I realized that he was the man who was responsible for its construction and organization. By all accounts he was a remarkable man, possessing as he did, a terrific drive of character together with a natural sense of

leadership. More than that, he expected others to do what he himself could do; where he could lead them they must follow, for he was as severe on others as he was hard on himself. He drew out plans and timetables for the training. How should they best become fit so that this sort of warfare could be rewarded with tangible results? . . . Wasn't there some story that in England parachute troops were jumping from moving lorries? He tried the theories out, one after another. He jumped from a truck travelling at twenty miles an hour and did a forward roll. 'All right', he cried out as he picked himself up, 'that's OK', and he put it down in the training syllabus. Then he jumped backwards from the truck travelling at the same speed, but in doing so he hurt himself. Accordingly the exercise was ruled out, for there was no object in causing more casualties than were necessary over the training itself.

This building up of a unit was hard work; and in speaking of it afterwards the men would tell me how every night they could see the light of the hurricane lamp dimly outlining Lewes's tent, while inside he sat at his camp table working away at fresh plans and schemes.

Jock continued to correspond regularly with Mirren and his parents but had indeed much of the daily administration and SAS training to attend to. He did injure himself and indirectly others in the process of parachute practice: three had suffered broken arms and others suffered more breaks by the first week in October. Jock's baptism of fire with the men was not over immediately: Pat Riley, who later became training officer, remembered that 'Stirling was away for most of 1941' and Jock, largely on his own, had much to prove to the men on his and Stirling's behalf. Perhaps it would have been less possible for David Stirling to be so soft-spoken, fair, firm and good-humoured without the powerful internal chemistry of the SAS, which under Jock's leadership was steadily developing and which Stirling was protecting in Cairo.

Parachute training and simulation for practice jumps had

originally been made from wooden platforms set on trolleys, and in mid-October tall towers were made. A miniature railway in an old quarry in Kabrit had been used for the trolleys. Soldiers pushed the trolley, which then gathered speed until it eventually came to a rise and a stop; a PT instructor would tell what sort of roll they wanted and when. This still did not simulate the appropriate force of landing, which was similar to jumping off a fifteen-foot wall, and therefore the detachment's designer (and much more besides), Jim Almonds, set to work on three forty-foot steel towers known as the 'Wedding Ring Assembly'. Advice from the parachute centre at Ringway, Manchester, was slow in coming, so the pioneers made do with the towers that enabled a parachutist to simulate landing in the wind; Jim noted that 'it gave you the impression that you steered'. The towers were attached to an iron ring around which the parachutist manoeuvred; the whole contraption was very heavy and, because the SAS lacked extra help, the towers were used and fortunately never collapsed, but they were potentially 'very dangerous'. The men ascended a small tower, put their harnesses on and jumped off with a big swing, descending slowly and finishing with a forward or backward roll.

Jock had already prepared practice jumps from 2,000 feet from the old Valentia plane that he had borrowed in June, and used in Bagoush. The SAS had acquired, for the same purpose, a Bombay, which was considerably more suitable than the Valentia. However, its tail was set too low in relation to the fuselage to allow safe practice, and it had ripped some of the men's chutes as they left the aircraft. On 17 October disaster struck. A fault in the clip attaching the static line to the rail meant that if the line twisted from the effects of the slipstream, that kind of line could detach itself. All the parachutists prepared to jump with this equipment. Two men to everyone's horror jumped from the plane and landed in front of Stirling, who with Jock, had previously made safe landings that morning. The two victims both died. The despatcher, Flight Sergeant Ted Pacey, and sometimes known as 'the Blue Orchid', was a man who was known to 'take you over'. On this occasion Pacey 'took over' the third man who was about to jump and saved his life. The morale of the whole unit was in jeopardy. Decisive leadership was needed in order to win back any lost confidence; parachute practice was halted for that day. In 1987 Bob Bennet remembered that:

> Lewes had us on parade, told us that . . . it was due to the fact that the RAF had put the fitting of the Bombay in the hands of the Egyptians. Lewes said this would be put right, 'the RAF would do it. Anyone that wants to leave is welcome to go.' This is when I found out I was with a unit that meant something, because not one man backed out.

Despite previous accounts to the contrary, Pat Riley, who jumped second in the next practice jump with a new clip that was substituted, recalled that on 18 October the first man to jump after stronger clips replaced the faulty ones was Jock Lewes. Stirling jumped too, but it would have been appropriate for Jock to jump first as Training Officer, and Pat Riley added, 'I know because I was right behind him.' Many accounts of the SAS have Stirling making that first drop, yet Bob Bennet's interview with Television South indicates that the first jump was entirely in keeping with Jock's mentality, character and role as Training Officer of the whole unit: 'He was that type of man. He'd make sure he was first out.' The morale of 'L' Detachment had been in the balance, but from then on training went ahead smoothly whilst Jock had different problems to solve. Perhaps seeing the two men die or taking the risk of dying himself whilst practice jumping after them was what may have prompted Jock to consider again the meaning of his life and that of those in his care. Two days after the two parachutists' funeral he wrote to Mirren: 'I do not have to die for me to feel the worth of my heritage, but when he dies [Jock's father] I shall also feel the responsibility of ownership. It was that phrase, read some weeks ago, its words forgotten, its picture remaining, which prompted some verses':

Inheritance

All the world is made of live men's bones,
And what we call the dead substance is no more
Than colour in our eyes, and in our ears the tones
Of melody, whose forms obey the law
Which is a pattern in the life of man.

That substance lives which gives itself to life,
And fears not to attach itself to things
Which it finds beautiful, to use with care the knife
Of reason, and with love of truth word's wings;
These lives are the architect's design.

The world's design is drawn in mankind's vision;
In seeing beyond the point that meets the eye,
And sketching out the form of classes and divisions
Which tones of sound and colour can't imply.
Each man builds who trusts to their reality.

The universe is built of what is known;
The homogeneous rock experience
Quarried by reason, striving to realize in stone
Man's images of separate existence.
Each stone conforms to and reforms the plan.

Each man whose hewn or shaped and polished
Transported, fitted, mortared, laid or set
A single building stone of wisdom has accomplished
More than his task, got more than he hoped to get.
He lives in the house he built with the friends he made.

And each man who in faith has drawn a line
On the quarry wall, on the picture that we live
In our thinking lives, has created more than a fair design
Or artistic pattern, given more than he hoped to give.
His bones are the world; his gift to men, his life.

By the beginning of November Jock conceded to his parents
that he had hardly written to them because his 'life had only
two interests beside food and sleep: My work and Miriam
[Mirren].' This was not entirely the case, because Jock kept
up with some books 'which are such friends to me'; he had
dipped into some John Donne and Rupert Brooke and was
'delighting' in *The Vicar of Wakefield* and Quiller-Couch's
The Art of Reading. He was also thrilled to receive some of
David Winser's writing in a copy of *The Spectator*. He
explained that his lack of correspondence was due to his
'wandering off into the wilderness alone, hammering at problems, imagining adventures, relishing achievement'. He was
not shut off from his parents, just unable 'to give any thought
or expression which fell outside the very narrow strip of my
life'. The wilderness of which he wrote was surely not the
tilting at windmills in his mind, but more likely the getting to
grips with the very real challenge of keeping up the morale
of the men. He graduated their training steadily forwards in
order to be ready for the onslaught of battle that would
beckon only too soon. The standards must never waver lest
those who passed began to lose faith in his system.

There was another 'wilderness' and Jock, as the SAS's
censor of soldiers' letters, wrote little of this to his parents, or
anyone he loved. 'Lewes Marches' set the SAS standard that
nothing was impossible, and he did this by setting himself
up as the guinea pig in the desert. During his training of the
men in Kabrit, Jock further developed his marches by gradually building up the distances that he travelled; he frequently
worked at this long after general SAS training temporarily
ceased. As he reached the limits of his endurance, each time

he calculated the best way to complete his journeys in the desert, which usually meant returning when he had consumed half his ration of limited supplies and water. Everything was timed and the loads of his burden were noted; they were increased as he managed to survive on the minimum water ration that was slightly reduced each time. Precise navigation was required, and he continued his method of transferring one small stone from pocket to pocket each hundred yards. His pace had to be kept uniform otherwise he would lose track of the distances he covered. The difference between his training and the men's own marching was that Jock had gained the confidence to know what was possible by trial and error; thus he gave the recruits abilities without placing their lives in jeopardy. In Jock's solo marches rescue had been entirely out of the question, because, as the parachutists realized, it was typical of the man that he did not want to adopt the wrong psychology and develop a march which had the safety net of radio, medical or vehicle support. Much was taught by this most exacting of tests in SAS selection.

Jock was clearly able to show the men that he could do anything they could do, and it was their turn to prove that they would reciprocate. Reg Seekings conceded that at first some of them wondered, after challenging Jock in the Lectures Marquee in early September, whether 'we might have bitten off more than we could chew'. Yet Jock exerted himself to give them confidence. Men were required to march and told they might have to repeat it if it wasn't done properly; their own knowledge of how they individually walked or marched was also assessed. After a thirty-mile Lewes March Reg Seekings recalled how each man's pace would be measured to check that his standard route march pace had not shortened during the night hike. Jock turned his art into a science: always attentive to detail, he tested the length of his own pace on different surfaces, and thus he enabled the SAS troopers to be always able to monitor their own marching capacity in any terrain. They began to appreciate the effort and time needed over gravel surfaces as opposed to sand. Parachutists were better able to determine distance, time and whether their rations would support their marches. With measuring distances and the time available came the all-important question of how to 'fuel' a particular length of march. Knowing how to use limited supplies of water and food would sometimes give a parachutist the choice of what type of marches were open to him in the untoward event of having to change his plans. Jock's self-discipline extended itself to every aspect of desert walking, and water rationing was a significant part of this potentially very dangerous activity.

For the marches to succeed, weight and water carried by parachutists had to be carefully measured and monitored in a strict SAS code of practice. Reg Seekings remembered how Jock first cottoned on to the fact that some of the men in the initial Kabrit marches were trying to evade the awful effects of dehydration by reducing the load, which could weigh up to sixty pounds or more (on occasions) in their packs. Jock discovered that the sand that had been used to weight the burdens was being deposited in small piles by several tents before marches began. Cunning was an essential quality needed by these soldiers but in this instance secretly reducing the weight of their pack would not provide them with the reality of the burdens they must carry in real operations. They were diluting the effects of training and unwittingly endangering their chances of successfully completing long marches. Reg noted that a simple solution surprised any wily SAS recruit: each man started a march by being lined up by an NCO, who issued him with numbered rocks or bricks that could be identified, counted and certainly not passed on to another. Jock insisted that water was to be used frugally, at certain times, never to be lent to a friend because it could cause chaos, resentment and many more problems than it temporarily solved. It should never be gulped but preferably saved until the cool of evening. Alan Hoe ably portrays Lewes Marches in his biography, *David Stirling,* and draws attention to the legend that was already being created out of them and their daring. On one march, Jock expressed satisfaction that none of the water bottles was empty after they had been checked as usual. Jock overheard one tired parachutist complaining, 'No one's checked his friggin' water bottle.' Hoe continues, 'Lewes called the unfortunate forward':

> Are you thirsty, man? Here, you can finish what's left of this. He passed over his own canteen. After about twenty miles of desert marching in the heat of the day, Lewes's water ration remained completely untouched!

Jock was creating a *corps d'élite* by enabling his men to respect each other partly because they were all gaining talents and abilities that warranted mutual respect. It was not simply marching the same distances as their officers with similar loads and rations. Jock led by example in a host of ways. Sgt Jimmie Storie recently recalled that 'Jock was the one officer who would get his hands dirty with the rest of the men.' As Alan Hoe recounted, 'There is no doubt that Lewes's dedication and professionalism set the psychology correctly, not only for "L" Detachment selection and training but also for the SAS today.'

It is the views of the original veterans of 'L' Detachment that explain the significance of Jock's own opinion that he had developed the unit 'within', while David Stirling had 'sold it' to the Eighth Army and nurtured it 'without'. Sgt Storie considered the relationship between Stirling and Lewes as a complex one, but regarded Jock as the 'father' and David Stirling the 'son' during the birth of the SAS. Stirling had to look to Lewes for much of the planning and preparation of the operations. Ernie Bond, Stirling's Platoon Sergeant in both the Scots Guards and the Commandos, corroborates Storie's view:

> With Jock everything was planned in detail. Orders were issued days in advance and everyone knew what was expected of

them. The administration and how everything was put together was left to Jock who was directing the line, and the other Officers were quite willing to leave it to him. Without Jock at Kabrit it would have been chaos.

Confidence based upon Jock's experience was again more important than knowledge alone. His vision of how to help shorten the war, and his actions in testing out his ideas to make that hope a reality, were far more important to him than simply being knowledgeable about MEHQ's outdated methods of combating superior numbers of Axis troops in the desert. When Jock had recruited the men who would eventually break Cambridge University Boat Club's succession of thirteen wins in 1937, he was convinced that enthusiasm was not enough to win: confidence was needed, and it was nurtured by experience based upon effective preparation. The training of the Dark Blues certainly helped to win the day for Jock's OUBC crew in 1937. It was the same at Kabrit with the hardy recruits. He wrote to Mirren at the end of October, sending his poem, *Inheritance*, and with it another pledge that it could not be said of him that 'This man decided not to live but know.' Experience was everything to him, and when he quoted the Welsh clergyman in one of Quiller-Couch's stories, he was characteristically asking Mirren to drain the cup of life dry: 'You will never enjoy the world aright till the sea itself floweth in your veins, till you are clothed with the heavens and crowned with the stars.'

11

Baptism of Fire

Don't drift into battle – J.S.Lewes

The SAS at first operated with the ability to transport itself around the Western Desert and return alive. Yet it was only a beginning for Lewes and his parachutists and marchers. Their rationale for existing in the first place was that they would be able to raid enemy airfields and logistical centres, destroying the Axis fixed bases and supply routes. They may have trained on thirty-mile desert walks with packs of at least sixty pounds, but their success and effectiveness as a small unit of about sixty men and officers depended on whether they could first destroy enough of their targets using their manoeuvrability and independence. Blowing up Axis aeroplanes was one of the first jobs expected of the fledgling SAS. Even with the careful positioning of a bomb, without the right kind of explosive it was possible that a parachutist might blow a hole in an aircraft but not render the vehicle irreparable. The litmus test of the unit's effectiveness lay in its ability to destroy Axis vehicles and installations. The SAS would not last very long if it did not produce some results after several months of intensive training, irrespective of Ritchie's benevolent support of Stirling's and Lewes's ideas.

Lewes's mobile troops were unlikely to be both successful in the desert and effective behind enemy lines without light-weight bombs. The technology then offered by MEHQ provided Jock with a bomb in two parts: an explosive device with its own fuse and an incendiary mechanism which would ignite the explosive with a separate fuse; it weighed at least five pounds and took ten minutes to assemble. Axis airfields often contained up to fifty aircraft including those in the hangars, and even if you used as many as one group of ten men in a raid they would be unable to destroy all the planes because enough five-pound bombs were clearly too heavy to carry there and took too long to assemble. Initially the small SAS sub-units meant only one detachment of ten men would be used per aerodrome. The whole unit of sixty men would then not be spared to carry five-pound bombs to an aerodrome because it was against the rationale of Lewes's 'new learning'. All the men would then be a sitting duck as Commando raiders had been before the SAS. Airfields were not always far apart, which meant it was more effective to attack a string of them on the same night, using several sub-units.

Every one of the machines on the airfield had to be blown up. Otherwise remaining operative planes could take off in hot pursuit of the saboteurs or other Allied targets; usually the enemy had the sense to remove any intact aircraft to the safety of a nearby airfield out of the clutches of the parachutists. The parachutists' pack had to contain water, dates, equipment and weapons as well as bombs, and it was imperative to mop up everything on the airfield if possible. Therefore the five-pound bombs then on offer from the army were simply not viable for successful desert raiding. The SAS did their best to operate 'invisibly' on an airbase, but putting together a heavy explosive and taking too much time attaching it to the appropriate part of a plane would also jeopardize the operation. That October MEHQ sent an Ordnance Major, whose name has not been recorded, to assist Lewes and Stirling. The Major informed Jock that what he was asking for was impossible and had already defeated the scientists: gelignite and thermite – or anything else for the matter – either exploded or ignited, but not at the same time. Many young officers might have been cowed into submitting to this viewpoint, but Jock refused to give in to the Major's assumption.

Without the relevant technology, the embryonic SAS unit might have faded away. For Ritchie's continued support of the SAS could only be based on its results. There was a dearth of manpower and the detachment could only exist and continue recruiting from other units if it could prove that ten of its men could destroy as many targets as 100 Commandos. At that stage of the war, without a lightweight bomb the SAS could only be very useful for limited raids and intelligence gathering; however, the LRDG had already been filling the last role for over a year. Ernie Bond remembered how Jock spent several weeks experimenting with explosives in any spare time he could afford. It must have been clear to both Stirling and Lewes that a solution to the problem had to be found and quickly. The pressures came not only from MEHQ, but also from the fact that, if the men had been asked to train for action in the desert, there had better be some of it.

Jock had already invested plenty of time on his understanding of chemistry with his brother David in Sydney, Australia. One of the most important lessons that David had taught Jock was the pleasure that could be derived from simply experimenting with different amounts of chemicals and their combinations. This type of enthusiastic enquiry was precisely what was required by a busy lieutenant under extreme pressure in every aspect of his job. Jock procured an old wing of a plane that he placed on some large oil drums, so that he could blow a hole in the wing and ignite the fuel in the tanks inside. In early October, it would have been normal for men at Kabrit to be training away or writing letters after exercises with very little peace during either activity: small explosions from Jock's makeshift laboratory punctuated the day, ringing out like a loose cannon. It seems that their Training Officer did not rest until he had made the 'impossible' possible.

Both David Stirling and Jock found great solace in inviting

back the Ordnance Major for a little demonstration. For Ernie Bond recalled how one day Jock 'erupted with joy shouting, "Oil! Of course oil!" and hugged several innocent by-standers'; the experimental wing had been blown up but also now gushed with fire. Jock had developed a bomb through sheer persistence; he had obtained some of the new plastic explosive that he then rolled successfully into a mixture of old engine oil and thermite from an incendiary bomb. A time pencil activated the explosion. It consisted of acid that would eat away through a wire connected to the plunger of a No. 27 detonator. Different strengths of acid gave time delays of between ten minutes and hours if need be. The plastic bomb was an unstable mixture and could be packed into the hollow tubing of an aircraft seat, so that the explosion might take place days after a raid. Jimmy Storie suggested this was another way 'to put the fear of God into the enemy'. The oil made it that much more malleable, so that the new bombs could also be shaped into tennis-ball-sized explosives, if required, and set up in seconds. A crowd of sceptical sappers and RAF officers saw small pliable lumps of explosive being quickly assembled and effectively used on an aircraft wing; a large number could be carried by one man. The Ordnance Major accepted that the latest weapon in his armoury should be called the Lewes Bomb. With the Lewes Bombs (or 'sticky' bombs) Jock had provided the first SAS with the 'teeth' it so badly needed.

A dress rehearsal of an actual desert raid was now a realistic ambition for the SAS unit. Much of the timing of Jock's training programme and invention of his bomb was in rhythm with the development of his men who were ready for the promised action. Within weeks of the Lewes Bomb's invention, another sceptic provided the fillip for more leadership from Lewes and Stirling and yet more daring from the men. A Group Captain of the RAF was sent by Ritchie to evaluate Jock's training methods and chances of successfully raiding an airfield. The RAF Officer, whose name has been lost, apparently decided that it was an impertinence of David Stirling to suggest that raiding an airfield was quite within the gift of the SAS. The Group Captain was certainly piqued when the Scotsman considered the real challenge lay in being accurately dropped on target by the RAF. Stirling, a clever talker and salesman who could talk anyone into anything, baited the RAF Officer to offer his own airfield as a target exercise for the SAS, as they had been recently inspired by their confidence to place charges on their objectives. Stirling, who always considered money should be used rather than saved, also lured the Group Captain into laying £10 that the parachutists could not get onto his airfield at Heliopolis at any time they wished in order to position stickers – rather than 'sticky' bombs – to prove that the aerodrome would be successfully attacked.

David Stirling and Jock Lewes worked well in tandem. Stirling was much more than a salesman for the SAS, although Jock thought he was 'too good sometimes and needed restraining', but networking in Cairo and MEHQ was clearly important in order to protect the new unit from the scepticism of the likes of the Ordnance Major and the RAF Group Captain. The experience of doubt and opposition that was shown to the exponents of the 'new learning' dated back to June 1941. Then MEHQ had sent their official report to a Captain Schott to inform him that Jock's parachute detachment would not be allowed to operate, because parachuting was not considered possible in the Middle East. It was Stirling's job to counter the influence of those opponents who might pour scorn on the unit if they were provided with an opportunity to do so. In the last quarter of 1941 the trained unit had yet to prove themselves in the field, and that included Stirling, who admitted that, unlike himself, many of the men had been blooded, even if they also were still somewhat green. George Jellicoe, who joined the SAS nearly a year after Jock and Stirling began founding it, recalled that David Stirling's 'persuasiveness and ability to get to the top' was crucial in safeguarding the new unit and allowing Jock's training to continue unhampered.

As the SAS Brigade, as it then still was known, was honed into a fighting force, Jock relaxed a little and wrote more frequently to his parents in order to share his enthusiasm for his unit, the fruits of his and Stirling's labour, the comradeship with his men and, in what remains one of the most balanced and full descriptions of his young war partner, a fine portrait of David Stirling:

At Largs I hardly knew David: I saw his great height and dark figure striding along the slippery waterfront but seldom. I could have told that he is six-foot-six, dark-haired and pale-faced with a thin black moustache, but I could not have told of his brown eyes, so dark that the pupils are invisible and which look like the eyes of one who has just taken off his spectacles as though they look out parallel and not focused on a point, nor of the gaze which he turns with them to whom he speaks with, direct but deliberately so, his conquered wish to look away showing in a slight wavering of the head but taking nothing from the penetration of the look, which is reinforced when he particularly wills to carry a point by a forward thrust of the head with its straight black unruly hair, small for his size, sharp-featured and with something elfin in the clear cut eyebrows and blue chin. On Arran I learnt that he is physically very strong and tough, delighting in mountain climbing, with great endurance. In the trip out I saw him first as the promoter of (to me) astronomical gambling at roulette and baccarat, willing to make or take a bet on anything in amounts which I would reckon in months or even years of work: clearly he does not think of money thus. And then as an invalid keeping [to] his cabin, wearing dark glasses, unable to eat or drink more solidly than water, appearing very occasionally amongst our brown bodies like a white ghost. He went straight from ship to hospital with a badly injured eye. I first began to know him when the Battalion was already beginning to break up and he wished to join me in the enterprise that I then had in intention. It was then that I saw his enthusiasm, his energy, his confidence, his courage in any undertaking to which he gave himself or, as he put it, which was sold to him. He jumped with me in that first glorious amateur experiment in the desert: he persuaded me to let him in on it in the last days when all arrangements were made. I did it as a means to a very proximate end, I see now that he appreciated the long-term value of my experiment more accurately than I and wanted to be in on it to exploit its novelty and future. I let him come reluctantly: he was interfering with my task in hand; I resented his colossal confidence of being able to do in a few days what had taken me weeks to prepare. He went to hospital for his pains but came out undaunted. He is an all-in fighter: whether at Ping-Pong, roulette, the paper war with GHQ, training or battle, he takes every advantage and gives none, uses every argument and admits none that can damage, takes every doubtful point, scores the adversary's uncertainty to his account, pursues victory relentlessly and without pity to the loser. The force of his will and character and enthusiasm is irresistible when he is inspired, and when he's not he's a pudding, no not that because he has a sharp wit at all times and especially then, but he is ordinary, idle, pleasure-loving, cynical and upper-class, though always country-bred, thank God.

Rarely hasty in his judgement and appreciation of people and situations, it took exactly two months of training the SAS before Jock wrote of his confidence in the new partnership:

> While I was in Tobruk, David took up the work and, when I arrived back, had this unit ready for me to train. It has been a wonderful vindication of my ideas on training, and, I regret to say, an exposure of the sterility and condemnation of the perversity of the accepted army ideas and system. Together we make a combination that could hardly be bettered and in which I am proud to play second string, confident that the training I am receiving in this role is worth more to me than premature command.

Jock had already experienced a dress rehearsal for fore-
going personal glory in favour of the good of his chosen
mission in his role as President of the OUBC. In 1937 he put
his friend David Winser in his own place at stroke, in order
to make the boat go faster. The President was a man of
vision then, and Oxford won the Boat Race for the first time
since 1923. In early November 1941 Jock philosophically
explained to his parents the significance of his enterprise and
how much bigger it was compared to the individuals that led
it. He describes his soul-searching before finally agreeing to
work with Stirling in early September 1941:

> It is strange how certainly I feel that I am still preparing for my
> life's work, how entirely unable I am to see an end to the road,
> how unshakeably confident I am that it is the right road. I have
> learnt to recognize it now by the fact that it has no visible end
> and that each side road meets it on a steep hill slope, the true
> road always leading up and over the top, the others running
> away to the green and tempting valleys. I could have chosen
> otherwise than this on returning from Tobruk, and longed to
> do so. This decision meant a hard hill climb when I no longer
> trusted my strength and I feared it. But I trusted God that night
> in Shepheard's Hotel: I read in Jeremiah : 'And seekest thou
> great things for thyself? Seek them not: for behold. I will bring
> evil upon all flesh.' And when David came again in the morning
> I said yes though I knew not why, for I had made no decision
> in the night.

In 1937 Lewes was above all concerned with the success of
the OUBC, and in 1941 the same could be said of his attitude
to his detachment. Exactly two months after arriving in
Kabrit, Jock wrote confidently and enthusiastically of the unit
and his fellow officer Stirling:

> I have a new tale to tell of a new unit that is going to win a
> Boat Race. I have often been reminded of those proud days by

the progress of this unit: we are a team and we are friends and we are soldiers. David and I are willing to back them against any unit in the Middle East, friend or foe. We have shown what we can do in training: soon, please God, we shall show what training can do in battle. And our men are brave: we have many who have often gone up to the sky in aircraft and have never come down in one yet. That surely is a record to be proud of.

The mock raid on the RAF airfield at Heliopolis near Cairo was a turning point in SAS morale and development. The 'sticky' labels representing the recently invented Lewes Bomb were carried by five officers and their men inside a sixty-pound pack, each containing supplies that included only four bottles of water and three pounds of dates for personal consumption during the three hot days and four freezing nights out in the desert. In groups of ten men Lts Lewes, Bonnington, Fraser, McGonigal and Mayne set out from Kabrit at night, camouflaging themselves in rocky escarpments in the day with the assistance of shadow and pieces of hessian sacking. Jimmie Storie, who was in Jock's party, remembers that the group managed to overcome the risks of hallucination and deprivation in the cloudless skies that burned the parachutists in the day and froze them during the night.

Jock's men entered Heliopolis airfield in a novel fashion: this time he did spend some time in a canteen, however short. Apparently Jock had decided that through the airfield's soft underbelly the men would have less wire cutting to do: once inside the RAF kitchen, they would 'persuade' the staff to show them the least conspicuous route in and out. It was a great success as were all the other sticks of parachutists: none of them had seen each other, but all the aircraft were labelled, some with several stickers from different groups; the ears of senior officers at MEHQ were 'blistered' by the SAS operation, because none of the daily spotter planes had observed the raiders. This made more gestures of despair and doubting from administrators at MEHQ indefensible.

The fledgeling SAS unit was ready for its first operational task, and Operation 'Crusader' seemed to be just what the Brigade could assist with. Auchinleck's plan for this offensive was to push Rommel out of Cyrenaica in the largest armoured operation undertaken by the British at that time. Auchinleck was under pressure from Churchill to begin the next phase of the desert war which was a renewed effort to drive back the Italians and Germans. The offensive would stand a greater chance of success if parachutists destroyed enemy planes before Operation 'Crusader', and if the raid failed MEHQ had only lost a handful of men with no great drain on their resources. The recently formed Eighth Army were to obtain airfields, partly to protect convoys to Malta after relieving the garrison of Tobruk. The SAS mission was to begin on the night of 17 November and the parachutists' role was potentially vital in reducing enemy air attacks during the following day. Auchinleck paid a visit to Kabrit days before the SAS were dropped near the enemy's airfields in the area of Gazala and Tmimi, in recognition of the parachutists' achievements, and no doubt also meant as a great morale booster before their first dangerous mission.

The Imperial War Museum's four-minute film of the Commander-in-Chief's inspection of the SAS Brigade on 13 November 1941 remains one of the best visual portrayals of Stirling and Lewes's different but complementary roles. In shorts, shirt and sunglasses a very dapper Stirling invites Auchinleck to view and talk to the parachutists, while Jock, in battle dress, casually waits under the wing of a converted Bombay bomber surveying the scene; he, like Stirling, had been yearning for such a moment after three exacting months. Jock shares a few words with Auchinleck, before ordering his men into the aircraft for what was by then a textbook jump from 2,000 feet. Inside the Bombay Jock sits calmly by his parachutists, occasionally checking them, and leads the first jump, after giving the cameraman a friendly nod and smile; they would drop at staggered intervals, in order to land within yards and seconds of each other. Jock's 'farewell' letters to his father and mother reflect his strong sense of purpose:

> We were visited today by the Commander-in-Chief who came to watch an exercise and spent much of the morning with us and spoke to every man. He saw that we are not unwilling, nor unskilled workers and he values us. He came not to give heart but to take it and when he went he thanked us not for a good show but for a good unit whom he trusts.
>
> How different is this from the despair of solitude and orphanage! How much man can give to man and how much withold! He is God's steward in his giving; his life is God's estate.
>
> Remember how you pressed me not to be too sanguine in my hopes from Schools. You were right, and I was not disappointed because you weren't. You felt the worth of my work and knew how to hope from it. But you never questioned the promise of the Boat Race . . . to sustain me in the labour. You may feel the same of this. We know how to hope for the bridge, because we have seen the foundations laid.
>
> I would be remembered to all our friends and, if I neglect them, say that it is myself that I'm neglecting, and tell them that the sacrifice means much to me and is my measure of the importance of this work.

To his mother Jock wrote with prescience and conviction regarding the long-term success and future of the SAS unit:

> David has perforce been absent from the unit more often than not, and I have been in command the while. We have worked splendidly together . . . We have fashioned this unit; he has established it without and I think I may say that I have established it within. His task has been the harder because he had to overcome frank opposition and deceitful obstruction. I have

had no more than human indolence and dissatisfaction to deal with and have found people at heart truly thankful for a task worth doing, however unwilling they may be to make the effort for themselves. And now we wait to prove ourselves and establish the only unmistakable demonstration of our position in the Middle East Forces and in the British Army. This unit cannot now die, as Layforce died; it is alive and will live gloriously, renewing itself by its creative power in the imagination of men: it has caught hold on life. Soon men will be seeking our company drawn by the irresistible attraction of good life, soon our name will be honoured and our ranks filled with those who come seeking honour and nobility. And, if for some reason that we know not, our work shall come to pass, our example shall not end with it, but hand on its legacy of inspiration to all who have ideals longing for realization. This is pride but I am not ashamed, nor do I fear a fall, for shame and failure belong to solitude but brotherhood is proof against them.

However, within days Jock's conviction was put through the greatest of tests. Brotherhood there may have been, but also the usual high spirits associated with 'letting off steam' the night before a dangerous operation. In fact, some of the men had 'acquired' RAF supplies of liquor and were somewhat the worse for wear. The service held at 4.30 a.m. on 16 November did little to improve their sobriety before Jock discovered that several men were far from fighting fit; he gave them a reprimand few forgot. Concern for safety that morning intensified, because at Bagoush the parachute commander was informed that the weather forecast was for windspeed of over thirty knots, which was twice the acceptable speed for parachuting. When Jock cautioned the men on the excessive intake of alcohol the previous evening, he told them: 'You are either habitual criminals or congenital idiots!' Reg Seekings remembered that they were all fairly shaken by his reaction, and the men decided that 'they had better not let him down'. It must have been a depressing first 'opportunity' for the two war leaders, who were told that, due to the poor weather, the SAS mission was up to them, but General Staff had suggested it would be suicide to continue with the task. The men were informed of the dangers, but it seems that all ranks agreed that, in order to maintain their credibility as a new unit, to resign from the opportunity to strike the enemy would possibly jeopardize their military stock with MEHQ. Stirling and Lewes were struggling for recognition and support. Whatever decision was made would involve great risks, as far as they were concerned. Yet as the leading officers they bore much responsibility for supporting Operation 'Crusader' against the advice of all meteorological reports.

Navigating the aircraft into the dropping zone would be difficult from the outset. The pilots were flying the first troops in converted bombers whose centre of gravity moved eleven feet every time a parachutist moved down the fuselage to the rear gun turret which had been transformed into a lavatory! Even if the force were dropped they might lose the cover of darkness regrouping their scattered and injured men. Stirling and Lewes had little choice but to take the only chance that critical rivals might give them from the administrative centre at MEHQ. The men wanted to continue despite the obvious risks, and their officers were not keen to cancel their first SAS raid, even though there was great chance of failure. There had been too many pressures from headquarters that suggested that any excuse could be used to disband the new force: the enemies of the 'new learning' drove the SAS Brigade between Scylla and Charybdis.

Five detachments of men were guided by the same officers that succeeded in the Heliopolis raid except that this time Stirling led his own group and Lt Fraser joined Jock. Sergeant 'Gentleman' Jim Almonds kept watch at camp, because he expected immediate recall to England as both his son, and wife, May, were suffering ill health. Jock would have missed the presence of Jim in his group because the two had worked well together in Tobruk and the latter was an excellent navigator. Like Jock, Jim was convinced of the promise that his unit displayed, and on the day of the operation wrote, 'Reality beats fiction for sheer, cold, calculating courage. More will be heard of the SAS should this raid go as planned.' Jock contented himself with the company of Sergeant Pat Riley, later the SAS RSM, also battle-worn from Tobruk and another staunch ally. Pat Riley was both very tough and physically strong, and it seems that the SAS was the perfect outlet for his considerable energy and flair in a brawl. Reg Seekings recalled that earlier that year, in scrapes with the military police, Pat had managed to flatten the Provost Marshal in Cairo. At the inception of the SAS unit, aggression was reserved for the enemy.

Jock's Bristol Bombay took off in winds of about thirty-five mph at about 7.30 p.m. on 16 November 1941 from 216 Squadron's forward base at Bagoush. He and all the officers in their respective Bombays checked each man's kit which included a small spade that every parachutist had recently been issued with. It could be used to bury the parachute or even dig a foxhole if necessary. The short implement was fitted inside the parachutist's waist belt and rested parallel with the soldier's spine. Before leaving the aerodrome, Jock had warned his men to compensate as best they could for what was now becoming atrocious weather. In his memoir, *One of the 'Originals'*, Johnny Cooper gives a detailed account of Jock's first officially backed mission. Cooper, then the youngest in Jock's party, recalled how his leader alerted them to the wind speed, which he would give the men minutes before jumping, and the way he prepared them for the landing itself: 'Now remember this lads, set the back bearing on your compasses and you will have the best chance of locating the man who has jumped before you.'

The pilot of the Bristol Bombay was aiming to clear the coastal strip with its Italian ground defences, which were always ready to gun the high-flying RAF bombers that targeted Axis supply lines and the port of Benghazi. Although

Jock's plane flew low to avoid the enemy anti-aircraft attacks, they were still pinpointed by searchlights. With magnificent flying, the RAF pilot avoided most of the armoury by diving and twisting. Johnny Cooper remembered the 'pale light illuminating the anxiety on our faces' when two searchlights simultaneously lit up the fuselage. The green light came on not long after the aircraft was hit, but the shell did no serious damage and by then the coast was clear. Jock warned the men that the plane's course was off target, because of the recent attacks combined with the wind speed that was by then force nine. The navigator gave the parachutists the wind direction and then the whole stick quickly jumped.

The force of hitting the ground would have been far greater than the impact of jumping off a 15-foot wall. Most men suffered a severe jolt throughout the body. After that, most were at first unable to gather themselves and their parachutes up, because the wind was dragging them at thirty miles an hour. Staggering neat landings was an impossibility, but every parachutist who left that plane had been reminded of their responsibility in locating the man who had just parachuted before them. Reg Seekings, in Lt Mayne's group, remembered that most of his exposed skin was scraped off by being dragged by a still inflated parachute over small rocks and gravel. His parachute straps had snagged around the end of his spade.

Few of the men were fully aware of why some of them had been dragged well after they had pressed the quick release box into which the straps of their harness were clamped. In such conditions, some had failed to turn to unlock the release button, others had actually followed the correct procedure but immediately encountered a problem that they may have been oblivious to. The small spades that were worn behind them had never been used in a training jump and, although some of the parachutists did release their parachute, the straps of the harness caught around the spade and its handle. Therefore, men continued to be dragged across the stony floor of the desert, and this proved fatal in many cases. Reg Seekings survived this particular ordeal, and one of many important lessons was learnt.

Jock led the only party of men where every parachutist was located. Learning by experience was the SAS's hard school. Johnny Cooper gratefully acknowledged his fortune in being one of the men who had not been lost with the forty who had been mostly killed or captured: 'I was lucky, I was with Jock. We all got together, the only complete stick of the twenty-two that came back.' Johnny Cooper walked along the compass bearing provided by the navigator and met one of the group. Sergeant Jimmie Storie found his friend, Jock Cheyne, also in Jock Lewes's stick; Jock Cheyne was tall and the ordeal had left him with injuries that meant he had a better chance of survival as an Italian or German prisoner. Jimmie wanted to carry him, but it was impossible, and so Jock Cheyne huddled into the blankets that were brought him, and later it was thought that he must have died there.

The original intention of moving forward to the escarpment, in order to attack the enemy airfield the following night, was out of the question. Even though Jock's men had recovered all their food, water, Thompson machine guns and equipment, bar two hard-cardboard containers, there was nothing for them to blow up. The only course left open to them was to try and locate their rendezvous point with the LRDG at Rotunda Segnale. After a night of torrential rain their compasses were redundant and Jock decided that his group had been dispatched far off their dropping zone. All the Lewes Bombs were destroyed with a timed explosion, but they may well have been rendered useless, because not long afterwards the soldiers ceased to be short of water: the whole desert was swimming in several inches of it. The worst hurricane and rainstorm had been recorded in thirty years. Electrical storms had affected their compass navigation. They knew they had travelled in a circuitous route, because, by the time the Lewes Bombs went off, the men could hear the explosion close by. Fortunately it became warmer and the visibility increased, which helped because the terrain around them remained featureless for miles.

In the white molten heat of the day they marched in a south-westerly direction towards what they hoped would be the Trig al Abd, a so-called road, running thirty miles south of the coast between the Cyrenaican and Egyptian borders. Fortified by chocolate, emergency rations, biscuits and, on this occasion, plenty of water, the men were led by 'the young eyes' of Johnny Cooper, who noticed a signpost on the horizon. Jock quickly asked, 'But will it be pointing in the right direction and will it have anything written on it?' Jock turned west in the direction of Benghazi, Sergeant Yates in Stirling's group also reached the Trig al Abd, but marched in the opposite direction towards Sollum and eventually into an enemy patrol. Jock met Stirling who was accompanied by Sergeant Tait, and with most of Lt Mayne's stick they counted the dead. The SAS had lost forty of the sixty-two men, and Jim Almonds reported that it 'must have been hell' for the survivors 'are a tight–lipped lot'. The loss of so many of the unit was a tragedy few could have predicted, and it seemed that its future was in jeopardy. Lewes and Stirling were now in danger of having their plans for the SAS shelved at a most vulnerable point of its development.

12

Cry Havoc!

Never run; once you start running you stop
thinking, now remember that! J.S.Lewes

Lewes's organization of the SAS enabled the force to win an
opportunity to stage another raid a month later. Most of the
parachutists who survived the treacherous conditions of this
raid foiled the sceptics at MEHQ by marching nearly fifty
miles across the desert to their rendezvous and established
that, under the most exacting circumstances, Jock's training
enabled them to be mobile behind enemy lines without detection. Also with the LRDG patrol's successful recovery of the
marchers, the new unit displayed a great strength in failure,
and this augured well for operations which could guarantee
better conditions and greater success. As they were able to
carry enough lightweight bombs, it seemed plausible that they
could destroy airfields and return to their rendezvous points
in the worst weather conditions. First, they had to take stock
of men, equipment and the lessons that they had learned on
the way. The LRDG could also help the SAS further by transporting the parachutists to a new base from where they could
achieve success in new raids. Lewes and Stirling needed to
overcome their recent abortive raid with an effective assault
on Axis airfields – before making contact with MEHQ, who
otherwise might conspire to suspend or cease SAS operations.

The Libyan Desert stretches a thousand miles southward
from the Mediterranean and even further west from the Nile
valley to Tunisia: west to east it is Paris to Warsaw, north to

south, Leeds to Barcelona. Most of it is desert with some areas of spectacular scenery, 'though', one *Independent* writer notes, 'you would need to travel long distances to see it, and to see it change.' Freya Stark, who had travelled through much of the Middle East and beyond, once wrote that 'there is a certain madness that comes over one at the mere sight of a good map.' In Libya the only wildness that the itinerant writer might have encountered if she had ventured there would probably have stemmed from disorientation: Major Ralph Bagnold, who formed the Long Range Desert Group in 1940, could only find one small-scale map that extended beyond the western frontier of Egypt, containing mostly information gathered by Rohlfs, a Victorian explorer. Wavell appointed Bagnold to create a mobile scouting force to gather information on the Italians, whose motorized units posed a threat to the Egypt-Sudan line of communication at Wadi Halfa. Bagnold had offered Wavell 'piracy on the high desert', and this was accepted in the LRDG's role, but, Julian Thompson writes, only officially from late November 1941 to help operations of the Eighth Army in Cyrenaica and to 'act with utmost vigour offensively against any enemy targets'. It is probable that the formation of the SAS in September forced General Auchinleck's hand in fully extending the use of the LRDG, especially as David Lloyd Owen had offered to ferry the SAS to and from their targets.

The LRDG had managed to create a 'sand-screen' of movement and attacks that exaggerated its strength in 1940 by appearing 600 miles apart, and it destroyed 2,500 gallons of fuel north of Kufra; at the time when Italian troops outnumbered the British by twenty-five to one. In his book, *The Long Range Desert Group*, Bill Kennedy-Shaw regarded the partnership between the LRDG and the SAS as 'ideal'; and Fitzroy Maclean, who joined the SAS after its inception, described, in *Eastern Approaches*, how Kennedy-Shaw and his colleagues were so experienced in desert travel 'that there seemed to be nothing they did not know about the desert'. Able delivery of passengers anywhere behind enemy lines could be fully exploited by the 'parashots' – the LRDG's nickname for parachutists – who the LRDG considered were 'fine artists in getting into – and out of – places at night'. The partnership between the two forces enabled the raider 'sand-screen' of the previous year to loom that much larger in the minds of the Italians and Germans, who were beginning to lose the psychological war in the desert.

If the LRDG could pick the detachment up from a raid it might be able to take the SAS within walking distance of their target in the first place and thus avoid the considerable dangers of parachuting in unpredictable conditions. If it was arranged quickly, the SAS might be able to attack again before MEHQ discovered the nature of their abortive raid. Explosives would have to be carried with time-pencils, as containers of each, once separated, would be of little use to the saboteurs; in the abortive raid only Jock's men had been able to locate both containers together. Captain David Lloyd Owen, who collected Stirling and Lewes, discussed the SAS's future prospects of transport, and between them it seems an agreement was reached whereby the LRDG generously provided the SAS with its 'taxi-service'. Jock and Stirling were also both fortunate because Brigadier John Marriott, ex–22 Guards Brigade, suggested that the SAS apply to Brigadier Denys Reid, who had only recently captured the Jalo garrison from the Italians. Reid, a giant of a man with a handshake to match, offered Jalo as the new SAS base. It was far from MEHQ and any unwanted attention; it also lay 150 miles south of Benghazi, in striking distance of the enemy airfields along the Gulf of Sirte. Both Reid's Flying Squadron and Marriott's force had already been ordered to link up in the area of Agedabia by 22 December, but there were German aircraft poised to attack any British troops at Agedabia, Sirte and Agheila. If Major Steele's LRDG squadron could operate as a 'taxi-service' for the SAS, then Lewes and Stirling could return a favour to both Marriot and Reid and reduce the threat of

Axis planes targeting the Brigadiers' forces by attacking enemy aerodromes in the fortnight before.

To boost the men's morale the film of Auchinleck's visit to Kabrit was shown in the aerodrome cinema a fortnight after the abortive operation and a few days before their new posting. On 5 December the SAS flew out from Kabrit at 2.45 a.m. and were in Jalo the same night. Jalo, in the Siwa Oasis, was about seven miles long and two miles wide with abundant water and a few palms. To the south of the dry heat and flies of Siwa lay the Great Sand Sea, a vast desert of huge dunes in a zone known as 'Devil's Country'. It lay within a desert that, including the Qattara Depression to the northwest, was approximately the size of India. The temperature ranges from 120 Fahrenheit in the shade in June to 0 Fahrenheit in the bitterly cold winter nights. The skies afford no cloud cover during the heat of the day or after dark. In most of this area the population averages one person per square mile, and in one area of 100,000 square miles there is no one. A few huts and Italian concrete camps were all that remained at Jalo, the indispensable centre of the Majabra Arabs who had once traded there. Johnny Cooper described it as 'a typical Foreign Legion outpost, straight out of *Beau Geste*.' It was from here that the first phase of SAS raids began, with the LRDG initially acting as its parent unit.

Before 22 Guards Brigade moved fifteen kilometres east of Benghazi in the last week of December, preliminary SAS raids would take place on 14 December against their prime objective of the Agedabia airfields on the Gulf of Sirte. More raids would follow in the last days of December when the Allied assault on Benghazi reached its climax. Rommel was running out of fuel, and overstretched Axis supply lines would be vulnerable to attack. Driven by Gus Holliman and his Rhodesian LRDG patrol, Stirling and Mayne left for Sirte airfield 700km to the west of Jalo on 8 December in 1.5-ton pink and light green camouflaged lorries. Spotter planes were the greatest threat to the mission, and within a few kilometres of their destination they were bombed after a visit from a Gibli, an Italian reconnaissance plane. Stirling had been leading a group of eleven, the standard sub-unit that he had up to then agreed with Lewes to take on such operations. Since they had been observed by the enemy, Stirling split his force into two and directed Blair Mayne to lead his men in an assault on Tamit, thirty miles away.

It is possible that from this time the idea of the substantially smaller SAS sub-unit was born, because in the circumstances it not only made sense to avoid jeopardizing the whole raid by keeping the men together after the Gibli sighting. It also increased the probability that more enemy aircraft would be located. With Lewes Bombs weighing so little, it required only a few men to carry and attach up to fifty on the entire target area. Each group of six men could then destroy an airfield. Stirling's gambit paid off, because, although his half of the soldiers had entered a minefield that resulted in an abortive raid on Sirte, twenty-four planes had been destroyed at Tamit by the other six men. The control panel of the last plane at Tamit has become part of SAS folklore because Blair Mayne had run out of Lewes Bombs and used his bare hands to disable the aircraft. On their first active raid the six SAS men had blown up half as many planes as the whole of Fighter Command on their most successful day during the Battle of Britain. The concept of a five or four-man patrol, which the SAS later adopted, gained credence, particularly after Blair Mayne's success.

Jock headed north-east into enemy territory on 8 December with eleven of his own men and Lt Morris's LRDG party. Their objective was the landing ground at Agheila where they hoped to bag a whole airfield. By night they had covered 120 miles on level sand and were only ten miles south-east of Benghazi. In daylight the going was rough with steep hills and rocky ridges, but the terrain, with its gazelles and herds of wild animals, broke the monotony. Two days after setting out they camped thirteen miles from their target area. Jim Almonds camouflaged the lorries after he and Jock had patrolled near the main road. Then Jock, with ten men, positioned himself by Agheila aerodrome, hiding until 13 December. The airfield was deserted and Jock blew up a mile of telegraph wire and several lorries along the Tripoli road, and brought in 'Sambo', a dusky Italian Corporal, as his prisoner. 'Sambo' had left part of his platoon behind – the Italians were all 'disappointed' when he was the only one taken!

Before arriving at Agheila, Jock and Jim Almonds had insisted on bringing a captured Italian Lancia lorry with them, much to the chagrin of the rest of the men. It had always been his intention to use the Lancia behind enemy lines as a ruse to deceive the enemy. Now the opportunity presented itself. There was an Italian station house nearby which could be entered using the Lancia. With Lady Luck sitting on the men's shoulders, it might well pass through any German or Italian road block. The Italian lorry unfortunately had a tendency to sink into the desert sands and break down more often than any other vehicle which Jock's men travelled in. Reg Seekings remembered it was 'the bane of my life starting the engine with a crankshaft that only I could turn on my own.' Before reaching Agheila the usefulness of the Lancia was not apparent, but now Jock and Jim held the vehicle as a trump card with which to turn disaster into triumph.

At dusk on 14 December Jock and his party travelled in more comfort on well-made Italian roads in order to find the staging post at Mersa Brega. Enemy traffic was busy on the Tripoli road, travelling in fleets of about ten vehicles. In the Lancia Jock led a shorter column with five LRDG cars behind; the Lancia had no working lights but Lt Morris's lorry shone full headlights onto the Italian truck. The SAS convoy was relatively inconspicuous, despite passing within a foot of the enemy on the other side of the narrow track. The plan was to attack the Mersa Brega roadhouse at night and destroy as many vehicles as possible, but all this was timed to happen after Jock targeted the roadhouse itself, which was known to sometimes accommodate senior officers. Jock hoped to capture some VIP prisoners to join 'Sambo', since the latter had not been a mine of information.

He had always instructed his men to act naturally when raiding behind enemy lines, as their light khaki uniforms would lend credence to their likeness to Axis troops; this was essential as Jim Almonds recalled that the SAS passed no less than forty-seven enemy vehicles. The raiders were 'in the best of spirits': some sat on the top of their vehicles, lit up cigarettes, smiled and waved at the streams of Italian and German lorry drivers travelling in the opposite direction. About midnight they reached a turning where a track led to the roadhouse, around which were parked twenty or more cars with their German and Italian crews, some of whom were waiting for a meal. Jock parked his own Lancia next to a number of others. The Breda machine gun on the back was primed and made ready.

Alongside Jock's lorry a driver got out of his Lancia and asked for a light, which Jock gave him. This was the type of escapade that he thrived on: he followed the tradition of 'Ludus Belli' that had just about survived the ravages of the First World War. Pranks played against rivals were undertaken with all seriousness when stealing a flag from the British fascist leader in 1935, whereas a cavalier approach that turned warfare into a deadly game was used by Jock against the Italians. Captain Derrick Harrison in his memoir, *These Men Are Dangerous*, describes Jock's audacity:

> 'Got a light?' he asked in Italian.
> Lewes flicked open his lighter and held it to him.
> 'Thanks.'
> 'I suppose you have guessed,' he said, 'that we are English.'
> 'Eh?'
> 'We are English – Inglesi!'
> The driver smiled. He threw back his head and laughed. 'You Germans have such a wonderful sense of humour,' he said. He began to walk over to the resthouse.

'Come here,' ordered Lewes.

The driver stopped and turned. The cigarette fell from his lips. Lewes was pointing a revolver at him.

'Get in,' said Lewes, nodding towards the back of the lorry.

Jock hustled him around the back of his own truck where the Italian went silent and then 'broke down and cried like a child'; hands were placed over his mouth to stop him 'spoiling the show'. The lorry was driven fifty yards to give sufficient room to operate the machine gun, but Jim Almonds found to his horror that the oil in the Breda had congealed in the cold night air. Armed with Thompson machine guns and revolvers, the SAS party planted thirty-eight Lewes Bombs on the surrounding cars. Then a 'sharp fight started' as the enemy recovered from their surprise, sheltering in the buildings around which they closed their gates. Enemy fire was 'poor and erratic' and this enabled the SAS to get away and move down the road without any casualties. Charges were placed on more telegraph poles, and after several miles Cpl Garven of the LRDG laid a few mines in the road before the convoy left it for a safe place to camouflage the trucks and lay up during the day. Their prisoner got drunk on rum and sang long into a night that was also punctuated by the reports of at least seven more explosions in Mersa Brega.

It seemed that Jock had been right to throw down the gauntlet to fate when he promised his mother in early December that her present to him, which had recently arrived, would be left unopened until Christmas:

> I sent you a cable to tell you that your parcel came to greet me from the battle. I said I am nailing my colours to the mast and keeping it till Christmas: a bold bet with Fate indeed so do I value it, but Fate is a good loser and it will be even dearer then. As soon as we have re-equipped we shall be off beyond the battle again. It will be won by Christmas.

By 18 December Jock was back in Jalo to discover that, although Stirling had found a deserted airfield at Sirte, the planes had taken off to land in what was considered to be the relative security of Tamit. However, Blair Mayne had been successful in destroying the twenty-four enemy aeroplanes that landed there. The next day Lt Fraser left with five men to attack Agedabia and was back two days later with the news that thirty-seven enemy planes had been destroyed. Two SAS men had been killed, but all Jock and Stirling's ideas had been vindicated in two weeks of fighting. Brigadiers Reid's and Marriott's gambit of offering Jalo to the SAS had paid off handsomely. Jock had little time to rest because on Christmas Eve he prepared for a new raid. Stirling and Lewes wanted to silence the doubters of the 'new learning' at MEHQ, so it was hoped that another significant strike was worth attempting before the SAS contacted Cairo in the New Year. Rommel was retreating and would need all the available air cover for his withdrawal, so any reduction in the number of enemy planes would markedly increase the SAS's military stock. The Germans were already becoming wise to the raids and salvaging wreckage from one plane to rebuild another, so the SAS placed their Lewes Bombs on left wings only to frustrate the enemy who were forced to wait for new replacements.

Jock sent a cable to both Mirren and his parents on 23 December: 'Back Today With Pullable Beard And Possible Medal. Off Again Tomorrow. Merry Christmas And All Love John Lewes +.' Stirling later wrote to Arthur Lewes that Jock had been recommended for a DSO for his work in Tobruk. He was everything a parent and fiancée might want him to be – except he was too far away, and they had only known him as a correspondent for the last year and a half. However, in England Mirren had at last accepted Jock's proposal of marriage; the letter of acceptance was on its way to his base at Jalo. He left for Nofilia aerodrome early on Christmas morning, a day after Stirling and Mayne called the enemy's bluff by raiding Sirte and Tamit for the second time in a fortnight. Jim Almond's diary records how Jock and Lt Fraser proceeded towards Marble Arch and Nofilia airfields. Jock and his men watched Stukas alighting and taking off from their bases on 28 December, when the party left their lorries and walked the eighteen miles to the outskirts of their target.

At 2.00 a.m. on 29 December Jock's party was within a few miles of their target, but the men were forced to make a few detours around escarpments used by Axis troops. The men covered themselves with sand and shrubs for, as Dr Pleydell, the SAS doctor, later remarked, 'There is no lesson which improves camouflage as well as a low level machine-gunning attack.' Jim Almonds wrote, 'Hope we don't wake up to find ourselves in someone's barrack square.' When they did wake, it was to the roar of brand new, brightly painted Stukas; the group observed forty-three planes on the drome, as troops sprang into life. They watched the activity and planned the campaign for that almost fully moonlit night. 'Jock thought we were going to have a real harvest.' However, all the Stukas took off and the only targets were two out-of-service planes which they then destroyed.

There was no raid like Mersa Brega to uplift the soldiers' spirits: no roadhouse was within striking distance before they travelled north-west to pick up Lt Fraser. At 10 a.m. on 31 December a lone Messerschmitt 110 fighter with four machine guns and two cannons passed overhead and appeared to go away and Jim Almonds noted that, 'everyone breathed a sigh of relief'. Its 20mm cannons could fire 650 rounds a minute from a 60-shot magazine. The men were more than ready for their journey back to Jalo, a clean-up and news from loved ones. Then one wing tipped down and the pilot brought the machine round and circled very near. The Messerschmitt made a low-level attack; Jimmie Storie remembered the hole down the middle of one of the trucks that was quickly evacuated. The soldiers played 'ring a roses' round a few rocks every time the plane circled and attacked.

Jim Almonds recorded that Jock had been wounded in the

leg, as did David Stirling in his letter to Arthur Lewes. Jimmie Storie finally found Jock with his back blown out by a 20mm cannon shell; yet he still managed a dying breath that Jimmie Storie recalls as 'Mirren'. Storie, who had trained with Jock from the inception of the parachute detachment, was the last to see him as he buried him in the desert. With no other casualties the men managed to salvage the pieces of one truck and limp back to Jalo. Jimmie remembers that New Year's Eve consisted of a subdued gathering where a lot of men shared one pot of jam and a few cups of tea. That night Mirren Barford attended a New Year's Eve party only to discover she was experiencing cold shivers down her spine and an ominous sense of foreboding; she quickly made an excuse and left. She had written in early October to Jock of her joyous acceptance of his proposal of marriage in a letter he never received.

In early December Jock had informed his parents that 'L' Detachment had achieved full Brigade status, 'after all you can't go on being a detachment all your life.' He also sent home 'our wings . . . an arrogant badge for you to see and imagine on my breast. They are earned only after long training has achieved its purpose in operation.' This was the precursor of Sgt Tait's Wings and Sword insignia with its motto 'Who Dares Wins'. The right to wear Jock's original parachute badge was after parachutists achieved three operations behind enemy lines. Some mystery still shrouds the origin of the wings that have an Egyptian appearance. Jock had noticed the outstretched wings of the symbolic Ibis in the foyer at Shepheard's Hotel; he removed the Ibis and substituted a parachute. The dark blue represented his affiliation with Oxford and the light blue another SAS officer, Tommy Langton, who had rowed against Oxford in the Boat Race of 1937. It is not surprising that the leader who by then had left his mark on almost every aspect of the SAS's character should also want to design its insignia. The parachute in the parachutists' badge had come to symbolize much of Jock's work in North Africa. One writer's description of these wings echoes the nature of Jock's role in the desert, which hitherto has remained invisible in more senses than one:

> The parachute wings of the SAS, unlike those of the Parachute Regiment, had a straight top edge and were worked in light and dark blue silk with, in the centre and almost unnoticed, a small white parachute.

In Arthur Lewes's *Hollyman*, his serialized tale to inspire his three children, the Fairy Queen and her fairy garden are gradually threatened by the dark forces of Earthman, who tries to wear away the positive forces of the fairies. There is only one person who can save the enlightened kingdom from disaster and he is Peter, a boy of ten or eleven. In the story there is no compromise with Earthman, no reconciliation. Peter is sent to destroy the creature. He does so without hesitation or remorse. The wheel of Lewes folklore may have turned full circle; Jock may have regarded death with the same attitude as that with which Peter slew Earthman; in his conflict Jock too was trying to bring the war to a swifter conclusion. Just as in the fairy tale, his actions were ruthless but not without success.

Jock was not interested in the limelight but only the facilities to carry out his task and create a lasting entity. Having spoken to many who knew Jock as a soldier, I have no doubt that the nature of the SAS, both then and in modern times, reflects his personality strongly, both in the rigour and standards which he first laid down and in the ethos and whole approach of the Regiment. It is easy to fail to grasp how remarkable Jock's achievement was. He was able to co-found the SAS because of a keen intelligence, deep insight and an awesome imagination. Whilst it is true to say that other people had developed military techniques similar in some respects to those of the SAS in World War Two, no examples of these were available to Jock during his short military career. There were certainly no soldiers with experience to guide him. It could be seen as not so remarkable that he was both devising and providing the training for soldiers within months of joining the Welsh Guards, because there was a dearth of experienced officers at this time. What is remarkable, however, was that there was no tradition of using these techniques prior to the SAS. With only two years' experience as a professional soldier – one of those in the Tower Hamlet Rifles and as little as two months of action in Tobruk – Jock was the author of a completely new way of operating in the British Army. Key politicians and generals of the time admitted that the actions of the SAS in Africa, the Aegean and Europe did much to help shorten the war.

Not only did he devise his methods in his imagination, he also used this same imagination to anticipate the circumstances and problems that such warfare would give rise to, and then to work out in considerable detail the techniques for overcoming them. Clearly there were problems that were not at first understood, and very quickly he learned from them. This is perhaps the most valuable legacy of his training: the anticipation of unforeseen difficulties and the need to comprehend them and make them part of the collective wisdom of the unit as a whole.

There is no doubt that in late 1941 it was a very heavy blow to the men left behind by Jock in the emerging SAS, when he was lost so soon after the unit had begun operations. Jock exerted a powerful hold on his soldiers in death as in life. Both Reg Seekings and Jimmie Storie remembered that David Stirling was very angry with the raiders who had left Jock's body behind at Nofilia, where they had been strafed and bombed. Incensed at the news of his colleague's demise, Stirling overlooked the fact that there was no room in the sole remaining truck. In fact, Jimmie Storie and the other survivors were following Jock's training to the letter, because recovering his remains would have used up valuable time that could have prevented the completion of their safe exodus to the SAS camp at Jalo. Why did Stirling want the body? He was seriously unsettled. Jim Almonds recalled in his interview with Gordon Stevens that David Stirling was 'very put out by it. They'd struck up a real rapport with each other and he was a serious loss to David.' Stirling, in the same set of interviews, remarked that:

> Jock was totally indispensable. You can imagine the disaster it was for all of us when he got killed in the second operation. By that time, he'd set a pattern of training, the basis of which exists to this day, and he invented the Lewes Bomb, without which we could never have accomplished what we did in the way of destroying transport.

One of the strongest tributes to Jock's contribution to the SAS lies in Stirling's strong emotional reaction to losing a powerful friend and partner, who had solved most of the unit's challenges up to that point. David Stirling had not had the time to focus on the minutiae of training and solving the technical problems of launching the unit. Jock, whom David Sutherland christened the 'SAS meteor', may well have seemed to Stirling and their parachutists to be more magician than man.

It was as if the remains of his body might be a touchstone of inspiration in what seemed another serious setback for the SAS. Reg Seekings later described the death as having a great effect on morale: 'In some ways Jock's loss was worse than the forty men in the abortive raid in October 1941.' There was no obvious replacement for the First Training Officer, as Blair Mayne, so brilliant on operations, was later to prove. In the end, the baton of guidance was already there to be picked up by the very capable Pat Riley. One can imagine that the men's feelings were akin to an infant animal being abandoned by its protecting mother for the first time: experienced enough to know there are lots of dangers and feeling barely able to face them without the support there had always been before.

As Jock himself wrote to his mother, he had done rather better for them than that. 'This unit cannot now die, as Layforce died; it is alive and will live gloriously, renewing itself by its creative power in the imagination of men: it has caught hold on life.' Although operations had not yet begun when he wrote this, clearly he was very confident that he had sufficiently instilled in his troops the core of his training. Once they had been shown the way they would always know it. Jock had the foresight to see that the SAS would go on to establish itself as one of the most renowned special forces in the world.

Appendix

Stirling paid his own tribute to Jock in a letter to his father:

20 November 1942
No 1 SAS Regt
Kabrit
M.E.F.

Dear Mr Lewes

I hardly know how to begin this letter. Any form of explanation is so inadequate as to be not worthwhile presenting.

Jock could far more genuinely claim to be the founder of the SAS than I.

He may have told you that we both served in the same Commando. In June 1941, after a series of abortive operations, Jock became impatient at the methods and poor training arrangements of the Middle East Commandos. He realised that the facilities for operating the large and clumsily organised Commando were insufficient in the Middle East at that time, so he applied and got permission to detach a section from the unit, and to train it on the lines required to enable it to cover an operation which he himself had planned. Although this operation was never executed owing to lack of decision at the top, there was never any doubt that it would have been successful. The whole conception, the thoroughness with which he trained the men and the beautiful simplicity of his plan seemed to eliminate the chance of failure.

After this operation was postponed, I think three times, Jock was included in a detachment of our Commando which went up to Tobruk. Although not in command of this force, he soon, by virtue of his astonishing qualities of leadership, determination, and skill in all field craft, established himself as the crack patrol commander in his sector of the Tobruk perimeter. So good was he that on one occasion a Brigadier responsible for another sector of the perimeter requested General Morehead that Jock should be loaned to carry out a vital mission in his area. I have frequently heard it said that in this period, Jock earned a DSO.

When Jock was fighting in Tobruk the rest of our Commando was disbanded. After this had taken place, I worked on a proposal that a unit should be formed to cover the undoubted operational opportunities of the Commando unit of a size that was consistent with the very limited naval and air force facilities. This proposal was largely based on Jock's ideas and was merely an application of them on a unit basis. Later, ME [MEHQ] instructed me to go ahead and form a unit on the lines of Jock's ideas. Inevitably, the first officer whom I applied for was Jock. In fact, I built the unit around him.

There is no doubt that any success the unit had achieved up to the time of Jock's death and after it was, and is, almost wholly due to Jock's work. Our training programmes and methods are, and always will be, based on the syllabuses he produced for us. They must show the extent of his influence.

Jock was killed while returning from an operation against Nofilia aerodrome by strafing from German fighter aircraft. He was hit high up in the leg by a cannon shell which apparently cut the main artery. The truck in which he was travelling also carried the medical orderly and his equipment so that Jock had almost instant attention by a trained professional. He remained conscious and continued to give instructions to his men until he died fifteen minutes later. He was buried twenty miles inland South East of Nofilia. On our next operation I hope it will be possible to visit the spot where Jock is buried and to build a permanent cairn to mark the place.

In five or six weeks time I hope to be returning to England for a five-weeks visit. If I may get in touch with you on my arrival I will be able to give a much more complete account of Jock.

Yours sincerely,
David Stirling

This tribute was written for the British Council

Lieutenant J. S. Lewes.

A friend writes:

All who knew Jock Lewes will be grateful for the tribute paid to his memory by "G.R." [Gilbert Ryle] in *The Times* of February 3. He was one of those who might have led his generation back to a saner world after the war, for he had that solidity and balance which men at once unreservedly trust.

No man had a greater capacity for the enjoyment of living. His Australian upbringing had given him, besides a fine physical presence, abounding energy and strength and great skill of eye and hand. He had the pioneeer's resourcefulness and the craftsman's patience: apart from his record as an oarsman, he was a first rate shot and stalker, indeed a born master of any sport, and his natural dash and high spirit, and his enormous zest for life, bore the rest of the world along with him. To such a man popularity comes easily, and a lesser man would have been content with it. Yet with all those gifts he was utterly without vanity, because he judged them by a stern exacting standard of his own – he looked on men and things with a clear eye and although his gentleness and understanding for others were without limit, to himself he showed no leniency. He had only one object, to give the best of himself to the service of the two countries which he looked on equally as home – Britain and Australia. He was indeed the living example of what each two has to contribute to the other, and his hope was after the war, to return to the British Council, and devote himself to the cause of Imperial understanding. In such a field a man of his character might have done great and lasting good; this beside much else, the madness of our times has lost to us. True to his standard he chose the hardest and most dangerous way of wars, and gave to it all his faculties of mind and body.

If such was to be his end, it was worthy of his country, his Regiment and of the man himself – But we can ill spare him.

Jock's Family, Friends and Colleagues During and After the War

Many of Jock's family, friends and colleagues survived the war.

Jim Almonds was captured in North Africa but later escaped. He received the Military Medal and became a Major. He still lives in Lincolnshire.

Dr Michael Ashby, FRCP, became a neurologist and lives with his wife, Pamela, in Sussex.

Mirren Barford obtained her degree from Somerville and joined a military intelligence unit. She later married an American Captain, Dick Wise.

Ernie Bond, OBE, was captured after the first abortive SAS raid. He was a prisoner during the war and went on to join the police force, later becoming an Assistant Deputy Commissioner. He still lives in Kent.

Owen Dibbs, OBE, joined the RAAF as soon as he left King's School, Parramatta. He flew in a Sunderland boat squadron in England and completed his career as a Group Captain. He still lives in Australia.

John Garton, CBE, became President of the OUBC in 1939. He lives with his wife Elizabeth in Berkshire and is the President of Henley Royal Regatta.

Sandy Gordon was awarded the Distinguished Flying Cross in the war and still lives in Scotland with his wife, Helena, on their estate at Lude, Blair Atholl.

Arthur and Elsie Lewes lived until the ages of ninety-three and eighty-eight years respectively.

David Lewes, DM, FRCP, trained as a doctor and became a Squadron Leader in the RAF. He put down an epidemic on the Azores during the war and was awarded the Cross of St Lazarus. He was later Chief Consultant Physician at Bedford Hospital. He became an inventor, and also an active member of the Cardiac Society. He died in 1997. His wife Daphne survives.

Elizabeth McArthur lives with her son, Charlie. She had five other children with her husband, Alistair, on their hill farm in Argyleshire.

Sir Carol Mather, MC, served with the SAS from 1942 and later with Montgomery in Normandy, retiring as Lieutenant Colonel in 1962. He was MP for Esher from 1970–1987 and lives with his wife, Phillipa, in Gloucestershire.

Pat Riley became a Major after winning the Distinguished Conduct Medal. He lived with his wife, Kay, in Sussex. Both died recently.

Reg Seekings was recommended a Victoria Cross and received the Military Medal and Distinguished Conduct Medal. He used Jock's training to help develop the Rhodesian anti-terrorist force. He died recently.

Frau Solf and her daughter were spared after the intervention of the Japanese government when the family was linked with the "good Germans" who were responsible for the failed assassination of Hitler. The rest of the Solfs were executed except Hans Heinrich.

David Stirling became a Lieutenant Colonel and was awarded the DSO. He was captured and incarcerated in Colditz. He survived there and went on to guide the development of the SAS after the war. He was knighted in 1990 just before he died.

Jimmie Storie survived the war and lives with his wife, Morag, in Scotland.

David Sutherland remained in the Army until 1955,

when he joined MI5, for whom he worked for twenty-five years.

Rex Whistler was killed in action in Normandy in 1944.

David Winser trained as a doctor and served as a medical officer. He was killed in action and awarded a posthumous DSO.

Abbreviations

BUF	British Union of Fascists
FO	Foreign Office
GHQ	General HeadQuarters
LMG	Light Machine Gun
LRC	London Rowing Club
LRDG	Long Range Desert Group
MEHQ	Middle Eastern HeadQuarters
NCO	Non Commissioned Officer
OTC	Officer Training Corps
OUBC	Oxford University Boat Club
OUOTC	Oxford University Officer Training Corps
RHG	Royal Horse Guards
RTU	Returned To Unit

Interviews and Documents

Author's Interviews
Pat Riley/ March, May 1994
Jim Almonds / April 1994
Bob Bennet / July 1994
Douglas Arnold/ September 1994
Ernie Bond / August 1994
Sandy Gordon / October 1997
John Garton / April 1998
Reg Seekings / May 1998
Phillip Warner / July 1998
Sir Carol Mather / July 1998
Jimmie Storie / August 1998
Dr Michael Ashby / August 1998
Brian Hodgson August 1998
Angelika de Guyon de St Prix/August 1998
Mrs Elizabeth McArthur / August 1998
Inga Haag /February 1999

Television South, 1987 / The transcripts of interviews by Gordon Stevens with members of the Original SAS veterans:
Jim Almonds / 18044/5
Bob Bennet / 18045/7
David Stirling / 18540/10

Documents

Family Papers / Collection:
The Letters and Papers of Arthur Lewes.
The Holiday Diaries of Jock and David Lewes 1925–1935.
Letters from Jock Lewes to his parents 1924–1941.
Letters from Jock Lewes to his brother, David Steel Lewes.
The King's School Parramatta Rowing Journal.
Hollyman by Arthur Lewes.
Essays and Poems by Jock Lewes.

Unpublished Diaries and Records:
Major Jim Almonds' War diary.
Dr Michael Ashby's Memoir.
The Hon Hugh Lawson-Johnston's *Berlin Diary*
Sir David Stirling's Scrapbook of Letters.

Public Record Office:
British Council: PRO BW2 117
War Diaries: WO 201/731; WO 201/732; WO 218/166; WO 218/170; WO 218/173.

Bibliography

Barnett, Correlli, *The Desert Generals*, (Allen and Unwin, 1983)

Bloch, Michael, *Ribbentrop* (Bantam, 1994)

Boston Sunday Globe (2 July 1995)

Bradford, Roy, and Dillon, Martin, *Rogue Warrior of the SAS* (John Murray, 1987)

Bucheim, Hans, *The Third Reich*, Kosel Publishing (Munich, 1958)

Burnell, R. D., *The Oxford and Cambridge Boat Race, 1829–1953* (Oxford University Press, 1954)

Greacen, Lavinia, *Chink: A Biography* (Macmillan, 1989)

Cooper, John, with Kemp, Anthony, *One of the 'Originals'* (Pan, 1991)

Cowles, Virginia, *The Phantom Major* (Collins, 1958)

Farran, Roy, *Winged Dagger* (Collins, 1948; reissued, Arms and Armour Press, 1986)

Gilbert, Martin, *A History of the Twentieth Century*, Vol. 2 (HarperCollins, 1998)

Harrison, D. I., *These Men Are Dangerous* (Cassell, 1957)

Higham, Robin, *Guide to Sources of British Military History* (University of California Press, 1972)

HMSO, *Combined Operations 1940–1942* (1943)

Hoe, Alan, *David Stirling* (Little Brown and Company, reissued Warner Books, 1994)

Independent (10 April 1999)

Isis (13 & 20 May 1936)

James [Pleydell], Malcolm, *Born of the Desert* (Collins, 1945)

James, R.R., *Chips: The Diaries of Sir Henry Channon* (Weidenfeld, 1993)

John Bull (9 March 1957)

Keegan, John, *The Second World War* (Century Hutchinson, 1989)

―――――*War And Our World: the Reith Lectures* (Pimlico, 1998)

Kemp, Anthony, *The SAS At War, 1941–1944* (John Murray, 1991; Signet, paperback edn., 1993)

Kennedy-Shaw, W.B., *Long Range Desert Group* (Collins, 1945)

Ladd, James, D., *SAS Operations* (Hale, 1986)

Lloyd-Owen, David, *The Desert My Dwelling Place* (Cassell, 1957; reissued, Arms and Armour Press, 1986)

MacDonogh, Giles, *Berlin* (Sinclair-Stevenson, 1997)

―――――――― *A Good German: Adam von Trott zu Solz* (Quartet, 1989)

Maclean, Fitzroy, *Eastern Approaches* (Jonathan Cape, 1949)

Mather, Carol, *When the Grass Stops Growing* (Pen and Sword, 1997)

Mazower, Mark, *Dark Continent: Europe's Twentieth Century* (Allen Lane, Penguin, 1998)

Nicolson, Harold, *Diaries and Letters, 1930–1939,* ed. Nigel Nicolson (Collins,1966)

Pitt, Barrie, *The Crucible of War* (Jonathan Cape, 1980)

Pollock, N., *Tobruk – A Personal Account* (Gooday Publishers, Thetford,Norfolk, 1992)

Rommel, Erwin, *The Rommel Papers,* ed. Liddel Hart (1953)

Richie, Alexandra, *Faust's Metropolis: A History of Berlin* (HarperCollins, 1998)

Scottish Daily Express (24 August 1944)

Shirer, William. L., *Berlin Diary, 1934–1941* (Promotional Reprint Company Ltd, 1997)

Strawson, John, *A History of the SAS Regiment* (Secker and Warburg, 1984)

Sunday Times (27 December 1993)

Sutherland, David, *He Who Dares* (Pen and Sword, 1998)

Taber, Robert, *The War of the Flea* (Paladin, St Albans, Herts, 1970)

The Spectator (20 May 1995 & 9 November 1999)

The Times (16 April 1937, 17 April 1937

Thompson, Julian, *Imperial War Museum Book of War Behind Enemy Lines* (IWM, 1998)

Warner, Phillip, *The SAS* (William Kimber, 1971; Sphere Books, paperback edn., 1983)

Waugh, Evelyn, *The Diaries of Evelyn Waugh* (Weidenfeld and Nicolson, 1976)

_____ *Men at Arms* (Methuen, 1986)

Ranfurly, Countess of, *To War With Whitaker: The Wartime Diaries of The Countess of Ranfurly, 1939–1945* (Heinemann, 1994)

Ross, Gordon, *The Boat Race: The Story of the First Hundred Races between Oxford and Cambridge* (Hodder and Stoughton, 1954)

Wise, Michael, *Joy Street: A Wartime Romance in Letters, 1940–1942* (Little Brown and Company, 1995)

Ziegler, Philip, *King Edward VIII* (Fontana, 1990)

Index